The Emerging Woman
The Impact of Family Planning

Th

An Informal Sharing

Emerging Woman

The Impact of Family Planning

erests, Ideas, and Concerns, Held at the University of Notre Dame

Edited by Martha Stuart MARTHA STUART COMMUNICATIONS;
CONSULTANT TO PLANNED PARENTHOOD–WORLD POPULATION, NEW YORK

with William T. Liu, PROFESSOR OF SOCIOLOGY
AND DIRECTOR, INSTITUTE FOR THE STUDY OF POPULATION AND
SOCIAL CHANGE, UNIVERSITY OF NOTRE DAME, NOTRE DAME

BOSTON *Little, Brown and Company*

Foreword

THE topic of the conference presented in this book, so ably and intelligently edited by Martha Stuart—who also thought it up in the first place—was by no means another variation on the eternal theme of *donna è mobile*. When we at Notre Dame agreed to sponsor the meetings, we knew full well that they would deal with social changes which have just begun to make themselves felt and which will have a very powerful impact on the future.

That woman has been steadily relieved by technology of chores imposed by housekeeping and family-rearing is obvious. There are still pockets in our social landscape where flatirons are heated on the back of the stove and sonny shoots and kills a couple of rabbits for supper. But the average American family eats more canned food than it does any other kind and washes more clothes at laundromats than it does at home. The vacuum cleaner and the rug shampooer have deprived spring housecleaning of most of its horrors. And so forth.

But the relationship between woman and child-bearing is quite different. For at least two generations the "hired girl" has been unobtainable, at least by the semiaffluent American family. As a result, the burden on the mother, particularly if children came in rapid succession, was very heavy indeed, in spite of gadgets. If henceforth the sanctioned use of modern contraceptives will result in the spacing of children, if not to a marked decrease in the number of those born, mothers and housewives will henceforth live in a different world. There will be far more leisure time in the lives of young married women. How will that time be used? How can it be used?

The prognosis is by no means automatically favorable, and it is this that the conference was really all about. On the one hand, we have enough historical evidence to give us pause. Not every contraceptive-using society—for example, France during the three decades prior to the First World War—has been distinguished insofar as the lives of women emancipated from child-bearing were concerned. Nor in an environment like our own, where the widespread conditioning of women by their use in entertainment is a major phenomenon, do the data seem to suggest much else than dieting and hairdos. For every woman who emerges into political or social leadership, there are a hundred topless girls or striptease dancers.

If the emancipated woman of the future is to make her contribution to a society so badly in need of sincere contributions in terms of thought and service, she will have to do a lot of thinking and self-appraisal. The fact of the matter is that nearly every woman wants to have children. It is not yet evident that she knows what else she really desires.

One surmises therefore that conferences like this one will be repeated again and again. But anyhow this was a starter; and if the reader finds the record half as interesting as did the participants, the effort will prove to have been really very much worthwhile.

GEORGE N. SHUSTER

Notre Dame, Indiana

To the Reader

I'm so glad you're interested in our conference and I hope you feel as though you are listening to the sessions from the observers section and that you get a feel of the people there and of what was said and what happened.

This book is the complete edited transcript of the conference on the emerging woman, not a compilation of after-the-fact papers nor, for that matter, before-the-fact prepared texts. The delegates were so stimulated by the communication within the group, among disciplines, and between men and women that they discarded prepared texts and spoke as they thought. You will see that much of the thinking was joyously original.

A good conference is like a good marriage or a good relationship. It starts with everyone stating his particular brand of expertise and moves on to real listening and exchange and finally to a common momentum. Don't be discouraged with the initial stiffness. You will feel the momentum when you hear Jacqueline Grennan, a Roman Catholic college president, say "The religion which should have produced Freud fought him!" or Joseph Bird, a psychotherapist and marriage counselor, say "Perhaps one of the finest things that we have going today is the communication gap. This will at least help some teen-agers not to listen to their parents." One of my favorite asser-tions is that of businessman Charles Lecht, who announced "Work is a bad habit." Virginia Johnson's statement that woman "sometimes confuses privilege with equality" is lovely.

During one of Harold Gibbons' great late parties (where most of the serious work of the conference was done), Michael Scriven turned to me and said, "This conference is really your toy, Martha"; to which I replied, "You'll have to admit it's a Creative Plaything!"

At that same party I suddenly realized what responsibility is—and at 37 that's not too bad—what the word *responsibility* really means. We cloak the word and the acting out of re-sponsibility in such a long-faced, almost pejorative, and cer-tainly authoritative aura. It was beautiful suddenly to see that what it really means and is meant to mean, I think, is one's *ability to respond.*

It was everyone's ability to respond that made this gathering so exciting. I hope this book gives you some ideas about women's ability to respond to their men, to their children, to their world, and to themselves.

MARTHA STUART

New York

Thank You

My special thanks to George Shuster and Bill Liu for sponsoring the meeting in the first place. Dr. Shuster understood the idea immediately, and I kissed him for it. Bill Liu trusted me enough to leave the country and give me carte blanche to invite my favorite thinkers to his meeting.

Thanks to Anne Sheffield for sharing so intelligently as the idea began to take form and for helping to raise the money.

Huge thank-yous to Jean King, who helped so much at Notre Dame; to Joanna Underwood, who unraveled the transcription; and to Rosemary Washington, China Zorrilla, Michi Kobi, and Frank Westbrooke, whose talents and involvement extended beyond the task of typing.

It sounds phony, but the conference never would have happened without Dick Cornuelle. He raised money and spirits and he got me started and finished in the editing process. But most important, he helped me create the loving and open atmosphere of the meeting.

Six million hugs and kisses to Sally and Barkley Stuart for understanding that their mother is an *emerging woman*.

MARTHA STUART

Contents

Delegates and Observers

Chairman: William T. Liu
Adviser: George N. Shuster
Program Coordinator: Martha Stuart

DELEGATES

DONALD BARRETT

Associate Professor of Sociology and Anthropology, University of Notre Dame, Notre Dame

FRED BELLIVEAU

Manager, Medical Division, and Vice President, Little, Brown and Company, Boston

EDGAR F. BERMAN, M.D.

Assistant to Vice President Hubert H. Humphrey; Chief Health Consultant for Latin America, Agency for International Development, Washington, D.C.

JESSIE BERNARD

Research Scholar, *Honoris Causa,* Pennsylvania State University, University Park

WINFIELD BEST
Vice President, Planned Parenthood–World Population,
New York

JOSEPH W. BIRD
Psychologist, Psychotherapist, Saratoga, California

LOIS F. BIRD (MRS. JOSEPH W.)

LEE BULLITT (MRS. JOHN C.)

JUNE BUTTS (MRS. HUGH F.)
Doctoral Student, Department of Home and Family Life
Education, Columbia University Teachers College, New York

CATHERINE S. CHILMAN
Research Director, Welfare Administration, Department of Health,
Education, and Welfare, Washington, D.C.

GEORGE CHRISTIE
Latin American Program Director, Communications Satellite
Corporation, Washington, D.C.

ELEANOR CHRISTIE (MRS. GEORGE)

RICHARD C. CORNUELLE
Executive Vice President, National Association of Manufacturers,
New York

WILLIAM V. D'ANTONIO
Chairman, Department of Sociology and Anthropology, University
of Notre Dame, Notre Dame

LORRAINE D'ANTONIO (MRS. WILLIAM V.)

ELISA R. DEBULNES
President, Red Cross of Chile, Santiago

LOUIS K. DUPRÉ
Professor of Philosophy, Georgetown University, Washington, D.C.

CONSTANCE DUPRÉ (MRS. LOUIS K.)
Attorney

HAROLD J. GIBBONS
Vice President, International Brotherhood of Teamsters, New York

MOTHER MARGARET GORMAN, R.C.S.J.
Professor of Psychology and President, Newton College of the Sacred Heart, Newton, Massachusetts

JACQUELINE GRENNAN
President, Webster College, Webster Groves, Missouri

VIRGINIA E. JOHNSON
Research Associate, Reproductive Biology Research Foundation, St. Louis

KERMIT KRANTZ, M.D.
Professor and Chairman, Department of Gynecology and Obstetrics, University of Kansas School of Medicine, Kansas City

WILLIAM M. LAMERS, JR., M.D.
Staff Psychiatrist, Ross Psychiatric Center, Kentfield, California

CHARLES P. LECHT
President, Advanced Computer Techniques Corporation, New York

WILLIAM T. LIU
Professor of Sociology and Director, Institute for the Study of Population and Social Change, University of Notre Dame, Notre Dame

WILLIAM H. MASTERS, M.D.

Director, Reproductive Biology Research Foundation, St. Louis

JOHN T. NOONAN, JR.

Professor of Law, University of California, Berkeley

HERBERT W. RICHARDSON

Assistant Professor of Theology, Harvard Divinity School, Cambridge, Massachusetts

ENE RIISNA

Associate Producer, Public Broadcast Laboratory, New York

REV. JOHN RING

Administrative Director, Larrain Inter-American Center, Catholic University of Puerto Rico, Ponce

BETTY ROLLIN

Senior Editor, *Look* Magazine, New York

JULIAN A. SAMORA

Professor of Sociology and Anthropology, University of Notre Dame, Notre Dame

SISTER MARY ALOYSIUS SCHALDENBRAND

Professor of Philosophy, Nazareth College, Kalamazoo, Michigan

MICHAEL SCRIVEN

Professor of Philosophy, University of California, Berkeley

JAMES P. SEMMENS, M.D.

Chief, Department of Obstetrics and Gynecology, Naval Hospital, Oakland, California

REV. CHARLES E. SHEEDY, C.S.C.
Dean, College of Arts and Letters, University of Notre Dame,
Notre Dame

ANNE SHEFFIELD
National Fund-Raising Director, Planned Parenthood–World
Population, New York

PIERRE SIMON, M.D.
President, Collège Médical; Vice President, Mouvement Français
pour le Planning Familial, Paris

SHIRLEY M. STONE, M.D.
Clinical Associate Professor of Pediatrics, New York University
School of Medicine, New York

MARTHA STUART
Martha Stuart Communications; Consultant to Planned
Parenthood–World Population, New York

JOHN L. THOMAS, S.J.
Research Associate, The Cambridge Center for Social Studies,
Cambridge, Massachusetts

PAUL H. TODD, JR.
Chief Executive Officer, Planned Parenthood–World Population,
New York

TERRY TODD (MRS. PAUL H., JR.)

RUTH H. USEEM
Research Professor of Sociology and Anthropology, Michigan
State University, East Lansing

SISTER M. JEAN WALLACE
Associate Professor of Biology, St. Mary's College, Notre Dame

OBSERVERS

ROBERT AMUNDSON
Loretto Heights College, Loretto, Colorado

FRED ARMSTRONG
United States Steel Foundation, New York

MOTHER JOAN KIRBY
Newton College of the Sacred Heart, Newton, Massachusetts

MARSHA NASATIR
Associate Editor, *Ladies' Home Journal,* New York

BETHAMI PROBST
Associate Editor, Women's Medical News Service, New York

VIRGINIA SHEPLEY (MRS. ETHAN A. H., JR.)
Reproductive Biology Research Foundation, St. Louis

Advance Statement of Purpose
The Emerging Woman:
The Impact of Family Planning

CONFERENCE HELD AT THE UNIVERSITY OF NOTRE DAME
NOVEMBER 20–22, 1967

THE purpose of this conference is to bring together a group of creatively concerned leaders in order to brainstorm about the revolutionary changes in the role of women around the world due to the widespread use of contraceptives.

The conference will take place at the Center for Continuing Education at the University of Notre Dame as a part of their program to foster population study and initiate social change. The delegates will represent many religions, countries, and disciplines, and they will be seeking some new answers to the new challenges offered by new feminine freedoms.

Some of the questions to which they will address themselves are:

What will women around the world be doing in the year 2000?

Is it possible for men and women to work together without forcing themselves into uncomfortable competitive roles?

What will happen to their relationships outside a working situation and to their roles as mother and father with, in many cases, fewer children?

Will our knowledge of sex and sexuality contribute to a better male-female understanding, enhanced by the concomitant personal freedom and responsibility provided by contraceptives?

How will men and women adjust to a relational rather than procreational sense of purpose?

How can we compare what is happening to women in the United States with the process of change in Latin America, India, or China?

How can we improve the quality of the mother-child relationship? How will this relationship be affected by the consequences of a contraceptive culture?

Will the underdeveloped nations make a faster leap forward to a kind of equality of opportunity for both sexes, minus tension?

With computers doing most of the time-consuming jobs, won't men and women have to learn to like each other?

What are the psychological implications of woman's search for identity?

In what ways can groups in society—church, government, labor, business, schools—help men and women adjust to change?

Each subject will be introduced and explored by a man and woman who are working together, in some cases a husband-wife team. This is a deliberate move to reinforce the additional dimension brought to a profession by male-female communication. The conference itself will be attended by both men and women in order to underline the joint responsibility both sexes share in the changes wrought by a contraceptive culture.

THE PUBLICATION OF THIS BOOK WAS MADE POSSIBLE BY A GRANT FROM THE ORTHO PHARMACEUTICAL CORPORATION. THE EDITING WAS FINANCED BY THE J. M. KAPLAN FUND, INC.

Contributors

The Emerging Woman
The Impact of Family Planning

What Is a Contraceptive Culture? 1

FATHER JOHN L. THOMAS AND CATHERINE S. CHILMAN

Monday, 2:30 P.M.

DONALD BARRETT: My name is Barrett, from the university here [Notre Dame]. My field is sociology and demography. I would like to begin by saying that this session opens up one of the broader dimensions of the conference. I would also like to bring up one thought out of my own experience at the Papal Commission on Population and Birth Control. Last year, as you may know, we brought in ideas from women, quite an innovation for the Catholic Church! There were to be four women on the Commission; actually only three were present. During the first meeting in 1965, they said nothing at all. Since I served on the planning subcommission, one of the first things I proposed was that the women be allowed to speak, and speak meaningfully. The problem was this: How could they speak meaningfully to theologians who were not only celibate but had lived in an ivory tower for many years?

Our solution was to contact these women before last year's

meeting and ask them to lock themselves up somewhere and write exactly how they feel about family planning—personally, honestly, and candidly. We set up the agenda of the commission to include two sessions during which they could express themselves fully to the assembled group of theologians, medical researchers, economists, sociologists, and demographers. Of the three women who gave reports, I think it would be fair to say that two found they simply could not fulfill the request. They could not talk about how they felt about family planning.

This was a very interesting phenomenon. It showed that some women become so involved in the organizational effort that they lose track of their own personal relationship to it, their feelings about what it means to them. They cannot speak from their own hearts, but are always talking about what women in their movement—the women of France, India, or wherever—need or want.

The world family-planning movement is an overly male dominated operation. This conference, however, presents an opportunity for women to expose their views. This is important, and I must say that in the experience of the Papal Commission, the one woman who did speak from her heart spoke so effectively that the theologians were completely upset in their thinking about the subject. I think this was good.

In my own research in Latin America over the last three or four years, the expression by women as to exactly how they feel about family planning, other than in purely substantial analyses, has been rare. For example, we talk about rising abortion rates and women using abortion as a means of family planning. This is being discussed a great deal in Latin America. How many of the research studies, however, get the qualitative meaning of the decision to use abortion as the solution to their family problems? Very, very few! The wholehearted, total expression by women of their feelings is rare. So I come back to my point. I think that on this beginning issue of what is a contraceptive culture, the open expression of viewpoints is important.

Our two speakers for this afternoon have agreed not to present formal papers, but rather to begin with an informal discussion of the subject between themselves which, after a while, will be opened up into general discussion.

First of all, we have Dr. Catherine Chilman, a psychologist who did her degree work at Syracuse University. Her main work experience has been in family social work, and she has taught in the fields of family and social psychology and social work. She has done six years of basic research with the federal government with a main emphasis on the family, especially families in poverty. For the past two years she has concentrated on sociopsychological research and the administrative aspects of family planning and, although this is not an economic announcement, Dr. Chilman is to be coeditor with Bill Liu, the chairman of this meeting, of a special family-planning issue of the *Journal of Marriage and the Family,* which is coming out this spring. Among her publications are the volume *Growing Up Poor* and a government publication on the life styles of very poor families.

The second participant is Father John L. Thomas. Father Thomas will probably ask me not to say much; he hears too many lies about himself now. But Father Thomas did his degree work in sociology at the University of Chicago, and for many years he was at St. Louis University. He has been involved in marriage counseling, has written extensively, and has many volumes to his credit. In St. Louis they finally caught up with him, however, and he disappeared. He is now in Cambridge, Massachusetts, where he is continuing his extensive work in family research and family development.

CATHERINE CHILMAN: As a woman and as a Unitarian, I feel rather doubtful about taking on an easy dialogue with

Father John Thomas, but I know him well and I am sure we can do this because we have had many discussions in the past.

FATHER JOHN THOMAS: Should I begin?

CATHERINE CHILMAN: Yes.

FATHER JOHN THOMAS: This is putting me on the spot already. If she started off I'd have some remarks to make about her remarks. This way I have to take the lead. The way we worked it out, we thought we'd like to spend some time first analyzing what we mean by contraceptive culture and then go into some of the aspects that feed into our specific problem. One of the points one has to keep in mind when discussing any one aspect of an ongoing society is that it can never be totally separated from the other aspects of that society. In social phenomena, everything is related to everything else. Everything holds together, or as the French say, *Tout se tient*. If you change one thing, such as limiting family size or the length of time the woman is involved in raising a family, you have to redefine and rethink most of the other relationships that involve men, women, the training of young people, and so forth.

We can look at a culture in a broad way as a blueprint for behavior. A culture provides a system of approved norms. We are all more or less raised with these. They are fed down through our parents, through the peer groups, and they tell us: "This is the way you do things." Ordinarily, if we analyze any beliefs and behavior at three levels there are, first, the underlying basic ideas about man and particularly about nature. What is nature? How does man relate to nature and what can he do with it? This is very important, it seems to me. In Western society, since the development of science in the sixteenth and seventeenth centuries, men have acquired a drastically changed view of nature. We see we can remake it, remodel it, reshape it, so that today practically everything that we deal with is man made. But in two-thirds of the world today, people still regard nature as something to live with, look at, admire, perhaps even study, to see how God operates in this world. But they don't see it or deal with it as we do.

Then we have the beliefs underlying what I like to call institutional objectives: the economic, the political, the sexual, the social. Are these objectives to be reached through the family system, through economic private property ownership, through politics—monarchy, democracy, or whatever—or how? Generally, the objectives are established according to the society's basic concept of man, what he is and how he relates to nature.

Then we have the third level of beliefs, those involving personal relationships, how people relate to each other. There are the normative standards: how we meet other people, how we relate in terms of sex, how we get into this hassle of marriage, what happens when we are in it, and how we get out of it. These are all more or less culturally defined although they are changeable. If you ask, "Well, why is marriage this way? Why does the family system operate this way?" the answer is that these systems *do* function in certain ways and they are needed for a viable family and a stable society. If you then ask, "But why must that be true?" the answer is, "Well, because men and women have certain characteristics. This is the way they are built; this is their destiny and purpose."

Any change in society makes its impact on one or all of these three levels of behavior. Relationships can change when a family moves from the farm into the city, or from a city into the suburbs, or (when there's a little bit more money) into the "shruburbs." The way of life changes. There may be an hour or two of commuting for the man, a new kind of role for the wife to fulfill, different preparation of the children for living in the world, and so forth.

We may also have change at the institutional objective level. We may decide that marriage is not or doesn't have to be stable. There are various forms of family relationships. We can make the shift, as we have done historically, away from the extended family system. We mustn't forget that in the past, for all practical purposes, the primary thing was the family, not the marriage. Marriage was very secondary. It came in as a unit inside the larger family system. To a great extent, in two-thirds of the world today, this is what is really still important—the family system, into which a young couple is united. Often their partners are even selected for them. Now we're moving toward emphasis on the nuclear family, the conjugal type, that is, husband and wife and immature children.

We may have changes in basic beliefs about man and his relationship to nature. We've had some drastic changes of this sort, new insights and views starting, as I said, in the sixteenth century. All I have to do is mention people like Marx and Darwin and Freud, and we can see that some very radical new views regarding the nature of man and the way he relates to society have been introduced into Western culture.

When we talk about a contraceptive culture, we are dealing basically with one aspect of change: namely, some form of regulating and inhibiting (or, if you like, frustrating) the normal consequences of marital relations. Our whole society tends to be reorganized and reformulated in terms of this change. That is what we hope to discuss.

CATHERINE CHILMAN: Since it is well known that men tend to deal with the abstract and women tend to deal with the practical, I'd like to make a few comments along the same lines. As we were thinking about the term *contraceptive culture,* it struck us both that an important question related to family planning is the tendency to take a unilateral approach to it. There is a tendency to see the problems of population and family planning as unique and separate from other aspects of society, to face the great challenge of solving these problems in too specific a way.

It occurred to me as I thought about this that one reason we have such a severe population problem now is that we took a unilateral approach to reducing the maternal and infant death rate. This was an objective looked at specifically rather than as part of the total culture. The larger question might have been asked: "If you reduce maternal and infant death rates what is going to happen then?" But it seems that in our culture we tend to look at things one at a time and say, "This is a problem; we will solve it," rather than looking at life, society, and human beings as having many facets, and realizing that if you make one change you will have to make many others.

The scientific revolution Father Thomas alluded to, as a very basic article of faith, is the idea that you can rationally plan and rationally change human life. Most of the thrust in science has been toward controlling and conquering some very basic life problems: toward freeing man from starvation, freeing him from the tyranny of hard work, freeing him from unexpected and sudden death or prolonged dying. And now contraception is freeing people from the tyranny of sex and reproduction out of control. This is part of the long scientific stream of planning, of rationally handling life. Our tendency toward specialization led us to take a unilateral approach to improving maternal and infant health. Now we are taking the same kind of approach to family planning without thinking of the many ramifications.

Also, we certainly have noticed that our culture is strongly achievement oriented and terribly materialistic. It is a "thing" culture. We tend to feel we can handle problems mechanically, as in the case of contraception with the pill or the loop. A very central problem to all of us today is how to respond with humanity in a culture that is mechanized, materialistic, rational, planned, and based on prediction and control. We need to respond mechanically to the mechanical, but how do we keep feeling, individuality, intimacy, and the tenderness of human relationships alive in a mass mechanical society? It seems to me that throughout human history man has struggled with good and evil, heaven and hell, love and hate. And just when you think you have solved one problem there is another with which to deal.

FATHER JOHN THOMAS: Yes, one of the things you run into, of course, is this matter of values. Even though you have a culture which agrees on definitions of sexuality, of nature, of man, of society, and of the family, many individuals may be acting according to very different views. Also, especially when we're dealing with sex or anything that affects sex, we are dealing with values and ways of behavior that are at the very heart of every culture.

Throughout much of the past, man's concern with reproduction has been, I would say, the major wellspring of organization and motivation in all society. A change of attitude toward sex and reproduction is going to call for drastic reshaping, rethinking, and reappraisal on a good many other levels. It is not merely a simple matter of regulating or limiting the number of children to be reproduced—the change is not only quantitative. There is also a qualitative change that comes about in all relationships, it seems to me, because of the uniqueness of sex in all its aspects. It is a very complex phenomenon.

If I may quote a great authority, W. C. Fields, "It may not be the greatest thing in life or it may not be the smallest thing in life, but there is nothing exactly like it." And I believe this has been the experience of mankind. You smile when I say that, but it's true. No culture has ever been very rational when dealing with sex, although they have worked out various values and social controls to deal with it. When we talk about the contraceptive culture, we are talking about a society that has asked for planning, for a rational approach to something which is 90 percent irrational, and therefore problems will arise in many unexpected ways. I think we have to keep this in mind.

I like to regard sex as an attribute of the human person. We are all sexed persons in one way or another, most of the ways being distinguishable and fairly determinate. We have a few "intersex" persons, but not too many, and they don't set up the cultural norms. In general, young people are raised to become adults who conform to the present generation's ideas of what the terms *male* and *female* mean and what men and women should be. In a rapidly changing society, however, by the time the young people are age 20, they will be living under conditions and circumstances which do not correspond to the models their parents set for them.

Why is the contraceptive culture important here? It certainly calls for a redefinition of the female role and the uprooting of some old models. In the past, the role of women could be fairly well defined as the domestic role. This was not necessarily a matter of intelligence or cleverness; it was simply a biological demand. In order to maintain the continuity of the society, the average woman had to spend a good deal of her life having and rearing babies. As her mother had done, she married and settled down for a life that mainly involved producing one child after another. By the time she was through launching the last child, she felt pretty much like the salmon when it gets to the top of the stream—ready for the cannery.

In America at the turn of the century (which is really quite recently), by the time the last child was launched, in 50 percent of the marriages one of the partners was already dead. Today the average woman has her last baby before she is 27 and her children are well along in school by the time she is 40. With the great increase in medical care and good health in our present-day culture, a woman of 40 is good for at least forty-three or forty-four years more. In fact, I've often felt that if we are given any more antibiotics the modern female will be indestructible (*laughter*). This means, of course, that we have women asking, "What is my role now that only a relatively small proportion of my time is to be spent in the matter of having and raising children?" I think Catherine allots about ten years of child care to most modern women.

We're touching here on something that previously was taken for granted as a key organizing principle of our society, and we're seeing the need to redefine the meaning of sex, the meaning of masculinity and femininity, and the status and role of men and women. In the past, the whole matter of reproduction and procreation, like life and death, was left as an untouchable subject. It was a thing that just happened to you. Going into the sixteenth and seventeenth centuries, science dared not only to tackle nature, but medicine also began to deal experimentally with the human body. It is very interesting, for instance, that the first school to give formal training in obstetrics, founded about 1725 by a French woman, was considered a great horror by the whole populace and was driven out of existence. It was unthinkable to take a subject like this, openly discuss it, fool around with it, and presume you could formally train for it. It was untouchable and unmentionable. Only very recently could we cold-bloodedly sit down and be rational about this, or hope to be. We can plan now, but, if we do that, what does this mean to the woman who formerly had her role pretty well defined?

CATHERINE CHILMAN: It seems to me there are some other aspects here too. Probably it has occurred to most of you that the invention of the pill and the loop caused a very earth-shaking revolution, not just because contraception became simple and relatively cheap and was no longer connected with the time of intercourse, but also because for the first time women alone could completely control reproduction without the man needing to know anything about it at all. The other methods of contraception (unless a woman decided to have an abortion) took cooperation between the man and the woman. But now, with the pill and the loop, reproduction has become the business of women only. In the past, women were always dependent upon men. It was women who had to stand up for moral standards, largely because they were the ones who got pregnant and faced the consequences if moral standards were not upheld. Because they are no longer risking pregnancy, women may not feel the need to uphold the same moral standards. Women, whom I have long suspected are the stronger of the two sexes, now get into this vital decision-making which, because women were supposed to be physically weaker, used to be basically controlled by men.

In my opinion, the implications of this revolution require a great deal of thinking. Since I've worked for the government and have had some responsibility on this, I really have had nightmares about it. My daughter says the government ought to pay me for twenty-four-hours-a-day work because I'm always dreaming about these problems when I'm not working on them. I'm concerned about the tendency of a number of the people working in the family-planning field to work through maternal and child health programs and thus work only with the women. When we have the kind of contraception that only a woman uses, and can use without the man knowing it or even being consulted about it, I think we have the potential for further separating the male and female worlds and further undermining (which society is already doing) the man's feeling of being the strong and competent one.

In our culture, men have a great need to feel like heroes. Maybe this is a basic masculine need anyway. But with so many other things taking away from a man's sense of being a hero, when he doesn't need to be consulted even about reproduction, his masculinity seems to be very fundamentally attacked. This question was worrying me when I was the only woman on a task force for HEW. The others were almost all obstetricians, and I didn't know how to bring up this point with the distinguished doctors. So once I took a very strong drink at lunchtime, and at a meeting right after lunch I finally got up the nerve to say, "Gentlemen, a woman shouldn't need to tell you this, but talking about contraception only with women could very much undermine the sense of masculinity in men." They all looked at me in great puzzlement. After all, why *should* men be consulted when the contraceptives are for women? I said, "Well, you know, gentlemen, men do have a very big role in reproduction." Suddenly the dawn lit on a few faces, and they said, "You mean this could make a man feel less virile?" And I said, "Yes." Really, it had not hit them.

This is part of what I mean by the problem of specialization. To hear demographers talk, you would never think there was such a thing as sex. To hear economists talk, you'd never think there was such a thing as love or parenthood. Of course, ideally, men and women would sit down and talk over together what kind of contraception to use, and when to have their children, and how many to have. This should be a mutual thing. But it doesn't have to be.

Father John Thomas: That's a good point. You're telling us something that I have really felt myself. When you make a change of this kind, then you have to rethink a good many other patterns. One of them, of course, is what happens to the man in all of this. He has been set up as the aggressor, the courageous one, the dominant and decisive one, and then he finds that he is not planning anything. Does he end up just the cuckold? This has been one of the great concerns of men in many other cultures and, I would say, one of the main reasons for strict premarital control. In many cultures even today men put great value on marrying virgins. There is a very, very strong insistence on that. Now that we have interfered (and necessarily it seems to me) with the process of reproduction and have changed the patterns of sexual relations and of the family, we need to rethink man-woman relationships.

If you introduce contraceptive control, then the meaning of marital relations necessarily has to change. The stress can no longer be placed primarily upon holding a couple together because they are involved in a procreative enterprise, in the raising of children and so forth. This aspect of marriage assumes less importance—not that it becomes unimportant, just less important. What then is the meaning of sexual relations in marriage? The stress now tends to be placed upon the purely relational aspect. Two people are using marriage as a means of relating, the assumption being that this is a relatively easy thing to achieve. But it is not easy to achieve. I do not know of any culture in which men and women find it easy to communicate.

I used to believe when I was a young man that we were well on the way because we were talking about it a great deal. We're still talking about it a great deal. If you go into marriage counseling, however, you'll find that one of the major problems is that men and women can fall in love, and they can love each other very much, but they don't necessarily like each other very much. Yet they have to live together and communicate, and they do not find it very easy. Successful communication, after all, is a great achievement.

How do you make marital relations meaningful in a society which overemphasizes, through such media as *Playboy,* that people have genitals and breasts? Modern life has moved to an impersonal approach to all relationships. This has now hit sex very hard. The sexual act then becomes just a genital thing. There need be no real relationship, no deep involvement or commitment, and this follows in trend with our thought. What happens to the stability of marriage and the sense of fulfillment for the husband and wife if the stress is off procreation? How do we maintain meaningfulness and significance in the sexual act so that it becomes a symbol of the gradual growing unity of the couple throughout marriage? We pay little attention to that. We have not asked ourselves what the consequences of this new stress might be on the premarital level and what the feedback might be to the marital level in terms of marital stability.

What does it do to the man to live in an increasingly pseudo society during the formative years of his life? By this I mean living in a school system which is an artificial society. I don't believe we've even started to face the implications of putting our whole population of boys and girls together through the long formative years, which has come rapidly.

As late as 1940, a relatively small percentage of people got through high school. In 1900, only 6 percent of those in the eligible age group were actually going through high school in America. In 1940, probably 30 or 40 percent were doing so. A high school diploma is now almost universal in the United States. Then they go on to college. This means, however, that young people are kept apart and don't participate in an adult society. Moreover, boys and girls in the same age groups are not the same age physically and emotionally. The average girl is a year and a half to two years ahead of the average boy right through grade school, high school, and college. So the boy is simply passing from his mother's warm arms to those of a little girl who is physically two years ahead of him and is willing to mother him all over again. Because he really has not become fully male, he has not held a job; he has just been living in his artificial society for an increasingly long period of years.

Just the other day, my secretary remarked to me that she and her husband had gone to a show at Harvard that a great number of Harvard and Radcliffe students had attended. The thing that really struck her was that the girls had their arms around the boys. Now a woman puts her arms around the baby, you see, and here is a continuation of this pattern, this shifting of roles and relationships.

We speak about this female aggressiveness. The male was supposed to be aggressive; the female was not. The female today, however, may be just as highly educated as the male. She has discovered that she can protect herself from pregnancy and that she may have the same right to sexual pleasure as the male. So why should she not be decisive and aggressive? She is concluding that there's no real reason why she should not be so. This trend in thinking is taking place both on the premarital and marital levels. But what are the implications from the point of view of human fulfillment, which is one of our basic concerns? And what are the implications from the point of view of the stability of our institutions?

CATHERINE CHILMAN: We want to give you some time to join our discussion, so I'm just going to make a few comments and then hope you will all plunge in with your thoughts. We've been talking a bit as if contraception has just caused a lot of problems. Naturally, it offers tremendous amounts of freedom and the possibility for a much higher quality individual and family than we've known before. It's not as if it were a bad thing, but it raises new issues. Some of the larger of these issues are: Can human beings find the psychological strength to live with the kinds of freedom that our scientific society is creating? Can we stand the stress of nonproblem problems? Can we stand the anxieties created by solving concrete problems, leaving us with more abstract ones? (We are sometimes not even sure when we've solved them.) The problem of relations between the sexes is an example. We're free and there are all kinds of delightful possible relationships. Can we handle them? Well, these are some of our main comments, and we'd love to have you people join in now.

JOSEPH BIRD: One of the points that struck me in what you were saying, Dr. Chilman, was this question of the masculine image. To any of us who are dealing with married couples all the time, this is a very real problem. It seems it will be an increasingly difficult one as long as we have some who are proposing, as a means of coping with the population issue, a male pill or a male sterilization operation. The problem shows up more and more, particularly as vasectomies are becoming more and more prevalent in this country. Men often psychologically view vasectomies as a form of castration, and you see it even with such operations as prostatectomies. As one patient I remember, who was in his seventies and had had his prostate gland removed, put it, "I am now a eunuch." I think that any attempt to approach population control from the standpoint of the male, whether by temporary or permanent sterilization, is going to have very severe psychological effects on our culture. I have encountered this problem both in an institutional hospital setting and in private practice, and I would like to hear some of the views of those of you who have had to deal with it in your work.

VIRGINIA JOHNSON: This is nothing particularly new or different. The problem applies also to the female who undergoes menopause without preparation, reinforcement, or . . .

CATHERINE CHILMAN: Yes, I felt like saying, "Welcome to the club, boys" (laughter).

JOSEPH BIRD: Except for one thing. I think in our culture we have carried over from the past the idea that women are not necessarily supposed to be sexy, whereas men have been given the image, you know, of being virile and sexy and proving their prowess. This image is still being reinforced by the Hugh Hefners and others today.

FATHER JOHN THOMAS: Yes, and I think in some of the developing countries of the world this is still the accepted image. The male is the one who is sexy. In fact, he is not expected to control himself. He may channel his responsibility toward one woman as far as supporting the children goes, but aside from that he's free. Although the woman may complain about the situation a great deal, as an anthropologist mentioned to me, "If you'll notice closely, she's also bragging that her husband is this way." In other words, she has the same concept as he does of what real male virility is. If we really don't want to accept the male and female images and roles as they were defined in the past, if we want to change the actual social function of sexuality today, then we need to be mature enough to rethink what kinds of self-image for men and women are important and what kinds of relationships between men and women are important. This is obviously a very challenging problem with some tremendous possibilities. But, if we merely talk about gadgets—if we have a fixation about them—without reappraising basic questions, then we will be in serious trouble.

VIRGINIA JOHNSON: Father Thomas, this is perhaps not a terribly important point but I would like to comment on the pride of the female you were talking about. You know, this pride in her husband's role and ability. Well, she must be proud of something, and if this is all she can find to be proud of, what else is there? So it's more of a make-do technique.

FATHER JOHN THOMAS: Yes, but you see this is part of a larger pattern in a totally male oriented society in which the prestige and social position of the female are totally involved in her man. And that's true in many cultures to a certain degree. Even today in this country, if both husband and wife have a career, the wife always knows that if the baby gets sick, she stays home; he doesn't. His career is seemingly still more important than hers. In the matter of moving, how often does a couple move because of the wife's job? It is the husband's job, you know, that determines where they live. So in a sense you still have the idea that the male is the leader and prestige is more tied up with him and his position.

VIRGINIA JOHNSON: Yes, I was agreeing with you. I just

wanted to suggest that here's also simply an indication of the female's resilience and ability to adapt, in other words, to make something meaningful out of any given situation or at least have a wish to do so.

FATHER JOHN THOMAS: You mean "you're not much, but you're my only," as Shakespeare said (*laughter*).

KERMIT KRANTZ: If you really want to look at the contraceptive culture, I don't think you can speak about it in broad terms. You have to consider the context, the social and economic groups you are dealing with. Certainly the problems we face in this country with our ethnic groups are completely different from the problems the Australians would have to face, or the French or the Indians. I think if we wanted to discuss this, we could start by speaking about our Judeo-Christian tradition as it affects this nation.

CATHERINE CHILMAN: I think that's a very important point. Did you all hear his comments? If you are going to look at the contraceptive culture in different countries, you have to understand the particular groups that make up each one, and the particular problems involved. Of course, in this country you have so many problems, so many subcultures, by nationality, by religion, by region, by social class. And I'm sure that everyone here is aware that the subcultures of the very poor are extremely different in their attitudes toward what life is for, what values are important, or what life can be. I have been struck, in listening to the international groups working on strategies for family planning, by their tendency to think that if something happens a certain way in Taiwan, then you ought to be able to translate that to, say, what is happening or may happen in Peru. Countries appear to have common cultural elements only when you don't know very much about them. When you study a country in depth, the social, economic, and historical situations vary greatly. We cannot impose ways of acting and thinking based on our history and ethnic background on other people. Even in this country, we cannot impose the outlooks and patterns of one religious ethnic group on another. Take, for instance, the Negroes. They have a very different kind of total historical tradition, a very different attitude about who they are, where they came from, why they are here, and what this country is about. We need a tremendous amount of subtlety in our consideration of who people are and what they feel makes their lives meaningful.

KERMIT KRANTZ: Following your thought further, it is not uncommon for us to see in clinics a young man from a lower socioeconomic group for whom a real sense of self-importance, a real status symbol, comes from having as many women pregnant as he can. This, of course, would be something to be frowned on in our middle class because a sense of social responsibility has to go with this, and there are other, better outlets for ego-satisfaction. How can you deal with a young man like this without literally removing him from his society or raising his economic and social level? The problem becomes more difficult the lower his intellectual capacity is. We deal with a great group of people who are uneducable; their IQs are 50 and 60. How can you cope with this group? How do you communicate with them? Many of them are just cast-offs from society. Society has turned its back on them. These people have sifted slowly down and, as we now know, some of them can perpetuate their own group rather rapidly. For instance, in our own mental institutions we have mongoloid idiots breeding mongoloid idiots. You try and deal with that group.

WINFIELD BEST: I was wondering, I guess, whether our concern here is for the normal or for the abnormal. It seems to me that there's enough to be concerned about in terms of the relationship between normal men and women and helping them with family planning without going into the abnormalities of the intellectually deprived or the abnormalities of the socially deprived. That area has in itself a whole different set of challenges and difficulties. I think we need to set a focus here on the problems of normal psychology rather than the problems of abnormal psychology in relationship to family planning.

FATHER JOHN THOMAS: One of the problems, however, is that in any society we have what we call the lower 10 percent. The people in this group have very few rewards in life. One of the few real areas in which they have a sense of freedom and human expression is in their marital relations and in their family life. We can help these people by introducing health care when their babies are growing up, but we haven't been able to enlarge their horizon, making it possible for them to find other meaningful goals and outlets for their lives. A large family fulfills a very definite, important function for them. It gives a significance and direction to their lives, and if we want to go in there and try to limit the number of children they have, then we have to replace the motivations and values we are taking away with others. We have to give these people other definitions of what it is to be a man or a woman or other concepts of responsibility in marriage and in bringing up children. I think in any society you can only destroy what you can replace. There's such a complex of things we have to deal with. One thing I've been worried about in our own society is the tendency of the state legislatures to force sterilization on somebody who shows irresponsibility. On the other hand, I do not ignore the frightening problems of the relatively large segment of the population that might decide to be irresponsible. If you were to take this into international relations, you might run into relatively huge segments of the international population and decide that, as long as you were helping them out, they would have to be responsible. This could raise some very serious problems from the point of view of the democratic approach.

ANNE SHEFFIELD: It seems to me that one thing everybody who has spoken has emphasized is the need for different approaches to different social groups in terms of contraceptive culture. But that is forgetting that one unifying theme runs through all this: the desire on the part of women using contraception to decide on the number of children they are going to have. They want to use contraception; they all share this feeling. Also, there have been several comments about the fact that we mustn't tear down values without creating others to take their place; we mustn't be destructive without being constructive. But, again, it seems to me that most women who want to use contraception want to use it for very constructive reasons. They want to make more of their lives and do more for their children. I really think that's a very constructive beginning already.

FATHER JOHN THOMAS: Well, I would have to differ a bit there. I think we have been fooled by seeing the statistics from other countries on the number of women who say they would like to limit the size of their families. Because it seems that although women will tell you, yes, they want to have fewer babies and so forth, it is doubtful how much real effort they will make to use contraception. After all, women are capable of reproducing over a very long span of years, and family planning except for sterilization takes a lot of cooperation and a lot of consistent effort on the part of individual couples. It takes a lot of motivation and responsible concern. We have to be careful not to oversimplify the problem when we are looking at the studies done in India, for example, where it seems that many women would like fewer children. But looking at the actual progress of family-planning programs, it appears that either they really don't want smaller families or they just don't have enough motivation to do very much about it. Of course, in some cultures, as in parts of India, it's not up to the couple; it's all up to the mother-in-law. She's the one who lays down the law. Even in our middle-class Anglo-Saxon culture, we have a great deal of contraceptive failure despite the fact that many relatively effective and easy-to-use methods are available.

I think also you could make a very, very strong case that many of our population-control methods which we have exported to other countries have gone to people who are already concerned about and practicing family planning and are merely interested in changing to newer, more effective methods, rather than going to those who really need motivation and decision. I believe a lot of demographers would go along with that. Don't you think so?

So it's a very complex problem. In the developing countries, which have very, very suddenly been hit with a population problem because of our introduction of health care, we need to find a way of measuring the motivation of women to practice family planning and to give them more motivation by creating new opportunities and some other rewards. I have a thesis (with which Dr. Bird will probably disagree) that in Western society the use of contraception grew and spread because mothers saw that if they had fewer children, the children they had would get more education and could move up in life. I call it the invisible revolution, because it had no support at all. It was against the opinion of all the important politicians, philosophers, and religious leaders. But this was because opportunities for advancing in society were already opened up, you see, in the sixteenth and seventeenth centuries. But if the opportunities are not yet offered to the people, as in so many of the cultures today, then practicing family planning, you see, is not so meaningful.

DONALD BARRETT: I'm not sure this is entirely relevant, but in data we've accumulated in the last four months for Colombia (I can't give you actual figures except from our coding experience), in a representative cross section of Colombian women, by far the vast majority in the fecundity ages have not only considered but have actually attempted some form of fertility regulation. I'm trying to support the premise that Anne Sheffield was suggesting here a moment ago, that regardless of social class, religious involvement, and such, there is consideration and evaluation of the need, the desire, the possibility, and the variety of ways to control fertility. In the lower classes a wide variety of methods are used. Some women will admit that they have used abortion as a method of control; they have used Meheral (a form of aspirin); and lemon juice. They use all kinds of effective and ineffective methods. It is also interesting that the men with fertile wives are also apparently highly motivated to control fertility. It's only the men whose wives have finished their fertility years who seem to be a little more unconcerned about this. They've been through this; they have had 10 or 15 children; they're no longer committed to considering fertility regulation or family planning in an effective way. But those who are actually involved in the process of what Reuben Hill calls the "development stage" of family building are strongly committed to it. But, as Father Thomas was saying, it has different meaning for different people. Some of these women have been contacted by doctors in Colombia concerning the use of pills. But this involves taking a pill every day, which is unfamiliar to them. They'll do this for a while and then it doesn't make any difference. They prefer ways that are familiar to them. One woman preferred to keep going to her healer every week for advice. He would give her some medication which would prevent conception. It turns out to be a calcium type of thing like chalk. As you know, there's a lot of eating of dirt among the lower classes.

Nonetheless, I think you've a point that the desire, the need, the perception, the understanding are there. There are different means, however, and the strength of commitment to innovations—what we might call technical contraception—is quite different from culture to culture. I do think that at a certain level we can discuss a contraceptive culture in a realistic way. I think women are trying to make their lives better.

KERMIT KRANTZ: If you want to follow that through, ever since man has been on this earth, he has been playing this game. The only difference is that technology, as you said, Father Thomas, has upset the applecart. We are now keeping these children alive, as Dr. Chilman said. Maternal and child health has now disturbed the balance, so more of these youngsters are surviving the first year of life. The studies coming out of the Congo right now, I think, show this beautifully. Where is it that only 1 out of 5 was surviving the first year? Then the World Health Organization moved in, and now it's 2 or 3 out of five. They don't even have food for them. We have been able to do this. This is a man-made deal.

WILLIAM LIU: I really hate to break this very interesting session, but the coffee's ready and the housekeeper is very worried. So let's have coffee. We adjourn till 4 o'clock, folks. At 4 o'clock we have another session.

The Impact of Contraceptive Culture 2

WILLIAM T. LIU AND RUTH H. USEEM

Monday, 4:00 P.M.

JULIAN SAMORA: We turn now to the impact of this so-called contraceptive culture. I am assuming that the impact our speakers will be discussing is the impact on the individual, the family, and society, but I may be totally wrong. It is my distinct pleasure to introduce to you my two friends and professional colleagues, Dr. Ruth Useem, Research Professor of Sociology and Anthropology, Michigan State University, and Dr. William Liu, Director, Institute for the Study of Population and Social Change, University of Notre Dame. The format will be essentially the same as that of the previous session. Dr. Liu will speak first.

WILLIAM LIU: There are many ways to assess the consequences of the mass use of contraception. After our conference here last December on the family and fertility, the *National Observer* published a special issue which evaluated the impact of the pill on various groups. To the reproductive biologist, for example, the pill has yet to be surpassed by any other known contraceptive device. It is important not only because of its effectiveness, which has been demonstrated, but also because of its revolutionary concept. That is to say, the pill, unlike most conception-prevention devices prior to it, does not require decisions and precautions prior to each and every sex act. Hence it is independent of the prevailing relationship between a man and a woman. It is completely controlled by the woman, and its usage is not affected by the dominance-subordination relationship between the husband and the wife before, during, or after the sex act. The new generation of contraceptives, therefore, will have a greater impact on the lives of women, not because of their technological and safety factors, but because of their immediate effects on the husband-wife relationship.

To the demographer the effect of mass conception control is the decline of fertility which usually follows the decline of mortality. To the economist this means fewer but better consumers. To the politician it means vested interest groups over age 65, pushing for welfare and other social legislation directly related to the changing phenomena of the elderly in a society.

In the past forty years, writers have described increasingly far reaching consequences of mass contraception and declining fertility. Back in the 1930s, Warren S. Thompson discussed the economic implications. I remember I used to read his textbook and be able to parrot it back to the professor during examinations. Later I began to think of other implications.

In the 1940s Ogburn and Nimkoff wrote on technology and the changing family and described wider effects on family life resulting from contraception. One of the rarest things that David Riesman demonstrated, using statistical evidence, was that there actually is a changing American character. This analysis probably came closest to today's discussions of the psychological or sociopsychological impact of contraceptives.

The type of population behavior is related to the type of social behavior and social character. I think it is about time for us to take a good look at many of these problems at closer range. Like many people, I am convinced that the growing pressures of family planning in all countries of the world will cause a much more rapid pace of social change everywhere, and many of society's institutional patterns, besides family life, will have to be altered. We will soon be confronted by problems which may not even have been considered in previous conferences.

It would be indeed presumptuous for me to make any forecast as to what modal interpersonal relations we can anticipate in a society characterized by a contraceptive mentality. That would be like graduate students in sociology wishing to explain what Max Weber has said about the Protestant ethic. When Weber talked about the Protestant ethic he did not mean merely those belief systems of people who are Protestants. Being a Protestant does not necessarily give the person the ethic that Weber was talking about. What he meant was that there is a peculiar motivation, a commitment to achievement—especially economic achievement—concomitant with the logic of the age of reformation. The specific combination of reason, rationality, and economic competition gave the era of the Protestant ethic its vigor.

I began to think about the contraceptive mentality in the same way and wonder how it might affect patterns of social and family life. Not all people in a contraceptive society practice contraception all the time, nor do they necessarily place conception prevention above other values. But the circular effect of family planning and conjugal relations, each reinforcing the other, will, over a long period of time, change the specific course of biosocial development in human cultures.

There are certain actions which satisfy biological needs and which have also acquired tremendous social implications.

Take eating, for example. It satisfies a basic biological need. However, when it accompanies certain religious holidays, when we invite people to our homes and make them welcome and celebrate with a special meal, such as turkey at Thanksgiving, eating takes on a biosocial meaning.

The contraceptive mentality, as I foresee it (I said I wasn't going to forecast anything), will generate a kind of cultural system which we can tentatively term a *contraceptive culture*. (I think Ruth is going to argue about that point. I really can't say I'm totally convinced of everything I will say here today, but I think it might be a good thing to say what kind of culture I think this would be.)

The cultural system which might result from the contraceptive mentality will be, if I may speculate, one in which the individual's reason does not increase as fast as the system demands. The individual is caught up in the affairs of everyday life and cannot reason about the greater ends he serves. In fact, he often carries out apparently rational actions without any idea of the end they serve.

For example, we talk about the inequality between the sexes, not only in this country, but also in many underdeveloped countries. We talk about how such inequalities can be removed by the mass use of contraception and by the removal of the unwanted burden of pregnancy. We also talk about how the socioeconomic systems of underdeveloped countries, as well as those in the well-developed countries, have imposed upon the lives of women in such a way that they always come out at the short end of the deal; they come out dependent.

To be equal simply means to be independent or interdependent, anything but dependent. By that I mean that if a relationship is not dependent—if it is independent or interdependent—it simply means that there is, and should be, in conjugal relations, a total separateness. Only such separateness can allow individual choice and freedom, the kind of conjugal interaction we have long desired. I will come back to this point in a minute. One condition I'm talking about is a particularly desired state in which men-women relationships can have their fullest expression. This condition is the development of self-awareness through empathy. This is exactly what we're talking about, since interdependence and reciprocal mutuality imply separateness, rather than oneness, in being. Separateness of the physical entities has been misidentified as what psychiatrists such as Otto Rank call "birth trauma," or the breakdown of primary relations as suggested by Cooley and Faris. The empirical concept of *anomie* is used by Leo Srole and other people who talk about the lack of integration of the individual into a society. That is to say, only in societies which allow maximum individual separateness can we have the fullest expression of equality between women and men in the marital state. I am not saying that I am making this point clear now, because I think it will take some time for me to elaborate it in greater detail.

The first condition under which this *can* happen (I'm not sure if we should ask, "Is this good or is this bad?"; I always say, "If this is good, for what?"), this independence or interdependence, is the maximum separateness of the individual in a society.

The second condition that would probably result in a contraceptive culture is the maximum expression of what I call spontaneous mutuality. By spontaneous mutuality I mean the interaction between any two individuals. It is always a contingent interaction; it does not follow any prescribed status, nor any division of sex or age. That is to say, there is no such thing as a standard response pattern between the subordinate and the superordinate. It follows that two individuals must maximize interaction because of the particular personality (or what Arnold Green has called the cult of personality) in conjugal relations, which seems to be valued in a contraceptive culture. So the second condition under which a contraceptive culture (or equality of the sexes) can have its fullest expression would be a maximum expression of spontaneous mutuality.

Having set these two conditions, the job is to find out some of the consequences. For one thing, privacy is very much valued, because in essence a relationship built upon spontaneous mutuality is an ever-changing one. It is a relationship of persons. Since persons are constantly changing and expanding, they must perpetually be building themselves new norms. A stable relationship is merely a relationship with a greater degree of shared experience, not a relationship of two stable psychological states.

There is no single, fixed form through which to express such relationships. There are perhaps a number of different forms for each successive state of the relationship. At each stage in turn, the memories of previous shared experiences define new relationships, such as deeper mutual trust or stronger conviction. Such relationships represent a set of successive stages of personal and emotional involvement, woven of explorations of the other's mind, of linguistic cues, and so on. Therefore, the important desired goal in a society characterized by a contraceptive culture is to know the other person.

This is much more important than anything else: to know a person, to share his experience, to establish a relationship based on mutual identification. I do not mean understanding the autistic world of the other person. I mean, rather, understanding the inner core of the person through the web of spontaneous mutuality over an extended period of time. Only through this extended period of time can the presentation of the self be the whole self. The identification of self is an identification with mutual experience rather than with the relationship itself.

Shared past experience entails continued interaction

through many functional activities which somehow are fused into a web of communication. A relationship based on one bond, one hinge, neither requires nor results in knowing or sharing. There seems to be a paradox here. On one hand, you want to know more about the other person. On the other hand, it becomes more and more difficult to get the precious things we seek in our interpersonal relationships. Therefore, this enhances our desire to know and, at the same time, to protect our inner self. In a way, it is difficult to know the other person because of the segmentary, ever-changing relationship.

It must be remembered that spontaneous mutuality originating in this type of cultural development has its roots in technological developments and in the value of individualism. Its form of expression emerges from ascetic Protestantism. It was transmuted into a sensitivity to the rights of others, the real ultimate goal of individualism. The insistence on privacy is manifested in skill in presenting the self, a self differentiated from the naked self with its conscious separateness and social character. Privacy now not only gives a person an assurance of individuality, but it also gives certain refinements and a moral penetration into marital relationships, including conjugal love. This development may be attributed largely to the peculiar importance of spontaneous affection in marriage. The voluntary nature of mutual responses requires a kind of relationship prevented by the insistence on privacy.

UNIDENTIFIED PARTICIPANT: Say that again. I didn't get that last point.

WILLIAM LIU: The insistence on privacy between husband and wife is, I think, obvious in this society. You can talk about it in terms of examples. In some cultures, privacy is not that important. It would be very difficult for a Filipino, for instance, to understand why each child must have its separate bedroom, or for a Chinese to know why there must be a door on the bathroom. Such privacy may not be important to these people. It is important to us because of our respect for the rights of others, because of our lack of dependency and because of our insistence on separateness. All of these, I think, are clustered together. I must say it gives rise to, and also reinforces, the concept of a contraceptive culture.

Finally, may I just very quickly say that the last implication of the insistence on separateness—of spontaneous mutuality, of privacy—is that it will give rise to humanitarianism, that is, voluntary humanitarianism, which can be found in the West and in the West only, not in the East. We need effective linkage, and when, because of our insistence on privacy, effective linkage is denied in the normal course of marriage, it is only logical that it find expression in voluntary humanitarianism, in organized humanitarianism. This is why some of my writings mention that humanitarian enterprises are only to be found in countries where a Protestant culture predominates.

So, my summarization is (I'm sorry I have to make it very short) that the contraceptive culture has these consequences and conditions: We become more aware of ourselves and yet we find it difficult to identify. We even find it difficult to identify what is femininity and masculinity. Psychologists use various tests, but the conceptual framework is still weak and lacking. For instance, in the semantic differential test used by psychologists we find that what is male or masculine is tough and strong in contrast to femininity which must be weak and tender, and so on. Usually, however, the results of such tests do not indicate that the opposite of maleness is femaleness. Our experience with many of the psychological tests on femininity and masculinity reminds me of the Chinese characters in which all the good words related to femininity are composites of the terms themselves and the word *child*. In other words, if a woman is with a child, it is always good. We can see how concepts shape the linguistic images of people in a culture which has persisted for many years. In other words, we find it difficult eventually to identify the self because of the separateness of the conjugal pair, on which we insist.

Second, the need for spontaneous mutuality does not necessarily bring a perfect state of marital relations. It is like anything else. Once you become aware of the deprivation, then its fulfillment is a relative concept. It has its snowball effect. (Again, I am saying this in terms of what we anticipate, not that this is bad or good.) Third, we have become more insistent on individual privacy, which is related to reason, to rationality. Fourth, I can forecast ever-expanding humanitarian enterprises in a society characterized by a contraceptive culture.

I think that will get me into all sorts of trouble (*laughter*).

RUTH USEEM: May I ask Bill a question? In the societies I've known, other than the United States, spontaneity in expression and keeping a certain degree of privacy has ordinarily come between persons of the same sex, between friends. I don't know of any society that does not have some kind of relationship along these lines. It usually is not the husband-wife relationship. What is unique is that American culture imposes this relationship on the husband and wife, not on the grandmother and grandchild, two friends, two women in a family, or two men in a family. What you've described is what is done by male homosexuals (and some of my friends are) who feel that they can have this kind of relationship without the other problems. It is a cheap form of contraception (*laughter*). Very effective.

WILLIAM LIU: Let me respond to the idea raised by Ruth. I think it's a very good idea. I think that one invariable result (which I think Ruth will touch upon) will be the age-graded relationship, which I did not talk about. I think in a society characterized by a contraceptive culture, the emphasis will invariably be placed on the conjugal roles rather than on the parent-child relationship. This is fine, except that in a society in which you have various types of relationships—sibling relationships, parent-child, husband-wife, friend and friend, authority-subordinate relationships—you cannot have an equal degree of emphasis. Certainly we are not talking about the same kind of relationship. Once the concern of the larger collectivity, namely, the society as a whole, has been shifted from the parent-child relationship to the conjugal relationship, then we know we are searching for a kind of relationship which is different from any we knew before. That is, we cannot take anything for granted. The relationship of these two people, the stability of the institution, does not depend upon the division of labor, on the economic complementarity of husband and wife. It depends primarily upon how well these two psychological entities can interact and fulfill ever-changing needs. Now what happens if this is the case . . . (I had one thought here which I just lost.) The emphasis on conjugal relations will, by and large, determine the kinds of family norms. This is something I don't know how to continue, but maybe I can come back to it later.

RUTH USEEM: Let me just say that I think it's good, but it may be that in a highly mobile world one person happens to be the *only* person who has any continuity with you. And you can explain it structurally: in a highly mobile world, your husband or wife is the only person left. If you can't get along, then you jettison that one and hunt another one. But in a . . . Well, maybe I had better give my talk (*stands*). I have to stand up because I find it is an American culture pattern that when you sit down you whisper, and when you stand up you talk loud, so . . . I am going to try to develop what I think is a different concept of culture. To begin with, as I told my husband, the very term *contraceptive culture* threw me for a loop (*laughter*). And it just so happened that Yuen Tien from Illinois was at our house on Sunday and he had a loop for a tie-clasp and so he gave it to me to wear here for this meeting (*indicates pin on her dress*).

KERMIT KRANTZ: You know it's no good there (*laughter*).

RUTH USEEM: At my age, it doesn't make any difference.

KERMIT KRANTZ: You never know.

RUTH USEEM: God forbid . . .

I would say that everyday life is so messy and so complex and so full of happenings that all the things that happen cannot be classified as culture. A culture is simply, to me at least, the significant summaries of experience which then act as guidelines for behavior, which is different from culture. And so I'd like to go back a long way in history and take a look at what we think of as a preliterate society. It was relatively small; almost all relationships were face to face; and family and society were one and the same. As a matter of fact, the society even got its womenfolk from outside or imported its men from outside. Within this society everyone was related to everyone else. It was small, and it was pretty largely based upon human energy. What I would call gender roles were closely related to sexual and procreation roles. Women in a preliterate society never lived as long as I've lived. They died in childbirth. They spent most of their life in the childbearing period.

Moving from a preliterate to a literate society does not mean that all behavior rises to the level of a literate society. So you have something like this. You have increasingly complex social organization, but at the same time not every person that comes into the social organization is knowing and caring. By the time you were age 6 in a preliterate society, you were an adult in every role except perhaps the sexual procreation role. Preliterate societies had what I call a reverse adolescence. You assumed adult occupational roles prior to assuming adult family roles, and you had a reverse adolescence. But as a society gets more and more complex, you increase the length of time that you have to socialize and bring persons up to the top of the society. But great numbers of them never make it, so I feel that what they call subcultures are really fall-off cultures. (It's just like poverty. The poor ones keep going around and around.) The mark of a civilization, in contrast to a preliterate society, is the number of parasites that it can keep alive. A preliterate society could not have anyone in it who was not either currently making a contribution or potentially able to do so. A civilization can keep alive those who do *not* make a contribution, including those who potentially will *never* make a contribution.

As we move in our complex civilization, family and society are not coterminous. (This is what I thought you were talking about at first, Bill.) We have the development of privacy, not of the large family, but of the small unit. This disagrees with what Father Thomas said, because I think much that is passed on in the modern American family is not culture but is uniquely related to the personal impulses and feelings of drop-off people, particularly women, who are cut off from participation in the culture and have the privacy of the small family in which to wreak havoc or wreak good on the small ones. This is why I think we have so many battered children and why we have so many hippies. The sheer small size of the family means that the children are thereby more tied up, or hung, on a woman whom we have left in the privacy of a home.

As I sometimes put it, I used to hate it when springtime came in Lansing, because in the long winters the windows were closed and I could yell at my kids to my heart's content. But just let the windows be opened and I had a different kind of relationship with my kids, because I felt the pressures of the cultural norms as to how mothers ought to behave. I think this is different from individual privacy. I would also argue that what privacy we have in the home is pretty much set by walls, by things you can't see through, whereas privacy in the Indian home (and I don't know the Chinese family) comes from having your body there but not your mind or your thoughts. So if you go into an Indian home people will sit and stare at you, but you are never introduced because you are not in their world. You are all in a 20 by 20 foot room—three generations, sometimes two or three brothers, sometimes unmarried women —and you maintain the privacy of the self by ignoring that which is irrelevant. So I have a feeling that our privacy here has enabled more of us to invade the privacy of the small child. I think this is what the hippies are rebelling against. This is what they are hung up on. The trouble with the hippies is they think all of us are their mothers, but their mothers are not part of the culture.

It seems to me that in addition to this, as we're getting a more complex society based less and less on human energy, we have to begin to divide gender roles from sex and procreation roles. Gender roles are what you might call masculine-feminine; and sex and procreation roles are what you might call maleness and femaleness. (I'll let our other friends take care of this.) These are learned, too, but gender roles are reflections of social organization, social experience, and, to some extent, culture. But gender roles, I think, are infinitely variable. I have a feeling that in the privacy of the home, and certainly some of our small-group people find this, the women are masculine and the men are feminine. The minute they close the front door, the man becomes masculine and helps his wife into the car, even though you know she just carried out all the garbage cans (*laughter*).

We have a difference here, and I'm saying that the cultural definition on the outside is not necessarily at work on the inside. I think that the contraceptive culture, if it is a culture, is very often a mighty small subculture of one person. It will become a culture, I think, when we make significant summaries of it, and this is what then will, in a sense, predict the future. So far, the significant summaries of these happenings have been made by economists, physicians, and others; not by social scientists, who have been trying primarily to summarize what's happening statistically but not to make a cultural phenomenon of it. In other words, they want to know how many do what, where. Until this is shared by the participants themselves, it does not become part of culture even if 100 percent of them do it.

Let me give you an example of this. We interviewed 190 Americans overseas in India, and 100 percent of them claimed that they were not typical Americans. They knew this because the Indians had told them. The Indians said: "You're not like the other Americans that come over here." Now, the thing is that the stereotype, the cultural myth, did go on, despite the fact that there was a 100 percent deviation. I think this helps explain why we can have a change in culture and no change in behavior. We can have a lot of change in behavior without a great deal of change in culture. (Did I say that right or reverse it? Okay.)

I think, in contrast to most societies of the world, our women are caught up in the kind of privacy which is spelled *lonesomeness* in which they are hunting what John Gagnon calls homosociality. This is found within the family in many other societies of the world. I think we are going to have both a masculine world and a feminine world. Certainly, as some of them break out, we are going to have a subculture within each.

Consequently, I am much concerned about the summaries which are made of this, in part because we are living in a highly interdependent world. What I see happening does not jibe with what others have said up here. What I see happening is a series of cultures which were separate now being connected by what might look like a moving band, and forming a third culture of highly mobile people. In this, sex is what we've got going for us.

It seems that people who have very different definitions of sex roles according to culture can still get together. I have one student who has just finished a study of 200 cross-marriages between Indians and Westerners in India, and the reports are that they have a little trouble with their gender roles because the gender roles are related to the culture. The sex roles they seem to be able to get together on.

Similarly, we have a number of children throughout the world who are, literally, bastards, being born now in Viet Nam and Korea, as we had them earlier in Japan. Because these children are what I would call the bastard children of this highly mobile worldwide population, I think this is going to have an effect on the way we take humanitarian responsibility.

When we separate sex and gender roles we will also separate progenitor and parent roles. We've done this for many hundreds of years in Japan where we have adopted a son when we don't have one. I think we will separate these two, that is, the sexual, progenitor role from the parent role. In many ways this is what we've already done in Kibbutzism in Israel. There we have a family with its own incest taboos developed among people who are not related to each other. I frankly think (Jessie Bernard's heard me talk on this one) that some of the so-called rules of marriage within one's own group are simply the social incest taboos of today. I think we have perhaps too many people who have made their summaries of it. These summaries are not yet shared by the people who are acting, but I think we ought to go ahead and do it.

WILLIAM LIU: I just want to clarify two points. I still insist that there is such a thing as a contraceptive culture. I think a discrepancy between external behavior and what one might believe is the right thing to do, or what one might do, does not mean that there is no such culture. If the discrepancy does exist more often than not in a society, I would say there must be something at work here. I don't exactly know what it is but I call it culture. I used to criticize David Riesman all the time, but I began to think that he did have something to say when he related population growth trends and the social behavior of individuals in the society. I think the discrepancy between one's belief system and what one might do precisely indicates the conformity of other-directedness. I think perhaps this is the thing we have missed in our evaluation of his early work, not to speak of the fact that I admire his writing style, which is terribly important in social science today.

I think Ruth said that the word *privacy* as she understands it, namely, privacy of the nuclear family itself, provides a very important place for affective exchange for members of the family. The privacy I mentioned earlier is mainly a matter of the individual's psychological behavior. I think the distinction is well made. However, my point was that privacy in both cases is valued in a society characterized by a contraceptive culture. In some of the societies I know about, people are not afraid to wash the dirty linen in front of the neighbors. They do shout at each other when the windows are up during the summer, simply because there's very little to be gained by hiding the secrets of the family. Moreover, external appearances, putting your best foot forward, does not make that much difference in the lives of people in such societies. There are enough black sheep in the family to make that unimportant. On the other hand, it is logical to think that when you put the emphasis on conjugal relations, vis-à-vis parent-child relationships, the family becomes the center of affective exchange, and this is more important than the economic function, which is supposed to be the function of the family in other societies.

Insofar as privacy is concerned, I think it is important for people to hide their feelings; for instance, when a man tells his wife that her dress is pretty, and all that. This becomes a routine response because of the demands of the culture, because wives expect it. I have never told my wife her dress is pretty because I don't have to. In Chinese families such affective exchanges are lacking in the language. (I can't find it.) Therefore, if you try to use the same standard to judge the husband and wife relationship in an American family and in a Chinese family, or in a Filipino family for that matter, you'll find there is a great difference.

I cannot convince myself that American husbands and wives are better related to one another, that such affective relationships are more satisfactory, than the husband and wife relationships in other cultures. Sometimes people are so tired they don't want to say anything, but that simply does not mean that the lack of affective exchange will be detrimental to family relations. This is why I have criticized earlier studies of marital adjustment by such people as Burgess. In their adjustment scales, they have such questions as "Have you kissed your wife this morning?" or "How often do you kiss your wife?" I think that this is very much a culturally shaped behavior pattern rather than an indication of affectivity.

RUTH USEEM: Well, I think the cultural norm is that homes are the place of affection. I think the reality is something different. Homes are the place where you have your problems. I find, for example (and I'd like to have other people check on this), among my young people, as the result of contraception possibilities, that they're asking for the perfect mate and the perfect children. They will have neither because they will not take a risk on anything less than perfect. I think this is going to reduce the size of families more than anything else, because unless young people can have the perfect child, they are not going to have any. I have seen this kind of thing develop just within the last four years.

WILLIAM D'ANTONIO: I'm Bill D'Antonio of Notre Dame. Sociology. Ruth, could you clarify your interesting finding on the mixed-nation marriages of Indians and non-Indians? If I understand you correctly, you're saying that they're well adjusted sexually, but their gender roles—that is, their culturally defined roles—are giving them trouble. Now does this mean that they free themselves from some prior cultural definition of their sex roles, or that you don't believe their sex roles were ever culturally defined?

RUTH USEEM: I don't think they were that much defined and were not open to some experimentation. (You know, if the Puritans were so puritanical they never could have had children.) At any rate, I'm trying to say that it isn't that they have trouble, but this is the place where they are creating new forms of the husband-wife relationship. The interesting thing about these cross-cultural marriages is that many of them are the second and third marriages. At first they tried the family type and it didn't work. They were divorced, or sometimes the wife died. Then, like Ambassador Reichauer, you try the other kind. Instead of having their own biological children, Mrs. Reichauer set up an orphanage. She has a new kind of parental role in her peculiar kind of cross-cultural marriage. These people are freed, let's say, of the Irish Catholic or Italian Catholic or Lutheran Protestant definition that only a person who is born to us can belong to us. These people, especially in their second and third marriages (some in their first), are creating new forms of relationships which I think will be culturally defined. The interesting thing is that they get together. This has been true in this country. We have organizations of GIs with their British brides, or GIs with their Japanese brides, or GIs with some other kind of bride. We have communities of Negro-white marriages. They are creating a new kind of group instead of an ethnic group. I'm saying these are just new forms, individually tried out, and when they begin to be shared, they become a kind of culture.

JULIAN SAMORA: Any other questions anybody?

JESSIE BERNARD: I'd like to say that I think this concept of spontaneous mutuality is terrific. It has lots of implications, and it ties in with some of the things Ruth is saying too. In the past, marital relationships were what some people called segregated. I call them parallel. Husbands and wives were not supposed to interact very much. Their roles were defined by institutional norms—she did what she had to do and he did what he had to do, and they had plenty of privacy. But we didn't think of it in those terms. They just didn't have much need for interactions. But now, we have a totally different concept of husband and wife relationships, one that women particularly want and men sort of hold back on because it's very hard. It is a kind of interaction. What women long for is this spontaneous mutuality for which we really haven't worked out patterns. It's very hard to achieve, and I agree it requires a withdrawal and privacy. You know, you have to extend yourself in this kind of thing. Then you have to reveal yourself and reciprocate. It's by no means an easy thing, and quite new. We haven't learned how to manage.

RUTH USEEM: I think spontaneous mutuality, by its very definition, is not cultural, or else it is not spontaneous. I agree with you on this one.

JESSIE BERNARD: No, the point is that culture makes it possible. In some cultures, it isn't even possible to have this kind of relationship. In our culture it's becoming possible to be acultural and to have this relationship.

RUTH USEEM: It is possible to be acultural, I think, partly because of the privacy. As long as you have this, you're all right. But, as you say, if you get into a neighborhood, your kids go off and tell your neighbors what you do. I feel much better about my spontaneous mutuality with my husband since I no longer have children at home.

JESSIE BERNARD: You give an awfully grim picture of your home (*laughter*).

RUTH USEEM: It never was. It was a ball! (*laughter*). But I never had any daughters so I don't know what might have happened. All I know is that boys are so physical that we wore out a good many bits of household furniture. But what I'm trying to say is that we do allow for this, but this is the only thing we can have with high mobility in a group that also uses contraceptives and family planning.

JOSEPH BIRD: Well, I have comparable difficulty with this phrase or concept *contraceptive culture*. If there can be so many different ways in which husbands and wives relate to one another, we have an infinite number of possibilities. Contraception introduces a very fundamental new technique and variable and value, as was said in the last session. Women can make the decision regardless of what the man thinks about it, and so on. I would raise this question. The question is not "Is marriage, is family perhaps now viable in our culture?" The question is "How is it viable? *How* is family viable in our culture?" If we look at it from an institutional perspective, the law has the function of trying to define the limits of acceptable behavior. Where do the limits of acceptable behavior come? As we try to answer the question of how family life becomes viable in this changing, innovative culture, we should perhaps be examining the indexes of abortion, the indexes of serial marriage, the indexes of venereal disease—perhaps among teen-agers—and various similar indexes, to see how this innovation actually begins to change the whole orientation of male-female relationships from an institutional perspective. The second question (which is related to this) is in the social-psychological dimension. We ask the brutal question: "Why should a young man or woman get married at all?"

UNIDENTIFIED PARTICIPANT: They don't.

JOSEPH BIRD: If we try to answer this question, perhaps we can perceive what this innovation of contraception really means. Then what do we look at here? If we take from an institutional perspective the questions what can be tolerable in a society, and then from a more social-psychological and personalistic point of view, why should we get married at all—these are the questions that are going through college students' minds right now.

RUTH USEEM: Yes. I wrote down something here I don't know the answer to, but I felt that throughout our talk there's a great feeling that we are making the assumption women do not want to be pregnant, do not have an impulse to be pregnant. I think this may be true after you have a number of children. But I find among the young girls of high school and college age that there is a real impulse, a need, to be pregnant —not to have children, but to be pregnant. Of course, there are a number of older women who are perennially pregnant because they don't want to be real mothers of children. They just want to have babies, because then they get a lot of attention and get out of PTA because they've got a little baby at home. They get out of carrying on the other gender roles of school teaching and working and all of these because they've got a little baby they have to take care of. Well, I think what you are raising here, then, is that since contraception has been thought (at least among young men) to be the duty of the girl, the girl can also use this to entrap a man. Clark Vincent has some studies of this. I have many girls who want to be pregnant and have a child who don't want a husband at all.

JESSIE BERNARD: Of course, a great many young people are living together outside of marriage and they only get married (they're very responsible, most of them) when they do want children. You mentioned measuring trends in terms of institutional outcome. Marriage is doing very, very well at the present time. If you want to measure our society in terms of what's happening to marriage, it's very successful. The proportion of people who never marry has gone down drastically. It used to be something like 10 percent. For this current generation it's only going to be about 3 percent for the girls. So more and more are getting married. With regard to divorce, there were fewer divorces in the first five months of 1967 than in 1966. The divorce rate has, of course, stabilized. So if you want institutional indexes, whatever is going on is doing good for marriage.

RUTH USEEM: I think another interesting fact is the new McNamara rule that Negroes in the Armed Forces can get specialized training now if they want to be school teachers. This is a new parent role which can be given to them, because they can't help but fail under the old system in which parental and progenitor roles were synonymous. Our studies of Negro men who cannot fulfill these roles successfully show that they still want to be with children and to be parentlike. And I think we're going to have more and more parent roles separate from the progenitor role. This to me is the most encouraging part of our whole society.

JOSEPH BIRD: It seems to me we've finally gotten down to something we're going to have to face which is right at the nitty-gritty of this. That's the thing you mentioned in terms of the need to be pregnant, wholly apart from any desire to have children. I think there are two aspects of this. One, of course, is the neurotic need to be pregnant, the need to carry a child, and the woman's feeling that this is somehow going to turn her into a woman. But there is also, and we feel this very strongly, a healthy aspect of this. There is a basic (you can call it the nature of man or the nature of woman or whatever) need to be impregnated by the person to whom one is giving oneself. No matter what we do with contraception now or in the future, or in the contraceptive culture, we're eventually going to have to face this.

MICHAEL SCRIVEN: Well, I deny it exists. Have you got any evidence that it does?

JOSEPH BIRD: No, I do not, if you're talking about evidence. I do not believe this is a dimension which can be measured.

RUTH USEEM: This is the first man I've heard who's said this. When we talk among women, so help me, this is what we talk about.

JOSEPH BIRD: And I don't believe it's a measurable variable.

KERMIT KRANTZ: But it's evidenced in the Japanese culture. That's why they will not accept the pill. And you talk to them. I've spent a great deal of time talking with these people. The woman will go and have the abortion. It's just that need to fulfill. Now we're seeing this in the single girl in this country who is on the pill who comes to us pregnant. We say, "Well, why did you quit it?" She says, "I wanted to be pregnant. I wanted to fulfill and prove my femininity."

RUTH USEEM: The whole history of the world is educating people to do unnaturally what they would otherwise do naturally, so I think we have a new kind of socialization process. But I think the impulse to be pregnant is just as strong as the impulse to impregnate.

KERMIT KRANTZ: Absolutely.

JOSEPH BIRD: I think this is not necessarily related to any need to fulfill masculinity, femininity, malehood, or anything else. It relates to the direct relationship of a particular couple at the time of the sexual act. He has a desire to impregnate her, she has a desire to be impregnated by him.

HERBERT RICHARDSON: It seems to me that Professor Scriven has raised my objection. You're suggesting, when you have this male-female level, that there is some aspect of human behavior that doesn't get aculturated. It's natural, the drive to be pregnant you're talking about. I thought in our earlier session there was the assumption, too, that there is something which is inevitable, and naturally and inalienably feminine. Women are more feeling, someone said, or they are more concrete. Now is this really the case? Why is it that all the other things people once felt were naturally feminine— that women were passive in sexual relations, that they didn't enjoy sex, that they're intuitive, not rational—have now been recognized to be relative to cultural systems, but not this desire to be pregnant? Why isn't even this desire, after all, something that can be played with in many different relations?

RUTH USEEM: I think it is. I think it's socialized. I think otherwise we would be continuously pregnant. I think it's like eating or anything else. It's there to begin with. It can be socialized; it can be perverted. But I do think that there is a body there and it isn't all cultural and social.

CATHERINE CHILMAN: I agree with a lot that's been said. I think it's very hard to separate what is culturally induced. That's what I meant when I said they could try to mechanize our culture so much that we could lose the basic human element. I believe there is not only a drive to get pregnant, there is to me also an element often of this man and this woman caring about each other. They would like to have a baby that is some of both of them. I think also that for a huge number of women, and this probably varies, and for men, there is a tremendous need to be parents, to cherish, to protect, to rear, to take care of, to be tender, to be significant. The most significant thing you can be is the parent of this little thing that regards you as the center of all life. Who would have more than one child if you were going to be rational? If you're going through it, if your mind were telling you what to do, you'd say, "Never again." It is a deep, instinctive feeling to socialize out. Otherwise, you've got far too many people in the world.

WILLIAM LIU: About the social aspects of pregnancy, I'm glad you mentioned that women want to have a child by a particular man, not just to be pregnant, period. The second thing is this: suppose you wanted to be pregnant, period. You have to let the world know you're pregnant. That's important. You can't just have a very privitized pregnancy and end it in a privitized abortion just to have the experience of having a physiological change in your body. I doubt very much that pregnancy is totally void of any social significance.

MICHAEL SCRIVEN: It seems to me that nobody's denying that some people want to have kids, and some people want to have babies, and some people want to be parents, and some people want to get a hold on a man, and some people want to have either pregnancy or children or something for some damn reason. What we're talking about is the question whether there is something you can replace the feminine mystique with, which you could call the pregnancy mystique. It seems to me that there isn't. At least there's no reason whatsoever to think that there is. It's not important that women constantly say they want to be pregnant. Of course they do, at that stage in their very advanced development. What's interesting is the extent to which we are responsible for women saying this. I absolutely support what was said down here (*motions down the table*).

If we're going to talk about a contraceptive culture, its potentialities and its actualities, we must keep an open mind on the extent to which the need to be pregnant exists independent of the need to demonstrate love for this particular man, the need to prove to the society that you're capable of it, or the need to avoid PTAs. There are plenty of secondary reasons for the need to be pregnant. The interesting question is whether the need to be pregnant is a primary one. It's extremely plausible from the evolutionary point of view that there's likely to be a primary need for motherhood, but whether there's a primary need for pregnancy is something that's unlikely, at any rate unsupported by evolutionary considerations. It seems, therefore, that we want to keep an open mind about this; and no amount of telling people about the phenomenology of femininity is going to make it one iota likelier that there is such a primary need. It is something we should think about. At any rate, I'm inclined to say we ought to bring all the forces of education toward not just socializing but controlling in all sorts of ways, providing surrogate procedures to achieve all these other secondary needs.

I do not think we can view contraception as kind of a gimmicky, gadgety affair and thus in some sense dehumanizing. I don't think that's the way to see it. I think it has the same status as clothes in a cold climate. It's not something we have to feel dehumanizes people. Clothes are not necessarily dehumanizing, and contraceptives are not necessarily destroying our love relationship. I think the tendency in some of the discussion here is to suggest that's so.

One final point: there is a certain tendency here to stress the cultural aspects of contraception a little too much. It's true and of importance that the mere creation of the pill doesn't solve the problem of population control, and the effect of the pill on different cultures will be enormously different. The technical creation of the pill has created these many different effects, some of which have a good deal of similarity, e.g., the reduction of birth rate among the middle class and the increase in the number of stable extramarital relationships. But it seems to me we ought perhaps to consider the possibility of the retroactive pill, or the male pill, because it's pretty clear that the technical discussion is going to start soon; I mean they're pretty close to having it as far as I can tell. Therefore, any sort of discussion we have here predicated on the idea that we've female control of pregnancy would be a temporary discussion if next month they announce the male pill, or the retroactive pill.

JESSIE BERNARD: Well, you'll still have female control

even though the male will also have control. I mean, she still has the pill.

MICHAEL SCRIVEN: Right, but she will not be the sole partner to have this, and the virility problem will no longer be quite so bad of course.

JESSIE BERNARD: I would like to raise two points. If women really have this desire for impregnation, do they get the same satisfaction from artificial insemination? Or is there more to it than simply impregnation, which sounds sort of far-out to me? The second point is that there might be all kinds of cultures which had the functional equivalent of contraception. For example, anthropologists used to tell us the status of women was closely related to the value placed on children and motherhood. Was a society that did not value motherhood or children, in which they practiced infanticide, in which they didn't want a lot of children, functionally equivalent to a contraceptive society? Shouldn't we think in terms, not of the specific way in which you implement the value, but of the value itself? That is, a contraceptive culture would be one of many cultures in which having a lot of children was not a great value. Do I make my point?

JOSEPH BIRD: May I take a stab at that first question you raised? When I originally threw in this point about the need for impregnation, I intended to indicate that this need is not merely the need of the women. There is a joint need here to impregnate. You raised the point of artificial insemination. What I'm referring to here is this need to be impregnated and to impregnate, a need that bears right on the relationship. It's this man and this woman, and it comes out of their relationship. He wants to impregnate *her*, not just impregnate a woman; and she wants to be impregnated by *him*.

JESSIE BERNARD: I think that is the point Bill was making.

RUTH USEEM: I'll take a chance on your second one. I think very often the procreation role is best got at indirectly by developing gender roles outside. Rather than trying to educate a woman on how to control this, you simply educate her so that she has a job or she has some interesting things to do.

JESSIE BERNARD: The point I was making was that if you're trying to characterize the culture, you'd call it a contraceptive culture. But if you wanted to find out what there is about this culture that characterizes it, then you have to include any kind of culture which has the functional equivalent of contraception.

RUTH USEEM: And this is what I call gender roles.

JULIAN SAMORA: Are there any other questions?

HERBERT RICHARDSON: May I just throw in an observation here? It seems to me it is possible at least to conceive that they might exist separately. Plato thought the desire to get pregnant was one of two alternative ways to have identity. A better way to fulfill your desire for an identity was to have spiritual children, or to meditate or to have communion with God. He regarded the desire to get pregnant as a desire to have continuous existence. And you can have continuous existence two ways. I think we might ask the question—I hope you will excuse the prejudice for suggesting this—what do we say, then, about virginity? I'm a Protestant. I don't have anything except a primordial loathing for the virginal state. But, as a theologian, I ask myself occasionally: What is it for a person to commit his or her life to virginity? Do they have diminished identity? Do they fail to fulfill themselves as persons? Or, let's ask it in a more modern mode: Do we really feel that homosexuals lack identity because there's no pregnancy and they don't procreate themselves biologically? It seems to me that in just these three or four cases we can see that it's perfectly conceivable that there might be identity apart from procreative sexuality, and I'm not sure that these alternative ways aren't fully as satisfactory as the one we are presupposing here, namely, that identity involves procreating oneself biologically.

RUTH USEEM: I'd like to take a chance on that unless somebody else does. I think the flight into fertility and the flight into marriage (in the reverse order, I hope) just after World War II was a direct part of a loss of belief in the future, a loss of belief that one belonged to something that would survive, would go on. Whenever you lose your sense of commitment to a larger kind of collective responsibility, you go back to the primordial kind of one-to-one relationship, to having children of your flesh and blood. In contrast, if you think you are part of a movement which has a future, or if you are part of a collectivity whose future is assured (we had the beginning of this for young people under John Kennedy and then it collapsed, with all kinds of problems precipitated), you are not so pushed to have these body, flesh-and-blood children because you feel part of a larger collectivity that you call *we*. If we developed a new Utopian notion that would catch the imagination, it would do more to reduce the birth rate than any kind of contraception.

JESSIE BERNARD: I'd like to speak to this other point. I don't think that humanity and sexuality can be separated. They're inextricably combined. I had the experience, the very delightful experience, last summer of being on a retreat with a Franciscan order of nuns who have taken a vow of virginity—the most feminine women! Their gender role was 100 percent; they were having complete fulfillment. I wrote this up for *Commonweal Magazine,* this discovery I had of what I call graceful, full of grace, sexuality. These nuns had a very graceful kind of sexuality. The editor said they all read it at *Commonweal,* and I guess it shocked them all. They couldn't take the notion of sexuality combined within nuns; so finally they reluctantly returned the article to me. I was so impressed that they were so feminine in our gender sense, and in every way delightful people. Their virginity certainly wasn't getting in the way of what I would consider very graceful sexuality. People who stand out with very great identities very often are celibate church fathers who surely have an identity.

KERMIT KRANTZ: Celibacy couldn't get in the way because, unless a person is introduced to something, how is he going to know it exists?

JESSIE BERNARD: Are you asking me? I don't know.

KERMIT KRANTZ: Unless a person has been introduced into the step-by-step activity that will culminate in coitus, it's only a fantasy. It can't be anything more, unless a masturbatory habit is developed.

JESSIE BERNARD: Are you talking to my point?

KERMIT KRANTZ: Yes.

JESSIE BERNARD: I don't see the relevance.

CATHERINE CHILMAN: He is interpreting sexuality differently than you are.

KERMIT KRANTZ: Sex is one aspect of it.

CATHERINE CHILMAN: She knows. By sexuality she meant an identification of being a woman and being a feminine person—being glad you are a human being, but also a feminine human being, and fulfilling a role that is not necessarily specific in terms of sex relations or procreation, but in the feminine way of living, caring for children or elderly people, or sick people in need.

KERMIT KRANTZ: Well, yes, everybody can have that to a degree.

CATHERINE CHILMAN: Well, I think this was what Ruth was talking about, that by a commitment to alternate forms of cherishing, you don't have to be a parent.

RUTH USEEM: Unfortunately, a society collapses if it does not have what Durkheim called mechanical solidarity. What I would call tenderhearted or affective solidarity—trust and faith and care and concern—will come from within a society, rather than from without.

UNIDENTIFIED PARTICIPANT: The feminine way of living was mentioned. All afternoon I've been asking myself the question, Is there a feminine way or a masculine way? It seems to me that the things we identify as feminine or masculine can belong to either sex, depending on the relationship. I don't think carrying out garbage cans, for instance, is masculine any more than I think it is feminine.

JOSEPH BIRD: If we knew what we're talking about in terms of identifying a certain mode of behavior as feminine or masculine, we'd almost have to ask why we are here.

RUTH USEEM: Well, I don't have the data to document this, but I'd like to have you think about it. I have a feeling that we have changed our notions of feminine and masculine a great deal, for a number of reasons. Masculinity became tied up with toughmindedness. Home became tied up with tender-heartedness and was considered feminine. But I think there are a number of men now who act out their commitments to this through their wives; and their wives aren't liking it because they have a new commitment as to what is feminine. But these men want their wives to be like Momma and they're acting out an earlier cultural definition, and this is pushing hard on many young women right now. You talked about the *feminine mystique*. We all call it the *masculine mistake*.

KERMIT KRANTZ: Ruth, who rocked that cradle, a woman?

RUTH USEEM: My husband. So help me, bottle-feeding did more than anything else to involve husbands in fathering.

JULIAN SAMORA: May I bring this session to a close by thanking our two speakers.

The Unchanging Woman 3

EDGAR BERMAN

Monday, 7:00 P.M.

EDGAR BERMAN: It has been suggested by the initial brochure tendered by the conference that we are here to discuss woman's plight and her potential. I must say I feel that the former is not taken as such by the average woman (mother and housewife) and the latter may never be more fully attained than it is right now.

Careful examination of this subspecies, average untalented woman, plain and unadorned by romanticism and fancy, shows her neither plight-plagued nor potential-ridden. Actually, she is rather medieval in her ambitionless contentment, little concerned about her position in society, about security or even domination in her most natural of habitats—the home.

Since Adam she has been an unalterable, immutable well

of genesis, periodically giving forth to the future, in greater or lesser numbers, as unconscious of her role as mother of us all as she was of her own genesis at her rather inauspicious thoracic beginning.

If she be, or can be, more, as has been suggested by the titles of some of the papers to be presented here, there is certainly a reasonable doubt from the historical evidence of those already liberated. Freedom or equality of opportunity endows no one with talent, ability, or capacity. Social laws and patterns will not change genetic failings. Sure, in every era there is a Cleopatra, a Jeanne d'Arc, a Madame Curie, or a Boulanger, whose feats stimulate feminist action groups. But this circling motion usually subsides due to a lack of continuity of talent, sometimes for centuries at a time. The rallying point today for the liberation of womanhood into the free world, for better or worse, is not a person, but a concept called contraception. This shall set them free.

But I would think before this conference spends too much time counting their liberated chickens they had better study their unhatched egg in the nest, and ask a few questions.

First, can this domesticated egg hatch out a "born-free chicken," and if not, isn't it highly doubtful whether it can be adapted once hatched? Actually, few women of any real feminine calibre, either addicted to contraceptives or abstainers therefrom, would exchange their subsidiary marital role (with all its faults) for equality and responsibility even if they could —which in itself is a point of some question. The average female goes along with little resistance to this type of benign domination, seemingly unconscious of a plight and pleasantly resigned to her dependency; and it has little to do with her surfeit of progeny.

Second, are women constitutionally adaptable to independence and equality? If so, this conference must consider whether it is possible to unshackle her by the mere negative means of reducing her number of offspring. Certainly this cannot redirect her urges and energies and state of mind that are so inextricably subject to basic hormonal influence, eons of social inferiority, male physical dominance, and the historical stigmata of being an instinctual life force. She has survived as a subspecies by these means, but, even if this change could occur, may this not create a male backlash that could in the long run throw women farther down the social scale than they are today? These latter considerations cannot be taken lightly, for the balance of nature, once disturbed, creates an uncontrollable chain reaction that may threaten her existing advantages. Woman's present unstimulated desire to be unaltered may be her survival instinct, if she be not too prone to the urgings of her so-called liberated half-sisters.

Are some children, over and above an unknown optimum, really the female shackles, or are they purposefully desired to use as a means to maintain an indigenous slothful female status quo? Isn't one child an anchor? Doesn't the rare female talent usually express itself regardless of family size? And, by the same token, doesn't the less than mediocre horde of females remain thus regardless of the limitation of family? In relation to size of family it is bruited, usually by the most fertile, that a woman is not a woman without fulfillment—meaning a child. This implies a degree of masculinity if a woman is barren. I am not so sure the fallow but fornicated and possibly fecund female is not the most feminine. Be that as it may, if, in the so-called contraceptive culture, the lowly device or pill is the freeing factor, child is deduced as the enslaving one. So if one child makes the difference between true femininity and part masculinity, how many does a woman have to limit herself to if she is to be female, but free?

Along these lines, in the terms of this conference, can woman be discussed as woman alone or must she be taken only when biologically productive and therefore one-third whole

—for she is then certainly dependent on two other components, man and child. So if in the ordinary view Madame One-Third is supposedly conceived in heaven, the modern feminist considers her just a minority stockholder in corporate bondage, managed and controlled by an unholy alliance of man and child—the child, according to this conference, being the critical factor. But is she really?

Is this freedom and equality a reality or a myth? Does a woman, by limiting her progeny and getting out into the world, become less or more emancipated? Does she enjoy it, and is it best for her and her family? I might ask, is a nurse less a menial? Is a factory worker less restricted? As a free woman is she a more loving wife, and are the children better off away from part-time mothers? As to the ultimate effect, Daniel Moynihan says the right answer may be crucial to our society.

I caution here even the leadership of the liberated to beware of an irreversible trap, baited by the male milieu, with fewer children cited as an equivalent to freedom and equality. In specious male terms this might be defined as freedom, but for whom? The free woman certainly works harder away from home with equal if not more responsibilities, under worse conditions, generally trading one service job for another. And to what end? The security of the male! By more readily filling the family coffers and cutting down on the expense of feeding more dependents (besides preventing the deterioration of his sexual partner) she makes more enjoyable his increased leisure time. In other words, he attains an even better of all possible worlds by this liberation of his spouse.

Consideration must be given to the fact that even women with a maximum of two children are still financially dependent for the first fifteen years and are usually tied to the household for this minimum period. At what period in life does the male-like freedom and equality come? Is it not then limited by the financial status, the preoccupation and depleted drive of motherhood, and, a few years later, by her menopause? Is the hue and cry worth the effort for these few declining years?

Another subsidiary fact to be studied at this conference is that, though it is known empirically that unproductive women and spinsters are supposedly in the realm of the free and emancipated, they somehow have not been up to either their equality or responsibility, nor have they fulfilled their supposed potential. There is enough history to prove this.

If the feminists and their supporters insist on dragging the reluctant ordinary woman out of her willful, heels-dug-in, entrenched thralldom into the changing-womanhood era (which I am sure the unenlightened ordinary woman will eventually fall for), they must be carefully instructed not only to see the immediate results but to anticipate the long-range reactions. To do this, you conferees must examine females in the laser light of rigid reason, strip her (if you can) of the gauzy shawl of the maudlin mother-earth delusion, which may be her true role and is usually flaunted by none other than herself. Analyze carefully the motive, authenticity and, yes, even the femininity of those females who roil the average mind of the average woman to anticipate a dubious female Utopia while denying them their only security and stability as a thing of Adam.

On the other hand, disregard and do not take for granted the special privilege, foibles, and frailties of the more female as a heritage (really a male indulgence for value received). For she will guard these greedily, shielding them with her body if necessary, and would not compromise in any bargain for any amount of male freedom and equality these hard-won chevrons; and she can't have both. These reverential trappings of the "anointed," the "chosen," must be torn asunder by this conference in intellectual cold blood. For if not, it must fail in its obligation to determine, through the knowledge of bare woman, whether woman can survive equality. This objectivity in itself is a difficult assignment. Even the most female of females can hardly judge herself. And, on the other hand, the unfeminine female is so distant from what she defines as the grubby world of the distaff that she could not possibly render an expert analysis. Even the unprejudiced male would be considered as evaluating from a jaundiced point of view, and accused of not wanting to lose the good thing he has so carefully nurtured to his own end. The difficult thing here is to disengage, and take a sharp, capon-eye view of the real woman and come up with an objective answer (if any) as to the relative merits of the home or office, not only for her but for her family and society. In this we must be scientific, clinical, and open, disregarding sensitivities and facing some rather animal physiological truisms and myths about females.

For instance, one that has bothered me is whether there is a maternal instinct at all, an instinct that must be satisfied, and that it is the natural function of woman to perpetuate the species. On balance, I doubt it. An endowed capacity, whether reproductive, intellectual, or physical, certainly need not be utilized because it's there. So why is child-bearing a natural function? Maybe fornication is the natural function and conception only a related ill—a disease. It certainly acts parasitic, and no one can say it is not physically and psychologically detrimental.

Are there really female procreative instincts? In the male it is pronounced lust as it was in Peking man. Do women, other than in their momentary sentimental ecstasy, actually think of propagation of the species even during the whole span of conception, gestation, and birth? And when one considers the number of abortions, infanticides, battered-child syndromes, the startling cases of neglect, the full orphanages and foster homes, one wonders about the maternal instinct.

More scientifically, when the possible period of conception is only three to five days out of an entire month, is the cycle not designed for sexual play rather than impregnation? If coitus is principally to satisfy the maternal instinct, wouldn't the human female be more like her lower primate sister, allowing contact only for conception? On the other hand, the human female is much more receptive to the male near the beginning and end of her cycle, her infertile period, rather than during the time of ovulation. Is this not intriguing?

On the motivational side, I give up. I have gone over about two dozen possible reasons for procreation. None is intelligent or rational. So we must all draw our own conclusions. My point is that women have been studied too superficially to make a judgment as to what they really are or could be.

To get back to the unscientific aspects, the superficial, off-the-cuff desires of the average woman for change of status may well be her bent. But if she looks closely at the examples of changed or emancipated women (Betty Friedan notwithstanding) there may be second thoughts.

This passive option must be offered at least to the sequestered and as yet uninvolved. The free and equal female must be viewed as suspect until she, her children, and their families have been carefully studied. The basic unit of society, the family, is already in shambles due to the indifference bred by wealth, the working female, the male defections bred by poverty, and other facets of our modern world. I believe that the family cannot stand more disruption without crime, illegitimacy, moral decay, and violence multiplying to vast, uncontrolled proportions.

One of the archetypes often cited as the new, changed female (and which may be a too-loaded example and to me most frightening) is the New York business executrix—as domineering as a Marine general, as driving and aggressive as any Budd Schulberg "Sammy," as shrewd and about as straightforward as a used-car salesman. Instead of the traditional mothers' triad of *Kirke-Küche-Kinder,* there is the office, the martinied lunch, and the bedtime child visit. In my opinion, family life is of tertiary importance to this type of female, with mixed-up children, estranged husband, and mounting hours on the couch with each succeeding rung of the emancipation ladder.

Her suburban counterpart is no less the bored barricuda— overdressed, either undersexed at home or oversexed abroad, a slimmed-down, cynical sophisticate, whose alcoholic consumption varies in direct proportion to her distance from the sink and diapers. Even in this economic bracket, the dependency at home on her sister female—the servant—will no doubt end with the coming new freedom. Then what?

At a lower level, we find the general office amanuensis who has been liberated from the home realizing too late that all she wanted was to fulfill her gregarious nature and be with people. Is she not more a slave in the office or factory with constant supervision, glinty-hard efficiency experts, sparse geometric cold surroundings, deadlines, and sorely needed coffee breaks? This, of course, does not absolve her from household duties before and after work. Most of these unfortunates would gladly reverse their present status, trading the typewriter and copier back for the mop and duster.

An even better example on a larger scale is the European, especially the French or Italian, woman. If freedom and equality are determined by the average paucity of progeny, European women are the freest in the world and have been for three decades. I believe that the noticeable changes in equality are nonexistent, the opportunities not challenged, and the extra time is troublesome and troubled for they know not what to do. The numbers of great women, or even lesser successes, produced in the arts, sciences, humanities, and the world of commerce by this freed female society are almost negligible.

Speaking generally of the already emancipated, for instance in the lesser pursuits such as technician, would any of you trust any of the so-called free and equal females to pilot you in a jet-liner across an ocean? No. And neither does any airline in the world. Would you want this type of changed woman in charge of the lending agency in your bank or trust fund? No. And hardly a bank anywhere in the world does. In these traumatic and trying times, would you want a woman such as those described in the seat of political power? I would doubt it, even though the one woman who, by a quirk of political expediency, is leading a major nation today may well be the last.

The fettered women of the world should take special cognizance of the women of the Soviet Union, certainly emancipated to full equality by any male standard, and strangely enough not by the contraceptive. They are probably the best brick layers, carpenters, and truck drivers in Russia today and have also attained the lower echelons of the professions. The many I have met wait patiently for their three-month maternity leave and look forward to retirement back to their tiny flats at the proper old age which is usually premature.

Woman, by every known criterion and by all history and culture, has not only been shown to be best suited in every way, but happier and most productive, as ancillary to male. But she may not stay a household being, much to her detriment, for she has been led by females who know not what they do and males who care little, knowing that this temporary glory can lead but to a more deadly type of indenture. But even so, it is highly questionable that the key to her fall is the liberation from that extra child.

I think that the average woman, led by her own instincts, would take the right course, for she knows intuitively that she is less than she is touted to be by her feminist half-sister. She knows she is limited in capacity, in responsibility, and in stability, if not by ability, by being rendered thus by the very essence of her cyclic nature. From pubescence to senescence, this creature is riven monthly by uncontrolled physical and mental gyrations, and is subjected at any time during her active sexual life to the shrill, unbalancing, and frequently debilitating effect of conception. The final insult and limiting factor is the shriveling of mind and body at a relatively tender age (usually the fifth decade) by that spectre of all female spectres, the menopause and its sequelae. I believe that woman is by nature neither free, equal, nor responsible. But she is all we have, and a vital complement to the compleat male existence, all too frequently his albatross. The male will continue to bear his burden nobly. But change her if you will—and can.

What Do Women Really Think and Feel About Themselves? 4

WILLIAM V. D'ANTONIO AND MARTHA STUART
DISCUSSANTS: Lee Bullitt, June Butts,
Eleanor Christie, Elisa R. DeBulnes,
Lorraine D'Antonio, Constance Dupré,
Ene Riisna, Betty Rollin,
Anne Sheffield, Sister M. Jean Wallace

Monday, 8:15 P.M.

WILLIAM LIU: This evening's program is the performance of two of my bosses—I've many. One boss oversees my
work as a sociologist. He's the head of the Sociology Department, Dr. D'Antonio of Notre Dame. And the other boss is a
person who sees that I do everything right at this meeting and
at least can pronounce the names correctly in a population
conference (*laughter*) . . . that's Martha Stuart. I'm sure
that neither one of them needs any further introduction. But
we do have a very attractive panel here. The unchanging
woman, Phoebe Berman, is not here; she's performing her
duties as the unchanging woman! We have June Butts, a doctoral student in Home and Family Life Education at Teachers'
College in New York City, and we have Eleanor Christie, who
is a woman of the twenty-first century. She is the female satellite, or she is really the wife of George Christie of the Comsat

Corporation. We have Mrs. DeBulnes from Santiago, Chile, who is President of the Red Cross of that country. We have Lorraine D'Antonio, whose husband is going to lead the discussion, and she's partly responsible for Dr. D'Antonio's enthusiasm in population conferences (*laughter*). And we have Mrs. Lee Bullitt whose husband works for the same organization that I am working for this year. He is with AID, and I'm never sure whether AID is not a part of CIA or vice versa. And we have Mrs. Anne Sheffield of the Planned Parenthood-World Population of New York; Sister Jean Wallace of St. Mary's College, Notre Dame, Indiana; Ene Riisna, a very important television producer; and Betty Rollin, a Senior Editor of *Look* magazine; and the lovely wife of Louis Dupré, Connie, who is also a noted attorney. And that's the line-up of a very strong team and I'm just going to turn over tonight's program to Martha Stuart.

MARTHA STUART: This is really for Edgar Berman and the rest of you are excused (*laughter*)! This session developed in my mind when Bill had the courage or temerity or whatever to invite me to a population conference at Notre Dame last Fall, when Virginia Johnson and I were the only women attending. I found that I was very suspect because I am a woman, and I was suspect because I work in radio and television and you know you can't really trust that—it's too *real*. I was also suspect because I work with Planned Parenthood, which was kind of *unreal* in this atmosphere at that time!

We began talking about lots of things and I learned that—and I don't say this disrespectfully except that after this afternoon I think you will understand what I mean—I learned that a "woman's goal achievement of her action potential" was whether her diaphragm worked or not!

I began to get more and more concerned about what women really felt and thought when one lovely priest got up and said,

"Really we don't understand experiences unless we've had them, so let's examine our own thoughts and feelings about that." And an equally lovely sociologist said, in another context, "Intercourse and birth are really the main experiences in life." So when Father Schlitzer called on me, I said, "You know, I'm a communications person and I'm not a part of any scholarly discipline, but I have a feeling that *if*, as you say, intercourse and birth are the main experiences in life" (I was sitting there as the only woman) "and if we only understand things if we've experienced them, then really, I'm the only authority in this room!" (*laughter*).

I don't want to talk any more because I would like to have you all, and my compatriots up here, hear on audio tape what some women do really think and feel about themselves, not because they represent any cataloging of data or any kind of statistical grouping or any attempt at a real cross-section but just because they're people who happen to be articulate and they are women and women are people—and because I think maybe they will be good discussion openers. My friends here will then continue with the discussion. So we will start the first tape. This is a lovely woman who told me that I could tell you who she is. She is assistant to the director of the Women's Unit for Rockefeller in New York. She's a Negro. Her name is Evelyn Cunningham. She's had a radio show in New York for a long time and she's especially articulate, I think. You can listen to what she says.

EVELYN CUNNINGHAM (*on tape*): I've always felt that as a Negro my problems were very, very unique and, certainly, they are very, very unique. There's nothing like them in the world. I've said to many people, as most Negroes have said, "You just don't understand my problems. You have to be a Negro to understand my problems." Well, in very recent years I've had to do a complete turnabout, simply because I have become involved in the whole area of working for and with and on behalf of women. And suddenly I've found that the problems are so similar that it's really kind of fantastic.

On the surface of it, I guess it's very hard to imagine that they could be similar, but let's take this one big, overpowering word that's used too loosely—discrimination. I'm not going to get involved in the clichés, the patterns of discrimination against Negroes, but the patterns of discrimination against *women* are just incredible! I had not realized that they existed to the extent that they do. As a matter of fact, recently I've been concerned with laws, legislation that is supposed to be discriminatory against women and legislation that has been passed to protect women. It's really *wild* to realize that many of the laws (I mean this on a city, state, or a national level) that are made to protect women are really in the books to protect men (*laughter*).

I'm trying to think of an example now. Well, let's take a law, and I'm not quoting the law accurately at all, and also the law varies in different communities—one of the most usual laws we find is a law that will prohibit women from working late at night; and in certain places women can't serve as barmaids, let's say. Well, this protects a man's job. Of course; it's not really protective of a woman. It's protecting a man, so that a woman will not get his job. Well, I hope I don't sound like a real feminist. New York State is the only state in the nation that has a Women's Unit on an executive level. Apparently, no one feels that a woman's judgment or philosophy is needed on an executive level. We have often found that we have had to face traditional resistance similar to that faced by Negroes. Here again I have to draw that comparison, and so often the men who work with us look on us with a little fear. They're frightened. I think they expect us to get out like Carrie Nation or one of those ladies who make noise and picket and demonstrate, and simply fight for womanhood.

This is not the idea at all. For example, consider a woman who's over age 40, who has a family, who's raised children, the children have gone away. She's been to college or she might not have been to college. Suddenly, here she is with absolutely nothing to do and she's got a wonderful, agile mind. She wants to do something. She doesn't know which way to turn. She doesn't even know where to seek employment. She doesn't know where her special skills are. She might have gotten a degree in sociology, for example, but now she says, "Well, I don't like sociology." Or she might say, "I'm certain the techniques have changed so and I am afraid I cannot compete with the younger people who have just come out of school, but I've got to do something. I do want to do something." She doesn't know where to go. That's just one of the little areas of our work here. Although we don't actually do the counseling, we know exactly where the counseling can be had. We're really a catalyst—a liaison between the government, or the governor, and women, all women's groups.

WILLIAM D'ANTONIO: Martha, what is her group? Who does she represent?

MARTHA STUART: She works for Governor Rockefeller and they have a Women's Unit in his office and she is the Assistant Director.

JUNE BUTTS: Who is the Director? Is the Director a woman?

MARTHA STUART: Yes, the Director is a woman! (laughter). This next voice is an environment designer of linoleum floors that are puzzles, tables that are cubes that can be modulated in many ways, and paper chairs, acrylic treated paper tiles for bathrooms, and even plastic rugs. She came to New York from Arizona with nothing but innovative ideas and redid a loft on Seventh Avenue where she works and lives and where I interviewed her. You'll hear some traffic noise and also the music she plays all day.

BETTY THOMPSON (*on tape*): Did I tell you, there's a good possibility I'll do lots of things with the Museum of Modern Art? This man is very excited about my environmental ideas and not having furniture as such. He was the first reasonable person I've talked to in one of those places.

Oh, I used to go into hardware stores and I wanted to learn about just what my craft was or what my problems were in design or hardware or about manufacturers, and I'd ask questions of a simple kind of the man who was running the store. I was paying him for his services and he would react to me as if I were really a formidable woman who was coming in and taking his place. He didn't want someone like me to come in, particularly since I know what I'm doing. So it took a while. I went through a lot of things like feeling very bad and feeling very hostile. You have to reassure men that this feminine person does know what she wants to do. You have to treat them like men. Hopefully they'll treat you like women and as equals. You just have to keep going back to the same hardware store (*laughter*) . . . and he finally becomes friendly. That is the answer. The world's hard enough to deal with, let alone to have to forage.

I came here with ideas that were too far ahead. Now it is beginning to be an incredibly perfect time for me. The first three years of sculptural work, or puzzle work, or floor work became a joke.

I don't want anyone to think that just because I'm a woman they have to like my work in order not to offend me. It's very fortunate, too, for me that this is New York. If it had been somewhere else, I very probably would have struck out, because there is no release of pressure in lots of cities. At least here I can say, "Forget the world; I'm going to stay here because there are some people who respect innovation."

At the same time that I was feeling better about the work, not feeling so lost because, you know, I'm trying to do something that is so new, I met a man who is almost ready to accept me as a person on my own level. He treated me like a woman and didn't have to have my work threaten him all the time. My having ideas wasn't threatening to him, and that's the most incredible thing! We talked about it. There are a lot of men who are nice people, but they don't know what to do with people who have something to do themselves. In fact, Merle is a little bit astounded, almost questions whether it's a hobby, something to keep me busy.

MARTHA STUART: You have heard this girl talk about what her work means to her. The next tape is by the daughter of a woman who is very busy and some of her thoughts will just give you a little bit of the other side of the situation.

GERI KAHN (*on tape*): Because your parents never brought up problems about sex, you never really felt too comfortable. It wasn't dirty or anything, it was just something that you didn't talk about openly. Of course, having an older brother helps and lots of things help, such as television.

The biology teacher can't start talking about sex with you very openly. First of all, he would be moralizing. I don't really think it belongs there unless you have had open discussion ever since you were in kindergarten. Otherwise, it's unnatural and the whole purpose is to be natural.

In the New York City school system we are constantly running around from one room to another and there's so much to do that there's never really time to talk. In school you're supposed to be quiet and listen to the teacher and out of school you're supposed to do your homework and go to sleep.

You do talk to your friends, but there's really never enough time. It really would be good if you had a class where you could just be yourself. We were discussing *Brave New World* once and all the implications to do with this book. I don't believe anyone really wanted to leave the class. There wasn't enough time. The bell rang and we had to go to our next class.

If we had a free period when we could continue such a discussion, we would have time to really think about these issues.

I have read *Summerhill* and also about a program in Chicago where the teacher really is just a guide. This seems to be a good idea. The kids would really talk. They still need a figure of authority—you do need someone to moderate and to bring out the questions. A teacher would do this and yet he then could become human to some degree, because he's not teaching us a syllabus. He's teaching about life, which is very human. I once had a teacher like that. He was very good. There were times when he was definitely a teacher and there were times when, you know, he would look at us and say, "Well, look, I don't know the answers either." I think that's very important, this kind of class.

It's crazy in my house. I see my parents so little. It's bad. I have a better relationship now with my mother than I have had for many years, but everybody in my family is so busy and we all have different hours. My father works at strange hours. All this is downstairs, so my parents are really never home or never really away. They're just around and yet they're in the office and you don't bother them. I learned many years ago that you just don't bother your parents when you have a problem. You can't, because they're busy and they're just not around. We have to work it out ourselves or with our friends, which in a way is pretty horrible.

I don't think it's enough that your parents are your mother and father. They have to start becoming people, because otherwise the conversation dwindles. When we were little we ran to mommy and daddy when we needed things, so we talked to them. When we are older, and especially if we don't see them that often, we have learned to be independent, and we don't talk to them. This is not good.

MARTHA STUART: On another tape that I will not take the time to play, another lovely girl, part Puerto Rican and part Negro, explained that she was an accident and her four sisters and brothers were accidents and that her mother would rather have an abortion than accept responsibility for herself. The plea that both of these younger girls kept making was that there is nobody with whom to talk. And the girl who was an accident said, very beautifully, "I can't talk to my mother because she says to me, 'I'm going to cut your curfew. What are you doing?' And I can't talk to my teacher, because she just passes out pamphlets, or says, 'You have to see me after class. That is something I can't discuss in class.' And I can't talk to my friends because they don't know any more about it than I do and I don't really want answers." She said, "I just want to be able to talk." So, let us talk.

WILLIAM D'ANTONIO: Shall we? Shall we first ask the panel to make remarks about this?

MARTHA STUART: Lee Bullitt passed me a note which said "We're all steamed up!" So let's start with Lee.

LEE BULLITT: I was going to talk about something very personal which is, apparently, the way women do things. How do you go about discovering yourself? I've spent thirteen years searching, as well as raising my children and finding ways to express my identity. Now that I'm more on my own my husband and I seem to have grown more apart. Maybe I should have stayed where I was!

SHIRLEY STONE: A woman who works must always put her family first. The job doesn't need you; it'll go on, but the child needs you.

ANNE SHEFFIELD: That's not always true. I don't know what kind of job you have, but in my job the responsibilities are as pressing as my responsibilities as a parent. We have to face the fact that job responsibilities will cut into time with one's children.

SHIRLEY STONE: Women have too much time and too little to do. Not every woman wants to work to fill this time, but once it is her choice to work, once she has made the step, she must devote equal time to her child. It's not the quantity of time but the quality of time that counts. The working woman must arrange time to be with her child. A child needs you, and if you put a child into this world, you must give of yourself to him. There's nothing wrong with a woman working, if she likes to work or needs to work, as long as she doesn't feel guilty about it. I took only two weeks off with each of my three children. If I didn't work I couldn't be a good mother.

ANNE SHEFFIELD: I don't know why you work, but I work because I need the money and I'm not the type to be on welfare. I must give to my daughter within the context of my job.

JUNE BUTTS: The unifying thing about what you both are saying is purely psychological. It is very difficult to think of women as just women. Here she is, either mother or jobholder. I think I epitomize this as a Negro woman, and I speak as the woman on the tape. Woman has been brainwashed as to what she is, a lowly creature, similar to the Negro.

EDGAR BERMAN: You panel members are speaking from a lofty peak. Ninety-nine percent of women are unknowing, can't think at all. What of the average low-level woman? I'm not thinking of the veneer of the species that you represent.

LORRAINE D'ANTONIO: Women who must work then go home and work, too. Should this be?

MARTHA STUART: The whole time schedule of the working world is bad for women. We have to feel more flexibility, so that we can take care of our kiddoes and work, too. Why nine to five? Why can't a man have two half-time secretaries? Why not use a corps of retired women to pinch-hit in a job if the jobholder has a sick child she wants to stay home with? We make a woman feel guilty in the working world if she doesn't perform like a man. It should be the other way around.

We should encourage and support her femininity at the same time we offer her a chance to produce something besides off-spring.

JUNE BUTTS: We do a double-take. We say we are women as long as we have babies. The compliment of the term *mother* gets lost somewhere when we consider women just a means of reproduction—when we are considered women as long as we do this. In a way I understand this as a black woman. There is so much similarity in what's happening to women and to Negroes. The protest and change is in society for the Negro, but it has to be an individual solution and worked out with one person for the woman.

EDGAR BERMAN: Have electricity and the wheel really liberated women?

CONSTANCE DUPRÉ: The idea that woman's place is in the home and man's place is out in the world hasn't been eternal. It came up only in the last century. Everybody's talking about it as though it were something new, but before man and woman *both* worked. They had their source of income in and around their own homes. For instance, they made things and had a sort of cottage industry, and men shared responsibilities in the home also.

With the industrial revolution men left the home, and then there was a sharp division of duties that there hadn't been before.

And now the woman is again entering onto an equal footing with the man in earning an income, so we're now back in the same situation we were in before when we shared responsibilities in both home and work.

Man was taken out of the home by industrialization and woman was left to do the work. Now that she is free to go, she feels guilty about it. She feels she is leaving a traditional role, when in effect it was not really hers alone historically.

FATHER JOHN THOMAS: We shouldn't ignore the healthy

or therapeutic consequences of working outside the home. She will be a better mother in the time she has to spend with the children because she is a happier, more complete woman.

CONSTANCE DUPRÉ: The current feminist movement is actually a reaction against a typical role. Women feel they are not doing what society really expects of them. One doesn't have to be completely involved in household chores to be a good mother. What we're reacting against is the typical role. Perhaps my natural self is not typical at all.

WILLIAM D'ANTONIO: There is very little public awareness of changing history.

RUTH USEEM: Women are, in fact, employed for pay for more years than men. We put you guys through school by working and we work after your retirement.

MICHAEL SCRIVEN: You can run a family any darn way and have success. The child should not feel the parent owes him a life-style. What the parent owes a child is honesty, affection, and hard work, not a style of life.

LEE BULLITT: What is our job? We are emerging as a force. Must we be in a competitive market with men or should it be cooperation? Shouldn't the job market include men and women working together each in their own way? The trouble with equality is it is so equal! When I go out into the job market I want a job because I am a woman and I can contribute as a woman.

GEORGE CHRISTIE: Talent is born in the world irrespective of sex. Let's think of political realities. We need women. How can we provide institutional mechanisms to exploit human potential we condemn to housework?

I don't care if she is a topless waitress or if she is a great physicist, she can work with us even if I have to put a screen around her office so the men can get their work done.

In our country we have been very wasteful. We have accomplished what we have by sheer good luck, despite our extravagance. Our problem is how we can put to work the potential that is woman.

CATHERINE CHILMAN: Our country hasn't used woman's brainpower and skills because we are just now beginning to make provision for her children so she can leave without worrying about them. Women must have special considerations so they can adjust their work to their families. Those kids in high school and college are different from us. We were educated but not at the same pitch. I wonder what these terribly pressured, terribly enriched, terribly educated children are going to do.

RUTH USEEM: I'm staggered by the expressions of guilt-taking in this group.

HAROLD GIBBONS: We must forget about exceptions for women. If a woman wants to take on the competition of a man's world, then she must forget about special considerations. She can't have these and freedom, too.

ENE RIISNA: If I have a good job and my husband has a good job, why do I have to be the one to get up and make the beds, fix breakfast, and dress the children and get them off to school? Would you be prepared to do this?

HAROLD GIBBONS: No more than any other man around here!

JESSIE BERNARD: You all talk as though there was no research on this. Since 1940, women have been going to work in droves. It hasn't hurt them or their husbands or the kids. The husbands do go back into the homes, help with jobs, though they may not like it. Many women go back however, who have never read a book, heard us sociologists, or felt guilty about it. She likes the TV set she has bought with her money.

JUNE BUTTS: Some of this guilt is my fault. My husband is a psychiatrist and psychoanalyst. He's the one-tenth-of-one-percent Negro in his occupational rank. I wish he were here because he could say it better, and I fear looking like the matriarchal Negro woman with the absent man.

BETTY ROLLIN: There are men who would just as soon not be threatened and women who would just as soon not work harder. When you decide to do anything, you also decide not to do something else. If you are a single woman and have something you like very much to do, you must make a choice —the choice of marrying or remaining single for a much better reason.

When I did a story on teen-age marriage, I had a feeling that many of the young women got pregnant because there was nothing else to do. They felt that it was better to be pregnant than to be a typist.

RUTH USEEM: There was a study in the Detroit schools that established that girls preferred pregnancy to school. They got pregnant so they could drop out of school, until the attendance law was changed. Now that we have changed the law on this, it should be better. Pregnant or not, you're in school.

MARTHA STUART: I think we'd better change the school, too, don't you?

ELEANOR CHRISTIE: Apropos of changing the school—all of these discussions so far have not touched on education, which shocks me, because Dr. Berman's prediction of the future and what it holds can horribly come true unless we start now, right now, with education for people to become people, not people to be men and people to be women, female and male. We've got to start educating our children to be people, real people. If we don't, I can see what Dr. Berman said will happen.

I think that the way we are struggling with these clichés and conventional ways of thinking about women and women's roles stem from what we were arguing about earlier today— culture. Our culture is pressuring girls and women at the present, and has ever since the Second World War, that is, pressurizing them into this business of "stay at home, this is the woman's role." It's changing, but when I was growing up and when I was a young woman, this pressure was pretty terrific, and apparently it's still pretty strong because so many of our young girls are getting married before they're even grown up. The pressure is there.

RUTH USEEM: One reason for the pressure is that we are producing a lot of very immature men who want a mother for a wife.

WILLIAM LAMERS: In fact, they always will.

RUTH USEEM: But then they grow up and they don't want a child bride.

WILLIAM D'ANTONIO: Ruth, I think, as you said this afternoon, items of behavior become part of the culture when they are summarized. Perhaps what we have here is that lag between a lot of empirical experience that has changed male-female roles and the society, summarizing it and distilling it so that it becomes part of a consciously shared culture pattern.

JESSIE BERNARD: The feminine mystique and all that has occurred is very exaggerated. The proportion of degrees that were given to women, the master's degrees and the doctoral degrees, are in inverse ratio to the birth rate. When the birth rate goes up, the proportion of women getting master's and doctorates goes down, and when the birth rate goes down, these go up.

CONSTANCE DUPRÉ: I disagree thoroughly that we should not educate women to be women and men to be men, because although I think men and women are people in the market place—in other words, they're interchangeable in jobs—they're not interchangeable in their relationship to one another as men and women. I think that there's so much confusion about this. I think that most jobs could just as easily have a man or a woman in them, but you cannot tell me, at least not from my personal experience, that my husband and I do not basically react differently on things, whether it's in the sexual sphere or in our way of dealing with people. You can say that this is cultural tradition. Perhaps it is. I think that being a man, as man toward woman, and being a woman, as woman toward man, is an art and it has to be learned. A woman learns how to understand a man. She learns how to live with him. The man knows only too well how hard it is to understand the woman and that it is a lifetime role to learn to live with her as a woman. My feeling is that if women would realize this and if men would realize this—that woman's entering the market place would not threaten their feminity because this is a different thing—then we would have much less of a problem.

JESSIE BERNARD: I would like to say that even if they did think and feel alike, they're reacted to differently, which makes all the difference in the world. A woman is reacted to differently.

RUTH USEEM: So, react right back!

WILLIAM LIU: We shouldn't forget that we are also human, too. It's already very late and some of you have been travelling all day. You probably would like to talk more informally and perhaps go down to the basement of the Morris Inn and have a drink. This whole evening I felt very hopeless and helpless, because I cannot participate in any way. The only thing I have to say is, in my experience, I think that this society and probably society in the world in general has overemphasized this sex-type behavior. We have names for men and names for women and we have genders in the language and we have etiquette which is defined separately for each sex. Moreover, I think that in a way it is true that women try to exploit their sex difference as they are talking about equality. A career woman in the East is not identified as a woman either by herself or by her associates, and she often retains her maiden name after marriage. She is not to be treated as a woman or a person of a different sex. For instance, you cannot tell a woman whom you know, who is the wife of your friend, that she is beautiful or that her dress is nice, because the moment you make that judgment you are treating her as a sex object and that is not allowed in the culture. All the cultural forces are minimizing the sex differences in sex behavior; at the same time the differences remain, and nobody gets really upset about it. I'm terribly amused by the desire to be equal and at the same time the desire to be different.

MARTHA STUART: We started dinner with Sister Jean's grace and she has a graceful remark that she wants to make.

SISTER JEAN WALLACE: Someone asked for a comment by a woman who wasn't married and I'm sitting here. I haven't ever been married and I doubt if I ever will be, and in this context I think of an essay written by a Catholic college student on the subject of birth control. It began with the idea that there is one method of birth control universally approved by the Catholic Church. The way that I live is somewhat like the song that Peter, Paul, and Mary sing about, "If I had wings no one would ask me could I fly." The theme of the song is "if you don't really understand, then I can't explain it to you too well." But I do think that the sociologists this afternoon made a marvelous defense of celibacy even though it's not too intelligible to Protestants. I do work with Jews, too, and it's very hard to explain it to them. I'll just do as the song says, "I'll just be me."

I would like to say that leading this life of celibacy doesn't make me feel that I'm any less a woman, and in a sense I do feel a dimension of freedom which I can't explain too well, either. As Dr. Liu said, he could come up to me and tell me he liked my dress and no one would get up and try to pick a fight with him. This is a very simple way of my saying that I can relate to both men and women just as persons and this is the freedom that I really appreciate, but I won't say that celibacy is an easy way of life.

I discussed this matter with a Jewish gentleman who drove me home from an airport once. He was asking me questions and I said to him "Well, it's hard for you, isn't it, to be faithful to your wife all the time?" And he said; "Well, as a matter of fact, yes." So then I said "Well, in a way, it's sort of the same thing." But I do appreciate this dimension of living, of relating to people as persons; and I think that, as women, we're missing the point just by trying to get into the labor market. I think the important thing is not just to get there but what do we take when we get there? We take ourselves, as persons and as women who should have love and concern and understanding, which all persons have but which I really do think is one of the special great contributions that women have to give.

WILLIAM LIU: Tomorrow morning's session will begin at 10 o'clock.

Female Sexuality 5

WILLIAM H. MASTERS AND VIRGINIA E. JOHNSON

Tuesday, 10:00 A.M.

FATHER CHARLES SHEEDY: I want to say good morning to everybody, both participants and the good crowd of observers. My own name is Father Charlie Sheedy, and I'm from here. I'm Chairman of the morning session. I'm not very well briefed on this subject (*laughter*). However, I do know something about the principal speakers this morning. Both are very well known. They have acquired a large—you might say sensational —reputation for their work in the last few years. They are co-authors of the very well known book *Human Sexual Response*. The subject of this morning's session is "Female Sexuality." They will make a combined talk in an informal manner. They are not reluctant to be interrupted if anybody wishes to ask a question during the presentation. Of course, at the end of the talk there will be time for discussion, questions, argument, agreement, and disagreement. So, I am very glad to be able to present to you Bill Masters and Virginia Johnson.

VIRGINIA JOHNSON: In going over the list of concepts and questions that was suggested as preliminary reading for this conference and contemplation during it, one of the questions asked was how men and women will adjust to a relational rather than a procreational sense of purpose. This appeared to us, perhaps, to be the most important area for thought. The quality of this relational sense of purpose will probably make a crucial difference in the quality of what was termed yesterday the *contraceptive society* in this country. We could not agree more with Father Thomas' plea for the evolvement of a realistic, workable system of relational values before aimlessly and mindlessly destroying tradition or traditional patterns. But we would like to suggest particularly that as the human female develops a sense of self, she may make the crucial difference in this contraceptive society. This we know (my one dogmatic statement of the entire conference): her sexuality, and thereby its contribution to society, is vested in her concept of self, in the way she perceives and values herself, or how she is valued.

Before we go further, however, since so little of what has been done in St. Louis has been published, it might be valuable to describe briefly the concept, progress, and level of return of our investigative process. For this I would like to defer for the moment to Bill.

WILLIAM MASTERS: She always gives me these nice jobs! I think it's best to tell you that work in the area of human sexual response has been going on since 1954. Three entirely different research populations have been developed: the sexually adequate, the sexually inadequate, and the sexually inverted. All these groups are highly selective. They are unique in that they represent established sexual units and a relatively high degree of intelligence—certainly not a cross-section of the population. Since 1954, individuals in the first group, the laboratory or sexually adequate population, called the *study-subject population,* have volunteered to work in the investigation of the physiology, anatomy, and psychology of sexual response. They now number well over 700, and recorded material in the laboratory represents something over 14,000 orgasmic experiences. It is important to emphasize that initially our interest was in two areas of sexual response: what happens—the physiology and anatomy of sexual response— and why it happens—the psychology of sexual response—as opposed to the Kinsey-type interest, that is, sociologically oriented, interpersonal interrogation to determine when, how frequently, or under what circumstances sexual activity occurs.

This does not mean, however, that a significant amount of material of an interrogative nature has not been accrued. In order to work with a study-subject population, a great deal of screening of volunteers has to be done. Although over 700 individuals have been worked with in the laboratory, the number who have volunteered is something over 1,400. The fallout, dropout, or withdrawal comes during the process of in-depth interrogation which is carried on with every volunteer.

From this intensive interrogation a large amount of material has been gathered and some concepts developed of the integrity and validity of the human female's concept of herself as a sexual entity. An average of four to five hours of interrogation of each volunteer unit has been necessary to get the job done. Interrogation has been conducted first by members of each sex and then by members of both sexes as a team, so that no material is collected solely on the basis of a single-sex concept. This factor, of course, has been one of the great prejudicial concerns of investigative evaluation in the past. For example, we studied the Kinsey operation in detail, hoping to learn from their mistakes (not that we haven't made a gorgeous crop all our own). In research, progress usually is based on learning from those who have gone before. We happen to think (retrospectively, of course) that the greatest mistake Kinsey ever made was not having a female interrogator on his team from the onset of his endeavor. Because of this oversight, the Kinsey volume on the female published in 1954 really represents essentially a male concept of female sexuality when interpretive elements of the text are considered separately. This work has great value, of course, but nothing compared to what it would have had if the Kinsey group had included a female interpreter.

In 1959 we began to develop another group, the sexually inadequate population, to provide the opportunity to apply clinically what was learned in the laboratory about the "whats" and "whys" of sexual response. In this second population, as of this moment, 412 individuals have been treated for sexual inadequacy—for such things as impotence, frigidity, premature ejaculation, and marked discrepancy in levels of sexual tension within the marital unit. A third population has been maturing since 1963, a homosexual population, that has been 80 percent oriented to the female homosexual.

From this background and this type of material, we're trying today to present some concept of female sexuality. Obviously, the laboratory material has been gathered from those who can function well in sexual responsivity or they wouldn't have been included in the study-subject population. There is contrasting material from those who are functioning poorly in true-life situations, at least according to their concept of adequacy. And there is material from women who have overt homosexual interests. All material is prejudiced, selective, and must be generalized. It is incredibly educative, however, particularly for the male, who really doesn't know what the female is talking about anyway when she speaks of her sexuality; who will never know anything about the physical aspects of her sexual response patterning because he will never experience it; who must observe, who must extrapolate from stated fact; and above all, who must have authoritative interpretation.

VIRGINIA JOHNSON: I'd like to add a footnote here. In spite of our concern for interpretation, our concern that the female must interpret herself and the male must interpret himself, we have been struck repeatedly from the beginning of our work by the similarities between the male and the female rather than the differences—the similarities in physiological response, in psychosocial orientation, and, most especially, in their requirements to live self-identified lives effectively and to contribute them to a viable relationship together—always the similarities, rarely the differences.

WILLIAM MASTERS: Yes, this is of incredible importance. I'd like to make one final statement regarding the background and work with the second great population, the sexually inadequate. We have insisted that there's no such thing as an uninvolved partner in a marriage in which there is sexual inadequacy. Therefore, both members of the marital unit must be present to be evaluated and worked with. Here again, there obviously is in-depth interrogation of the marital unit.

Our clinical work in the treatment of sexual inadequacy was nine years old in December, 1967. However, the findings will not be presented until the work has been carried on one more year to provide five years of follow-up on enough couples. It doesn't matter how successful therapy is in reversing the symptoms of sexual inadequacy rapidly (this is now being done in approximately two weeks). The important thing is how effectively the symptom reversal is maintained over a period of years. So our material will not be presented until we have five years of follow-up.

As a male, I have learned something about female sexuality. But I've learned it just as much from males as from females —trying to work with their stumbling blocks, their lack of concepts, their inability to verbalize their concerns, their feelings, their observations. As a male, I've learned even more from this opportunity to work with the marital units because I have had female suggestion, direction, intellectual hand-holding, and support from my partner.

VIRGINIA JOHNSON: Now, to go on. The first obligation of the investigation has been to compile a scientific body of knowledge on sexuality. Many popular theories of human sexuality, male or female, have been based on superstition and fallacy; they have never been based on physiological fact. So establishing physiological fact was certainly a major commitment of the total research program. Some of this superstition turned out to be accurate; but so often, and in terribly divisive ways, it was inaccurate, and whole theories of sexual behavior or expression were based on these misconceptions.

We have never believed—we couldn't believe it because we couldn't work with it—that physical fact is the be-all and end-all of sexual response. It's quite secondary; it's only a part of a total-body involvement. But we happen to think it's terribly important, for professionals especially, to have a base line of knowledge in the area, because those who are faced with the transition currently taking place in sexually oriented tradition and activity do well to establish a base line of scientific knowledge and social awareness from which to handle the sexual problems presented to them. They need an edge over the general population that considers itself expert in the field of sexuality. It's fortunate that people do feel themselves expert, because it's from this point that they derive the courage and the sense of identity which leads them to the successes that do occur in those total relationships of which sexuality is a component.

What then constitutes the edge of knowledge for the individuals dealing with problems in the area of sexual response? First, it is being aware of what exists in the realm of physical fact, knowing what really happens to the body during all forms of sexual stimulation. The fallacies existing in this area alone are legion. The physical reaction of the body to sexual stimulation can be the quantitative component of sexual response. Second, the edge of knowledge is completed by the awareness of a wide range of variability of those factors which influence the currents of sexual response in each individual. This is terribly important, and yet it is such a cloudy, fuzzy area of thinking in this society. Those things which are important to the individual make up the qualitative components of sexual response: affection and regard, acceptance of sex per se. These factors are conditioned socially and environmentally. They have a primary effect upon the sexual dimension of human personality. These factors will be discussed for the rest of the morning.

There are two definitions that should be thrown in at this time in order to clarify what may be discussed. They relate to the way we use the terms *sex* and *sexuality*. Most people working in the field have come to accept some differentiation between these terms. Arbitrarily we have defined sex as sexual activity per se—masturbation, intercourse, deliberate sexual excitation—and all the variables therein—heterosexual activity, homosexual activity, and what have you. Sexuality has been defined as a dimension and expression of personality. It is the quality of being a sexual, reproductive entity. *Reproductive* does not necessarily mean actively reproducing. This quality exists in, colors, and controls all individuals, even those living celibate lives. It is a viable part of the establishment of identity. This quality is the crucial factor in how individuals will adjust and adapt to the transitions that are taking place in society. Since we're primarily considering the female, let us talk then about the identity that has to be brought to a viable affective relationship with a man, that which supports the relational as opposed to the procreational role which seems destined to be woman's pattern of life for the next few hundred years.

WILLIAM MASTERS: Specifically, for the sexually responsive woman the double standard ceases to exist. The woman expressing sexual tension, the woman responding to sexual stimulation effectively, loses herself in personal demand. She continues, of course, to be concerned for her partner's satisfaction, but it is inevitably true that for any man or woman to reach orgasmic release, a significant degree of selfishness or personal demand must be expressed, must be enjoyed, must be lived. It is fascinating to watch the human female in severe orgasmic experience—in multiorgasmic experience, in driving, demanding, interpersonal exchange that still is primarily centered in "I-Me"—and then to see her revert, as she relaxes after orgasmic expression, into the analytic concept of woman's passive role in sexual expression, a role that she completely rejects as she's responding to effective sexual stimulation.

Perhaps an example is in order. In the last few years a good deal of observation of sleep has been done. There also is a general awareness of the human tendency after male ejaculation or female orgasmic experience to relax and go to sleep, particularly if the partners relate. The female reacts in an entirely different way from the male during the first hour of sleep after orgasmic experience. She may have been driving, demanding, concentrating totally on her own satisfaction; and yet as she sleeps, for the first hour after successful sexual expression she frequently does two things. She moves nearer to the male, the male body. If he is removed from the bed and she is not awakened, she may hunt for him. She will reach out; she will move toward the spot he occupied; and, at least half the time, she will curl up in the spot where he was. If exactly the reverse experiment is conducted and the female is removed, the postorgasmic male stays where he is; he doesn't cuddle up or

hunt for the female partner. We're talking dominant percent-
ages of reaction, of course, but it is fascinating to see. As the
female's sexual tensions are satisfied, she reverses—she suc-
cumbs—to an innate demand to identify, to orient at an incredibly personal level and, obviously, at a subconscious level.

VIRGINIA JOHNSON: Well, woman is and always has been
a sexually responding being. Her orgasmic response is as identifiable to her as ejaculation is to the male, even without the
ejaculatory phenomenon. Psychologically, it is a subjective perception of a peak of physical reaction to sexual stimulation. It
is a total-body response. It is only through centuries of restraint and adaptation to the role to which she has been assigned that . . .

WILLIAM MASTERS: Yes, of course, the tragedy of our
particular society is that Victoria had so much more influence
here than she did in England (*laughter*).

The analytic concept of woman as passive and receptive
sexually is a male concept only. In actual fact, the sexually
effective female responding to male stimulation is certainly
driving and demanding satisfaction as a total entity. The
female who says, "Here I am, you lucky fellow," in short
order loses the lucky fellow. However, the interesting reactions of the female as she sleeps—demanding identification,
demanding body contact—give great food for thought.

Of course, the male's erective processes during the rapid
eye movement (REM) periods of sleep have been well established. What is under investigation now is whether the female
does the same thing. Measuring the production of vaginal
lubrication may be the procedure of choice because the process
of vaginal lubrication in the female, in response to any form
of sexual stimulation, begins just a few seconds more slowly
than the erective process in the male. The male erection is,
in fact, a mounting demand, while female lubrication ex-
presses a mounting acceptance. So vaginal lubrication pro-

duced during the REM periods of sleep is being measured to see whether the state of psychological eroticism associated with the rapid eye movement is reflected physiologically by the female as well as the male.

JESSIE BERNARD: Have you been able to stimulate orgasm in either males or females while they're asleep, by music or other kinds of stimulation?

WILLIAM MASTERS: This hasn't been attempted. For the present the investigation is focused on what the individual does naturally. And that "naturally" is always conditional, because there's nothing natural about the laboratory. However, some concept of what really happens physically must be established. For that reason, no stimuli have been employed that the individuals don't provide, innately or involuntarily, on their own. For instance, no work has been done with drugs or any chemical entity that theoretically might stimulate or depress sexual functioning. However, experiments have been conducted to provide evidence of the female's subjective appreciation of sexual function.

For example, an experiment has been going on since 1962 which has not been published but has been described a couple of times recently at medical meetings. The magic number 400 was established for this experiment, heaven knows why. Anyway, progress currently rests at 352. A physiologist is placed in a room with the equipment necessary to record the orgasmic experience of a woman who is in a separate room. He has no idea of who the individual is and no concept of what form of stimulation is to be applied. As Mrs. Johnson has said, orgasmic expression is absolutely as identifiable for the female as ejaculation is for the male. It is also absolutely identifiable with the physiologist's recording equipment. (If an intra-uterine electrode has been placed, a specific tracing pattern is produced.) The physiologist is asked to grade the orgasmic experience in terms of intensity and duration—how severe it was, how long it lasted—with gradation from one to four. The individual female, too, grades the same experience in terms of her subjective appreciation of its intensity and duration. The two gradings are then correlated to see whether the physical recording techniques are beginning to express the sum correlations of the subjective appreciation.

In order to make the experiment more objective, any recording of multiorgasmic return was eliminated from consideration simply because such a recording would be absolutely identifiable by both participants and obviously would improve the percentage success of the experiment. The correlation between the intensity grading of the single orgasmic experience by the physiologist in one room and the woman experiencing orgasm in the other has been 82 percent. The experiment wasn't terminated with these observations. Taking advantage of the above-average intelligence of most of the female study-subjects, investigative interest was focused in addition upon their subjective appreciation of the orgasmic interlude—how they valued the experience—to provide yet another dimension of understanding.

An example—on Wednesday Mrs. Smith, in the laboratory after three days of continence, experiences a masturbatory orgasm that is overwhelming. Masturbatory orgasmic expression is usually stronger and lasts longer than coital experience. And on Saturday, with again about three days of continence, she's orgasmic during coition with her husband. On Wednesday she might have rated the intensity and duration of the experience a grade four. On Saturday, orgasm might be a very minor physical experience—two or three or four contractions at the most—a grade one by mutual agreement between the individual and the physiologist. Yet the low grade for physical intensity and duration doesn't necessarily describe the level of the woman's subjective appreciation of the two events.

VIRGINIA JOHNSON: Of course, this has to do with what was termed earlier the *qualitative variable*. In other words, she values subjectively according to the qualitative component, which has to do with the regard for the individual, the interplay and exchange between partners. However, to be objective one must also evaluate her fantasy patterns during the masturbatory experience. They will be indicative of the value placed on the experience. She may simply be summoning prior time and place of success with her husband, and therefore making it somewhat subjectively comparable to coital experience. A case is being made primarily for the female's naturally occurring sexuality—for the female as a sexual being—in order to redefine her role.

WILLIAM MASTERS: Actually, this is exactly what she's expressing. Usually she will say that, although the intensity and duration of orgasmic return was minor on Saturday, she enjoyed it more, it meant so much more to her. This differentiation is hard for the average male to comprehend, because for the male an ejaculation, from a physiological point of view, is a rose, is a rose, is a rose sort of thing. There is rarely the tremendous swing of physical intensity and duration of experience that the woman feels.

Males now are acknowledging what women have known for centuries: that there's no comparison between the two sexes in terms of biological potential, *biological* in this case meaning only the physical ability to respond to sexual stimulation. The human female is an infinitely more effective sexually responding entity than the male ever dreamed of being.

VIRGINIA JOHNSON: Many cultural developments in the civilizing process have imposed controls and demands upon woman which have altered her basic ability to respond sexually in direct parallel to the extent of her ability or inability to adjust to the controls. Many women, historically, have been responsive, have been able to function within marriage in a totally contributing role. (It seems impossible that this has occurred just in the last century.) But there have been other cultures in this country and abroad in which women are considered chattels. This concept has caused women to be seen as second-rate citizens, as secondary members of a double-standard society, and many women have not been able to adapt and yet remain complete individuals. May we refer in this regard to Father Thomas' statement yesterday about Latin American women. He said that some of them have even vested their own sexual interests and their own sexual capacity in their husband's virility—in other words, in the marks he makes on the wall. Certainly, this is an adaptation: this is simply building their own identity, sexual or otherwise, around their husband's sexual claims to fame. (I hope this doesn't sound like dogma.)

The problem (the hang-up, if you will) occurs primarily when the female member of a partnership maintained under the double standard is needed for participation beyond simple domesticity, or if her own golden dream reaches beyond second-rate citizenry. Either resentment or insecurity probably will undermine her sense of personal identity, so she needs to fulfill the larger role. We're not talking necessarily about her need for freedom of sexual expression, just the knowledge that she's free to be what she has identified herself to be.

WILLIAM MASTERS: Possibly the reason so much of the writing about female sex and sexuality has been done by males is the fact that the female has just not had the opportunity for equality or freedom of sexual expression. But now that she has the opportunity, she's hung. She has grave difficulty expressing herself, particularly if she has to express herself under pressure. Maybe this social insecurity is just a passing stage in a changing society in which she is given the maturity of a role and the responsibility associated with such maturity.

VIRGINIA JOHNSON: Well, in transition she does make some notable mistakes. She sometimes confuses privilege with equality. Ideally, this will be counteracted by the establishment of a real sense of identity. Some very fine sociological work has noted that the female significantly dropped the ball in pursuit of her own identity once she achieved the vote, once her legal rights were established. Suddenly she failed to pursue and establish her personal requirements. She failed to continue to support her own social viability in this regard.

Sociologists, in seeking to explain this, have come up with the bit of knowledge that the human female, when pursuing one particular goal, works very, very well. However, once she achieves that goal, she tends to drop the pursuit. This has primarily to do with the fact that most of her inner action, most of her personal life, is oriented to the opposition, if you will. In other words, it's spent with a male and not with females who share common concerns and problems.

It is our impression that there is a new impetus entering her life. This impetus is not inherent in herself but in the changing cultural requirement of her partner, who now desires her to be a participating entity. In other words, she no longer can remain a nonresponsible member of the relationship, the passive one, the one in the "here I am, you lucky fellow" role. The intelligent male today seems to be demanding a more personally secure, effectively participating woman. It is our hope that he will continue to do so.

I want to honor one person. When we remark upon the fact that almost all interpretations of female sexuality or female identity have been done by men and then imply that they really don't know what they're talking about, I would like to suggest that you follow up on Dr. Abraham H. Maslow's concept of women. (He actually applies it to all people.) But he perceives more than anyone else that I am familiar with, in his concept of self-actualizing people, the need to know yourself, the need to be something before you can give something.

JACQUELINE GRENNAN: I was fascinated with Virginia's statement a while ago, "She sometimes confuses privilege with equality." I was wondering at that statement, and then you referred to Maslow's application to the human person. It seems to me this has terribly important implications for the whole notion of dominance in groups, or in what we call categories, in our time. If you have a dominant category, and that's the status quo, actually the first movement against it seems to be antidominance. I think there are great reverberations on the race issue, on socioeconomic issues, on all kinds of things in this same line, and that until you break down the notion of dominance, you get a counterdominance before you get the kind of egoistic input that may have a mutuality in it.

VIRGINIA JOHNSON: It's really a "give-to-get" sort of thing, but it so often becomes the flag of competition. Any attempt to participate is always suspected as competition.

WILLIAM MASTERS: If we carry this just a little further, we might move into the concept of the female homosexual. Here is a dominant-passive type of relationship, particularly if the relationship is on a relatively permanent basis. And yet— despite the fact that this dominant-passive relationship certainly exists in sexual activity, in which male and female roles are played out—observing these individuals in sleep after mutual, multiorgasmic exhaustion, if either female is removed from the bed, no matter which has played the dominant role, the one remaining seeks her partner. They seek as females regardless of their conscious role-playing. This is suggestive support of the concept that even when one accepts a pattern of dominance at a conscious level, subjective response is yet another subject.

JESSIE BERNARD: With male homosexuals, does the one in the female role also seek the dominant partner? And do dominant male homosexuals also seek the passive partner?

WILLIAM MASTERS: This can't be answered with security now. The impression persists that the females are female while asleep in the first hour after mutually effective sexual release. Males are male regardless of how they choose to express their sexuality. However, too little has been done in this area to allow a dogmatic answer.

VIRGINIA JOHNSON: There are so many directions to go. I do make a further plea for accepting the facts as they are. As recently as 1957, a textbook in psychosomatic gynecology stated quite clearly that the female has neither the capacity nor the desire to respond sexually. There's an awful lot of this type of thing in the literature. Another reference is more pertinent to this particular setting. In 1966 a widely used reference book was published of a symposium on woman that was really quite superb, but for some unusual reason they chose a nonscientifically oriented male to establish the biological facts about women. He is a brilliant and frequently compassionate man, but he embodies so much of what I like to term *archaic man*. On the one hand, he seeks to give woman a role of social equity, but on the other, he repeatedly lessens her chances for achieving it with phrases such as: "Her own self-identity and self-development as a person should be of greater importance than her heterosexual orientation"—separating her out from herself. This, of course, shows the need to place interpretation with people who can interpret rather than with erudite, compassionate people who simply don't understand women.

What kind of thinking must seek to separate woman's self-identity from her sexual role? Unless she learns to value her sexuality as she develops the other facets of her personality, how can she securely direct the course of her life and how can she select the partner, if any, with whom she wishes to share it? If, indeed, you do not establish the fact of the individual's sexual identity and then allow the person to choose a way of living that to her or to him has greater value or greater destiny, it would seem to rob a choice of celibacy of its value.

WILLIAM MASTERS: Sexual response certainly is a naturally occurring phenomenon. Yet it can be delayed indefinitely or denied for a lifetime, as in the celibate life. Sexual response does have this unique facility. What other physical response can actually be delayed or rejected voluntarily? For example, respiratory and bowel responses are forever with us.

VIRGINIA JOHNSON: But sexual expression cannot be denied, not without physical manifestations of the rejection.

WILLIAM MASTERS: Of course not, but this is all part of the concept of sacrifice.

HAROLD GIBBONS: What are the physical manifestations of sexual rejection?

WILLIAM MASTERS: You mean on the long-range basis? They vary completely with the individual's personality, Harold.

VIRGINIA JOHNSON: Yes, and also with the individual's inherent requirements in this regard. Each person copes with celibacy achieved by voluntary selection or involuntary social rejection in a different way. Just one little passing example (and do remember that there are so many that we could turn this session into a clinical, medical discussion)—the female who has chosen celibacy at a very young, undeveloped stage, when she has not identified her sexual capacity, will for the rest of her life cycle develop her sexuality—her responsiveness —along rather standard, identifiable patterns. Of course, the intensity and degree of sexual response are always individually variable. If she rejects, or if her social commitment causes her to reject, all manner of release of the normal development of her sexual being, she may experience the distress of chronic pelvic vascular congestion. Over a long period of time, the symptoms of this physiological distress may or may not cause her major physical manifestations. In other words some women can, and some can't, sublimate the pelvic discomforts, the physical restlessness, of sexual need.

WILLIAM MASTERS: Pain sometimes.

VIRGINIA JOHNSON: Or pain, yes, might come to the surface. If this woman were someone who had had babies, the pelvic vascular congestion probably would be far more severe and far more a clinical entity to be dealt with than would be expected from the sexually inexperienced celibate. The sublimation of the physical distress may be quite difficult. It depends on that individual woman's ability to discipline herself —again, a variable. The male who has chosen celibacy for a period of time, or indefinitely, frequently has nocturnal emissions as a physical manifestation of the social "putting aside" of sexual tensions.

Certainly the prerogative to choose a celibate life must be retained. We would never deny this choice of destiny. But in view of such a choice, we would like to be able to help the individual cope with physical manifestations that might develop.

HERBERT RICHARDSON: You suggested that the permanent delay of some kind of sexual activity is harmful. I think that's the impression that was gathered here.

WILLIAM MASTERS: No one suggested that.

VIRGINIA JOHNSON: It was not implied at all.

WILLIAM MASTERS: We were asked to specify some of the physical symptoms that develop from celibacy. I think celibacy can be physically harmful, certainly, but this has to do with a specific situation. There are many men and women who cannot, despite their initial orientation, continue their life in celibacy. For others there may be no untoward physical result.

HERBERT RICHARDSON: Well, now, let me ask you—how can it be harmful?

WILLIAM MASTERS: It may be more psychological than physical.

HERBERT RICHARDSON: Good. Now what kinds of psychological investigations have you made to determine that this can be harmful?

WILLIAM MASTERS: Psychological investigations have been conducted of a very few individuals whose lives are devoted to celibacy and who have been referred to us for relief of the basic physical complaints associated with this strain.

VIRGINIA JOHNSON: Clinical study, primarily, in the structure of our research. But in our particular design, one plays itself back and forth into the other. When we pick up a manifestation, it is played into a structure.

HERBERT RICHARDSON: Good. Now is the harm that was done the result of some kind of failure to exercise the biological function of having sexual intercourse or not?

WILLIAM MASTERS: It cannot be confined to the statement of intercourse. Let's say that some of the distress engendered in a few pathological situations that we've encountered basically reflects an inability to orient to, or acknowledge, or receive, some form of sexual release. I certainly wouldn't confine it to intercourse.

VIRGINIA JOHNSON: Or it depends on the adaptation of the body to the imposed chastity.

HERBERT RICHARDSON: In other words, what you're really saying is that you have no evidence from your biological study that even permanent delay of engaging in sexual activities causes harm.

WILLIAM MASTERS: Again, no. You're interpreting. As Mrs. Johnson has repeatedly said, we have worked with women who have developed distress contending with major degrees of unresolved sexual tension. Not infrequently, these women develop clinical symptoms such as menorrhagia or metrorrhagia. Some of the celibate women in our series have a history of coming to hysterectomy to control bleeding. The etiology of this functional bleeding distress primarily is hypothalamic as far as we're concerned.

KERMIT KRANTZ: I think that's the whole point. There's

no question that when it begins to move into the hypothalamic area of the brain, damage can occur. There's some beautiful work that's been done about this, and there are excellent data supporting it. There is no question about it. Degradation is a proof of this. Blocking can get to the point where, with degradation, it can lead to adenocarcinoma or cancer of the uterus.

HERBERT RICHARDSON: Now, I'm a layman here and technical jargon has been used here . . .

KERMIT KRANTZ: Well, I'm not using technical jargon. You know what the word *cancer* means. You know what the word *degradation* means.

HERBERT RICHARDSON: I don't know. I'm stressing this question because I think you are making assumptions which go beyond the biological studies you're doing, and are making statements about social relations between men and women, what is good and bad, functional and dysfunctional.

WILLIAM MASTERS: Just a minute. We haven't said any such thing. We have said only, in answer to Harold Gibbons' question, that there have been cases in which it was felt that the individuals referred to us who had been leading celibate lives evidenced both physical and mental distress in their inability to cope with the demands of their own celibacy. In no sense was an open statement intended. If we have been misinterpreted, we apologize because it was not meant that way.

JESSIE BERNARD: I think that the fact that you are dealing with extremes of distribution leads to a good deal of the confusion. Since you have used a correlation technique, I presume that you assume a normal distribution in your population, and that you're dealing with people who can become ill from this celibacy or who can develop symptoms, a "clinical population."

WILLIAM MASTERS: Exactly.

JESSIE BERNARD: Yes, but the fact that there is a great gap between the clinical and the very active multiorgasmic sex characters shows that it is not something about which we can generalize. I would also like to point out, regarding this in-between population, that when you compare the never-married male and the never-married female, the female shows up a thousand times better, in terms of mental health, in terms of education, occupation, and any index you want to use. Not all of these are celibate, and not all of these are virginal, you know. They may be having regular sexual experience. But some of them are virginal and celibate. So, the fact is, it isn't hurting them any. We have evidence that it can hurt some. But it doesn't have to hurt everybody.

WILLIAM MASTERS: I don't think we have ever suggested that celibacy would hurt *everybody*. In answering a specific question raised here, I would only argue that there certainly are individuals, male and female, who are in major physical and mental distress as a result of living celibate lives.

JACQUELINE GRENNAN: I think this argument is very interesting, because I just heard you say very distinctly that you were answering a very specific question as to what are some consequences of rejecting sexual activity, at least my filter heard you answer that way. I think that in times when people feel very threatened by those who say, "there can be no human fulfillment without conjugal fulfillment," and this extreme sort of thing, if any evidence is given that there are important empirical symptoms of problems with celibate living, then we immediately go on the defensive and say, "you must not say that, because then there's nothing left." I think this argument is terribly important. But unless we are willing to admit in the individual case, or in the category, that there can be severe problems, it seems to me we can't even begin to see with clear eyes whether it's possible for anyone to live a full personal life in complete celibacy. I really don't know the answer. It's very difficult.

VIRGINIA JOHNSON: Jacqueline, people must address themselves to the wide range, to the poles. We have learned that material of sexual content evokes first and foremost, regardless of profession or age, an emotional response first and an intellectual response second. If the emotional response is intense enough, it will preclude the intellectual acceptance of the material, for at least a given period of time.

JOSEPH BIRD: I think what we're faced with along this line is that many of the terms we use—of necessity perhaps because we haven't had anything else—should be discarded. For example, the term *frigidity* has caused many problems and has impeded much of what we have been attempting to do in this area. If you were to use the term *frigidity,* at least as we would operationally define it, I would estimate that the vast majority of American women, married or single, are frigid. The women's magazines have been very guilty of augmenting this, coming out with all sorts of articles saying, "No, this is nonsense; women aren't frigid," or, "Yes, all women are frigid," and so on and so forth. You could define it, I suppose, ranging all the way from whether or not a woman felt some sexual response through masturbation all the way up to total fulfillment, multiple orgasmic experience in marriage.

VIRGINIA JOHNSON: The range is phenomenal.

JOSEPH BIRD: Yes, it is phenomenal, and we get absolutely nowhere as long as we use the term, because it is so loaded that women back up against the wall and say, "My God, I'm not frigid. Don't talk to me about it."

WILLIAM MASTERS: Actually, the term has an incredible range of application. We have seen 103 marital units with the distress of sexual inadequacy on both sides of the fence when the unit was referred for treatment. In 4 of the 103 marital units, the problem turned out to be that the men were primarily impotent. By primary impotence, we mean that these men had failed at their first opportunity at a mounting process, homosexual or heterosexual, and continued to fail every time thereafter. Not one of the four men had ever mounted. Of the four wives who came in with their husbands, three presented and believed the basic complaint that they were frigid (*laughter*).

JESSIE BERNARD: I'd also like to make a point that the double standard was a protection toward men (*laughter*). Because men can't equal women sexually and, therefore, to give some kind of disgrace to women, you had the double standard. I think it's something to consider that if you do emancipate women to become driving, demanding, sexual beings, it could have an extremely traumatic effect on men (*laughter*).

WILLIAM MASTERS: You know, one of the greatest difficulties that the male has, double standard or not, is coping with his sexuality as he ages; this as opposed to the female partner, who has much less difficulty with this problem.

VIRGINIA JOHNSON: It's where he places the emphasis.

WILLIAM MASTERS: Exactly. His great concern is for his demand for ejaculation. This demand decreases as the male ages. However, his facility to achieve and maintain an erection does not unless he talks himself out of it. There's no reason in the world why he can't repeatedly satisfy his wife and ejaculate when he wishes. This is something we have to educate the male to. The male has the ability to cope as long as he doesn't presume he must ejaculate with every female orgasmic experience.

VIRGINIA JOHNSON: I don't think it's coping, I think it's equalitating.

WILLIAM MASTERS: That sounds like a better word.

HERBERT RICHARDSON: I'd just like to draw attention to something. You've been talking about double standard. Now double standard is not a biological category. I would think it belongs in the realm of sociology, psychology, and those things. You've been quite condemnatory of the notion of the double standard. Now, I'd like to know on what biological grounds you can be condemnatory. And I'd like to ask you whether you've reflected on what kind of social function the double standard might play, as well as perhaps ask what the double standard *is*? In addition to this, I'd like to ask, when you affirm categorically that the man's primary demand is for ejaculation, do you mean . . .

WILLIAM MASTERS: I said the aging male.

HERBERT RICHARDSON: The aging male, yes. Now, do you mean that this is the demand that takes precedence over every other demand, such as, for example, eating, or sleeping? Does it take precedence over the demand for social prestige in the neighborhood? I think that we should, at least, not allow the discussion of the total set of problems—sociological, psychological, economic, and so forth—to be pressed simply in terms of the special perspective of the single discipline.

WILLIAM MASTERS: I think you're right, and I will withdraw the statement.

MICHAEL SCRIVEN: I think Herb is being too tough about this. Dr. Masters is talking about a male's sex life. He's not assuming that somebody's dropping his status symbol when he becomes 50 years old.

WILLIAM MASTERS: As a matter of fact, it's a very good perspective to maintain. We presume to express competence in but one area. The ejaculatory function is a male's concern as he ages sexually. The most threatening thing to the male as he ages is his considered loss of effectiveness, his loss of facility for frequent ejaculation. Here he doubts himself. I'm competent to say that. Beyond that, you're right.

VIRGINIA JOHNSON: The aging male is living in doubt. His value system has said that ejaculation is the expression of his sexual capacity, of his success, of his identity.

WILLIAM MASTERS: We're not talking in terms of the social context or in terms of economics either. There is evidence of this biological reaction to aging, and a facility for counteracting this on a biological basis only has been developed. This will have not only tremendous physiological implications but psychological implications as well.

JAMES SEMMENS: Bill, excuse me. I know that in counseling patients in this particular area, in the aging group, I've been impressed with the fact that we all learn that the female has to have everything going for her emotionally, with identity and all this, in order to respond sexually, at least, in our new middle-class concept of it. I'm saying that the male who is unable to respond all of a sudden needs these things going for him, too. When he's young, he can respond physically; this is part of his makeup. But later in life, he needs these other things going for him. This is where we see impotence. Maybe thinking about this might help us.

VIRGINIA JOHNSON: Jim, the similarities rather than the differences—always, always, always, always.

JAMES SEMMENS: That's right.

MARTHA STUART: The truth is we need each other.

VIRGINIA JOHNSON: Martha or someone should restate the purpose of this conference. Having been in this work for eleven years, we know the emotional impact of this field. Jessie knows it too, and many of you have also been fighting this battle, seeking only to get through the transition, to redefine the interaction between males and females in order to bring something more to the viability of the marital relationship. It has been very hard. Until such time as all of us begin to learn a smattering of the other disciplines' vocabularies and semantic implications, until such time as we can keep our defenses down and develop a whole new mutual vocabulary that applies to the here and now—and get away from a vocabulary that is historical, biblical, and no longer either applicable or sensible —until we can do that, we all must try and keep to a minimum the emotional impact of sexual material or we are going to stalemate over and over again as we have in the past.

JESSIE BERNARD: I would like to raise one more point. I

know that people are not fish, but Konrad K. Lorenz, in the study of the cichled fish, found that when females were aggressive, the males just faded out; they couldn't function. There may be a cultural equivalent to that in human society. Women may have had more or less a hidden wish to protect male sexuality because they could conceive, aroused or not. However, they couldn't be impregnated unless the men were aroused. So women may have accepted, by sort of an unwritten compact, that if sexual satisfaction had to be given up, they would do it, because it was more important for the male to retain his sexuality than for the female in order to conceive.

VIRGINIA JOHNSON: This has to be true, because it couldn't have been done by sheer imposition of strength of mind. There are too many variables. They use a lovely phrase on the West Coast: they talk about "trading vulnerabilities." Perhaps this is what women seek to do—and actually men too—when they are not alienated. But apropos of this condition, this attitude, that Jessie mentioned, maybe a breakthrough is possible. After all, the civilizing process does look forward. Progress has been made in other fields. For example, we have had to reorient our whole thinking about living since better nutrition, medical care, and health programs have greatly increased our life span. So, on the basis of the civilizing processes here, isn't it feasible that we might be able to reorient our thinking in this threatening area of female sexuality too? We are seeking a new way. We don't have to duplicate history.

JESSIE BERNARD: I think almost any woman, if she had to make a choice between her own orgasmic experience and her husband's, would want her husband's, wouldn't she?

VIRGINIA JOHNSON: Well, she would, for the very reasons you gave, but if in the civilizing process there were a changing of requirements—in other words . . .

JESSIE BERNARD: But you can never change the requirement that he has to ejaculate.

VIRGINIA JOHNSON: No, but the requirement he has for
achieving the erection in the first place.

WILLIAM MASTERS: This is the important thing. We're
talking about a contraceptive society here, theoretically.

VIRGINIA JOHNSON: Consequently, we're saying that perhaps this gives the male the impetus to be masculine, to
fulfill his male role. Perhaps this is changing. Perhaps he now
requires a more contributing, a more viable woman. I wish
some other women would jump into the argument with me.

MARTHA STUART: I don't have any special brand of expertise in this, Herb, but I just wonder if female self-sacrifice
isn't a special kind of put-down, too. Because what is it that a
man really gets the most from, in a sense? Honestly. What is it
that I, as a woman, get the most from, but this give-to-get relationship we've been talking about? I'm a little suspicious of
this self-sacrificing thing. What really is that? It may be unwillingness to share, to let him be a man.

JESSIE BERNARD: Well, now you're talking about contraception. But she wants a baby, you know. This is what she
wants.

MARTHA STUART: Oh, well, if she wants just the baby,
then that really is a put-down. I think she wants that man,
doesn't she?

JOSEPH BIRD: It seems that what we're talking around all
the time here, the irony we're facing with this conference, is
that we're talking about the changing woman, and you simply
cannot talk about the changing woman without bringing in
the changing man. In whatever future we're going to have
here, women certainly are changing, but if their husbands
don't also change, the mess is going to be even worse than it is
right now. I'm interested that you mentioned not taking one of

a couple without the partner. It simply cannot be any other way. If a woman comes in frigid and you somehow can give her help which will enable her to overcome frigidity, but you do not help the husband change at almost exactly the same rate, they're going to be in even worse shape. Or, as one husband told me, "I was very, very threatened when my wife didn't find any sexual fulfillment, but when she started becoming fully a woman, I thought I'd go off the bridge."

WILLIAM MASTERS: The same thing applies to a man, you know. When a male seeks help with a complaint of impotence, if his wife is not reoriented and reeducated, when he is sent back into the threatening home environment his impotence will return in a high percentage of cases.

KERMIT KRANTZ: One of the questions that has come up here is: Does a woman want a man or does she want a baby? Well, one of the problems we are seeing in this society today comes from the conflict within the woman as to which one she really does want. First, she becomes child oriented. Then, in her emancipation, she finds that she really doesn't want the child. Instead, she wants that man back again. And so she finds herself in one hell of a dilemma. This is something we see very, very frequently; and it's growing very rapidly in our society. She just cannot decide which way to go now. It can only begin to be solved by her complete reorientation to a new role in society, and a different relationship with the man. And that's not going to be easy. She's had something to fall back on all the way along. Religious dogma has been able to give her all the bolstering she wants, but now religion is going through its own upset and revival. With this tremendous technocracy that's come along with it, she has nothing she can go to immediately. About three weeks ago, I went to a conference concerning these problems in our society. It was probably on as high a philosophical level as one could get. The real purpose of the emotionalism of the woman came in—the right to live, the right to die, the right not to be born, the right to be born, and so on. It was very interesting to see their ambivalence on the subject. Before this, there was little question in the woman's mind, but now, these are no longer male decisions. They have become hers, because she literally controls immortality; the male does not. That's the main thesis I want to get across tomorrow morning. It is in her hands.

JUNE BUTTS: I am still interested in this sleep period immediately after orgasm. It seems to me that if the female is seeking out the male figure, that's an active goal. I don't think it's passive.

WILLIAM MASTERS: It wasn't presented as a passive action. No interpretation has been drawn as yet. The demand for touch, for body heat, for physical relation is woman's expression of a twosome concept; the male doesn't do this.

ANNE SHEFFIELD: Then it goes from the I-me back to the we?

WILLIAM MASTERS: Yes, to the us—the identification, warmth, the figure contact.

CATHERINE CHILMAN: I think this has all been tremendously interesting, and I am very impressed with the way you both do this. Thinking about this sleep pattern, I would like to know your reaction to what is often talked about as a basic problem between men and women, the fact that a woman seems to feel not only sexy, but also involved in this interpersonal love relationship virtually 100 percent of the time. She always wants her man. Even with fulfillment through sex, when she then sleeps, she still reaches for him and actually tends to become much more involved with him, more dependent, whereas it is often said that once the man has completed the sex act, he then feels, "That's fine; that's over with, it's time to go to sleep." And the next morning, it's time to go to work, while the woman is still clinging to him, thinking, "Don't you love me anymore? You didn't kiss me this morning," and so forth. She is wanting to absorb so constantly. That's a pull that has been observed so often between men and women.

VIRGINIA JOHNSON: These are the many ramifications. You've swept them nicely. What condition does woman find herself in as the result? It's the cause-and-effect thing Father Thomas was mentioning yesterday, the female who will take any situation and turn it to a positive reinforcement of her role. Don't be misled by the sleep situation. It has a physiological component as well, which ties in (and we won't get clinical and scientific again) with the refractory period of the male wherein satiation is present. The female has a far greater response capacity. Consequently, even after sexual activity, when she sleeps she continues to manifest her natural inclination to be a sexual being, to express herself sexually in this interpersonal relationship. She reaches out because physiologically she is capable of return, whereas the male reacts in varying degrees according to age, health, fatigue, preoccupation with the demands placed upon him or the demands he places upon himself "to achieve." The result is a very natural sort of response. It's what Kermit Krantz and Jim Semmens have been dealing with in clinical situations in volume. It's also what the Birds are reflecting as well. The ramifications of a situation which is so transitional at this time appear endless. It's going to take a very great deal of understanding, and a great deal of backing and filling, to change this.

CATHERINE CHILMAN: Wouldn't you think that this problem would decrease as women have more children? The periods of pregnancy and taking care of infants would take up a considerable portion of this need for humanness, and could provide another way of expressing sexuality, so that the dependency on and involvement with her husband could be less extreme with larger families.

VIRGINIA JOHNSON: That's a little hard to answer. If freed to establish her own identity, ideally a woman starts having fewer babies as well. There is a control situation which can be brought to bear. Look at the woman whose children have all grown up and left and you have the control situation which shows the real fallacy of such a premise. Because the woman usually has a total sense of loss, or—total may be too extreme—a varying sense of loss. Statistically she gets far more out of a viable relationship, but she doesn't have it anymore because she has invested herself only in her children, which is really a displacement of the sex relationship. The women I choose to term *successful* are those who raise their children with their husbands. The sense of responsibility must be mutual, but time expenditure is apportioned according to whatever the socioeconomic demands are. That's just a realistic, practical thing. They both must invest themselves in the children. Then the woman hasn't used them for an extension of herself to the annihilation of herself. If she has used her children in this vague way, when they are no longer there she and her husband look at one another, and what is there left?

JOSEPH BIRD: She's multiorgasmic, but is she happy?

MARTHA STUART: Wouldn't the man be multiorgasmic, too, if he weren't working so hard? Isn't this almost what we're saying about women in reverse? Possibly when we're all working less, we'll . . .

WILLIAM MASTERS: Beautiful assignment, but he simply doesn't have her capacity.

JESSIE BERNARD: Don't you get any, like the biblical men, who go from the chamber strong for the race? (*laughter*). Is this enervation the universal male reaction?

WILLIAM MASTERS: Oh, no.

VIRGINIA JOHNSON: It's the circumstance, the state in which you've endowed eroticism. It can range from anger to a whole variety of emotions. But this is a whole new area and we shouldn't open up this box right now.

RUTH USEEM: During the sleep period, is this female search for warmth primarily breast-arm oriented?

WILLIAM MASTERS: Not enough work on this subject has been done to allow us to state specifically. The interesting thing is that she will cuddle up in his warm area as a total body. There is no evidence to date that it is just breast and arm.

RUTH USEEM: Well, there might be an alternative explanation: the return to the breast-arm, mothering warmth. I mean, this is just a possibility.

VIRGINIA JOHNSON: There are so many possibilities.

RUTH USEEM: Because it may not be the male object that is caught, but the total agenital sexual warmth. I'm just speculating.

JESSIE BERNARD: Just one other thing. We have been saying that women have the greater sexual capacity, but haven't they also greater tolerance for abstinence?

WILLIAM MASTERS: As has been pointed out previously, we don't know anything about abstinence (laughter).

MICHAEL SCRIVEN: Do you have any evidence on the side of sexual excess problems? One of the possibilities emerging here is that the emancipated female will place more demands upon the male than she has in the past, and, in terms of her physiological capacity, with some justification. But now, do you have any sort of paper at all about clinical cases in which this leads to difficulties of its own?

WILLIAM MASTERS: There is some suggestive evidence only. As mentioned, we always interrogate the individuals in our study-subject population. No one can work in the laboratory unless he or she has the facility of orgasmic return, both from masturbation and during coition. Inevitably, in taking histories the male's masturbatory frequency is checked and his concept of masturbatory excess is interrogated. If the male masturbates once a month, he thinks that an excessive rate might be two or three times a month. If he masturbates once a week, he thinks the excess rate is two or three times a week. If he masturbates once a day, he thinks the excess rate is two or three times a day. Out of the hundreds of males we have interrogated, we've yet to find the one that felt his own masturbatory rate was excessive (*laughter*). Remember, the old concept that the male or female can masturbate to excess is in truth only a concept. From the biological point of view, excess is easily defined. The female stops masturbating from utter physical exhaustion, and the male stops when he no longer achieves or maintains an erection. As far as is known, there's no residual in terms of physical distress from masturbatory activity.

MICHAEL SCRIVEN: This is with respect to masturbation. But where you've gone into personal situations, the demands of the partner may be such as to produce certain psychological effects.

WILLIAM MASTERS: Certainly, but when the male learns that it is not necessary to ejaculate at every mounting opportunity—ejaculatory control of quality necessary to satisfy the particular female partner—he returns to himself very real control of the situation because his refractory period doesn't occur after penile erective reactions.

VIRGINIA JOHNSON: I hate the phrase, "he can satisfy." It sounds almost like a service. I think it's far better to restate, to refocus, to remove the total value from ejaculatory capacity.

WILLIAM MASTERS: That's a better way of placing emphasis.

VIRGINIA JOHNSON: In other words, this is like saying merely the intake of food is all that's required by the body. Just get it down. This is removing all of the contributing factors. I think they are very important. There's too much to be said here, too much that needs to be thought through in this volatile area, for us to oversimplify our concepts. This concept, that the male needs to be threatened by identification of the female's greater capacity, is really somewhat unmindful of what her sexual responses really depend upon. It is not just a physiological entity. We will acknowledge the fact that she has a greater physical capacity, that her body is constructed and wired for this, if all of the other requirements are met—but you must not segment out the physical. You cannot. She is still going to need his requirement of her. There is a naturally ameliorating tendency here.

There are many specifics that must be inspected. The most sexually effective woman in creation, placed with the male of her choice, with whom she has responded over and over for years, may be unable to respond if there is the unfortunate introduction of some rejection of him on any base line which she has endowed with value, such as her regard for him, his treatment of her, his requirement of her. Or it may be as simple as physical manifestation. She happens to be terribly sensitive to odor, and he has transgressed in this area. This is enough to abort her capacity to respond sexually. So we must always be mindful of how it is with women psychologically before we consider female sexual capacity a threat.

DONALD BARRETT: You have been emphasizing two principles. One is that we must recognize the similarities of the male's and the female's sexual orientations rather than the differences. Secondly, that there are, however, substantial differences. For example, the female has greater capacity for response, and so on. This confuses me. I was thinking of the fact that in certain Arabian cultures they have a theory that the female is a stronger sexual person. Consequently, institutional and legal arrangements have been developed to control this. This is what we call sociologically the double standard. Right. So now it's incorporated institutionally. However, in the way we've been talking here, the important thing is that there be mutual understanding rather than male control of the female. The question in my mind is, have you found any limits of adaptability, male to female, female to male, other than the extraordinary, such as homosexuals?

WILLIAM MASTERS: I don't think we can answer that.

DONALD BARRETT: You've developed something of this sort in the institutional arrangements, and it's very difficult to conceive.

VIRGINIA JOHNSON: Institutional arrangements develop. We need to be mindful of other cultures, and yet we have such vastly different systems of value. Our whole criminal code, our ways of legislating these controls, are so vastly different, it's so hard to impose one culture onto another.

DONALD BARRETT: I'm sure you would be quite critical of our own criminal code in regard to sexual orientation.

WILLIAM MASTERS: Yes.

VIRGINIA JOHNSON: But this is another factor in great transition.

DONALD BARRETT: What sort of hopes do you find that we can change the base line? That's my question.

VIRGINIA JOHNSON: Perhaps we are seeking to build it around maintenance of the family, meaningfulness of a one-to-one relationship, the qualitative relationship. I realize that these are very abstract things, but this is the direction we're all attempting to follow.

WINFIELD BEST: As Martha began to say, perhaps we all need each other. Maybe that comes tomorrow. But today, with particular reference to this, the one unspoken thing seems to be the direction the Birds and others touched on. Certainly we're all in this thing together, and if we're going to give a better opportunity to women to adjust to the changes which, in effect, we've already recognized or even made, then we have to change the male role too. This brings me back to your interrogative material. I was thinking about this personally, that is, the ways in which an individual's ability to respond sexually is limited. There are so many external pressures, preoccupations, and demands constantly facing each man and woman. What have you found out concerning the effects of these factors on sexual response? Is there any sort of correlation you can make, let us say, between the extent of female response and the preoccupations of the temporal context she lives in? What kinds of problems did the woman face before she came to the laboratory? What problems will she face after she leaves it? It seems to me this would help define the whole cultural context within which we must deal with the question.

VIRGINIA JOHNSON: Precisely. But it's so hard to reflect on that in a brief period of time. This constitutes a separate body of information. The interrogation has not been just immediate facts; it has also been deeply historical; and there is a follow-up counterpart to what is happening.

WINFIELD BEST: But certainly we can assume that there is a correlation.

WILLIAM MASTERS: There's a day-to-day correlation. In the past it was presumed biologically that there was a correlation between the female cyclic menstrual pattern and her sexual response. To a degree this is true. But now reproductive biologists are aware that to a greater degree it is not true. During interrogation, it has become apparent that the greatest level of sexual interest for most women occurs during the week before menstruation. The next greatest concentration of sexual interest develops in the first few days after a menstrual period. There is a certain percentage of women, much smaller, who have the greatest sexual interest during the ovulatory period. And as a matter of fact, there's an even smaller but identifiable percentage of women who can define the higher levels of sexual interest or demand primarily *during* the menstrual period.

The interesting thing is that even these generalizations about patients get thrown a curve by innumerable variables of cultural or interpersonal relationships. Let's take Mrs. Smith, who *says* that her sexual tension levels usually are highest the week before she menstruates. If, right after a menstrual period, her first or second sexual exposure is overwhelmingly successful for both partners—a thoroughly delightful experience—her tension levels and sexual demands will run a lot higher throughout that entire menstrual month than is reflected in her usual response patterning; specifically, her level of response will not just be focused on the last week of her menstrual cycle. Thus it is obvious that all the interrogation in depth has given concept only. Certainly, nothing that can be supported without variation has been established, because there are so many variables.

WINFIELD BEST: I should quickly add that I recognize there is another very large question among the others we're not going to open this morning involving the fact, or at least the good working hypothesis, that individuals can create a lot of preoccupations in order to have a good alibi for lack of sexual response. There's a whole cause-and-effect relationship here which also has to go into the cultural adjustment mix.

VIRGINIA JOHNSON: This is the spot for a perfect line. It is a reflection from the particular experimental therapy techniques developed in St. Louis: "We seek to establish motivation for not responding."

WINFIELD BEST: Yes. Right.

SISTER JEAN WALLACE: I've been sitting here listening to this as a scientist, because that's my background and training, and I'm sort of reminded of what Chardin said in his book *Phenomenon of Man.* Over and over again he said that he was explaining things as a scientist. But anyone who reads this book knows that he has gone far beyond science and has given us a really meaningful concept of the universe, and of man in the universe. It has been the scientists who have shot holes in his book, because he really has some mistakes in it. Dr. Richardson mentioned earlier that both of you have made most of your remarks on the sociological and psychological aspects of human reproduction, of female sexuality, from the biological scientific point of view. I think that a lot of what you've said is just pretty well known or can be looked up, although I haven't looked up *coitus* in the encyclopedia, and I think your contribution is more than sociological and psychological. I had hoped you would speak a bit more in a scientific vein. That's what I really hoped.

WILLIAM MASTERS: The great difficulty is that this group can talk physical sex till we are all blue in the face, but as long as we consider just anatomy and physiology, we're presenting at best half of the picture. Inevitably we really rebel against any concept of presenting a one-sided coin.

SISTER JEAN WALLACE: Well, what I meant to say is, most of what you said has been meaningful above the anatomical and biological level, considering the whole person. And I do think the discussion on celibacy was very kind to the celibates. I disagree with Dr. Richardson. You really didn't imply that this type of life is harmful. But what I'd like to say is that you've obviously gone beyond your training, and I think you have probably learned a lot more.

WILLIAM MASTERS: Wouldn't it be a tragedy if after eleven years we hadn't?

FATHER CHARLES SHEEDY: I would like to make a remark from what you might call the outfield. I've been coping with the problem of celibacy myself one way or another for years. However, I don't want to talk about that. I did hear last night some remarks made about industrialization breaking up sexual intimacy in the household, that industrialization of man's work and gadgetry for the woman has separated them in the house. This morning I heard something about the double standard. I get my knowledge from very peculiar places, and I wonder how many of you people know about a funny little sexy French novel called *La Jument Verte*. It's in English under the title *The Green Mare* by Marcel Aymé. It's really a green filly. In this novel, there are two brothers. One of them is a farmer. The farmer and his household, including the children, have a very integrated sexual life. On the other hand, his brother is a town guy, a veterinarian, a politician, and a devotee of the double standard. He thinks of himself as "in" sex, and his wife is left out of it. Much of what I have heard in the last couple of days in this conference is very well handled in this little book, at least with respect to sex life in France in the country in 1924. I enjoyed this morning's session very much. I enjoyed last night's, especially jumping around with the tapes.

MARTHA STUART: Thank you. I think you're the only one who enjoyed it.

FATHER CHARLES SHEEDY: These speakers, Dr. Masters and Mrs. Johnson, have helped us a lot. I think we have all gotten a lot out of the commentary, the disagreement and everything. It's a very lovely conference; and now I think we'll adjourn until after lunch.

Perspectives 6

HERBERT W. RICHARDSON

Tuesday, 12:00 noon (luncheon, Morris Inn)

HERBERT RICHARDSON: The pushmi-pullyu is an imaginary llama whose natural habitat, so the tale goes, is the Himalayan mountains. He has a head on each end, one facing front and the other facing aft. This arrangement can be explained as an evolutionary adaptation peculiarly fitting him for life on the steep mountain slopes. When climbing, the end walking backward *pushes* while the end walking forward *pulls*. And so he is his own best helpmeet, a permanent "you push me while I pull you" arrangement. His unique body structure also sustains his dwelling in those barren regions where there are few, if any, living souls. For the pushmi-pullyu is never lonely. The two ends, each with a mind of its own, are able to talk to each other. Sometimes they argue. Sometimes they even fight. But pushmi-pullyus are never lonely.

In the hands of a professional raconteur, the pushmi-pullyu story would have, as its purpose, the catching of attention or the exemplification of a moral. In the hands of a philosopher, its purpose is rather to call attention to a selection from Plato. In the *Symposium,* Plato records the tale of another remarkable four-legged beast who resembles the pushmi-pullyu, another two-in-one affair. This is the marvelous androgyne. It seems, goes the tale, that all of us were originally androgynes or, rather, that each of us was *half* an androgyne. However, long ago the androgynes were cut in two, severed half from half. So each of us today has only two legs, not four, though we use our two legs, most of the time, chasing after two other legs, seeking to reassemble ourselves with them into our original androgynous four-leggedness.

Though Plato presents this tale as a myth, there is a great deal of evidence to support it: psychological, physical, linguistic, and even biblical-versical. There is, first, the *emotional fact* that we do feel lonely and are moved by the passion of love to seek out some other two-legger with whom we can be (as it biblically versically says) *one flesh.* Then there is the *physical evidence* that the protuberances and cavities of our bodies do, in fact, fit together. This suggests an original unity which was, like some jigsaw puzzle, cut into pieces whose purpose it is to be reassembled again. Then there is the *evidence from ordinary language* whereby we hear persons speak of their "other half" or "better half." Surely they are referring to another person when they say this: a person who is, however, a piece of their own androgyne. Most conclusively, *there are Bible verses:* "So God created man in his own image, in the image of God created he him; male and female created he them" (Gen. 1:27). It is seen here very clearly that the original man whom God created is not some solitary two-legged creature. As the greatest theologian of our time, Professor K. B., has explained this Bible verse:

The *whole man,* i.e., the whole man whom God forms and animates, . . . is not solitary man. In isolation man . . . would not

have been the being with whom God willed to enter into a relation and to have intercourse . . . God the Lord willed to have
dealings with a *twofold being*.

We see that, according to this explanation, *the whole man is
not solitary man, but a wonderful being,* for man was originally created by God as a kind of pushmi-pullyu, a "two-
folder." We should also point out that this agrees with
Plato's tale when he explains that the twofoldness of man
arises from the fact that he is a *sexual being*—shades of Alan
Watts, of Yang and Yin, of D. H. Lawrence! This is Professor
K. B.'s exegesis of Bible verses: "Men," he says, "are simply
male and female." Whatever else they may be, it is only in this
differentiation and relationship. This is the peculiar dignity
ascribed to the sex relationship.

As the only real principle of differentiation and relationship,
as the original form not only of man's confrontation of God,
but also of all intercourse between man and woman, it is the
true *humanum* and therefore the true creaturely image of
God. Man can and will always be man before God and among
his fellows only as he is man in relationship to woman and
woman in relation to man. As he is the one or the other, he *is*
man.

I do not pretend to fathom all the wisdom of this statement,
failing to understand how that intercourse, which depends on
the sexual difference between male and female, can be carried
on by men with men and by women with women. However, I
believe that, after close textual scrutiny, I have discovered that
Professor K. B. is referring to what is esoterically called "the
secret of Noah's ark." This is the principle that Noah adopted
in order to save all the creatures of this earth, namely, that you
can't have *another* giraffe or polar bear or pig unless you first
have *two* giraffes, *two* polar bears, or *two* pigs. One of these
two must be a male and the other must be a female. Step two:

if we must have two giraffes in order to have *another* giraffe, it
follows that there had to be two giraffes in order to have *any*
giraffe. Step three: whence it follows that every giraffe is *essentially* what it was *originally*, i.e., "a twofold being."

Today's higher wisdom is, of course, yesterday's common-
place, namely, that we learn *what* things are by asking how
they originated. So, since it always takes two to get one (the
secret of Noah's ark) and because each one is moved by the
passion to find his other half and reassemble the four-legged
beast (the mystery of the androgyne), a twofold, relational
being—alas, O reader, you thought until this moment that you
were truly a human being; but no, O solitary two-legged one-
folded thing!—your true humanity, the *humanum* of every
one of us, is in your potential and actual sexual relatedness,
your desire for whole, four-legged, twofoldness! And this is
why, O reader, when you spoke of your "other half," you
were speaking literally. And this is why, when the Bible
speaks of a sexual union of "one flesh," it is speaking scientifically. And this is why it is an economic fact that two *can* live
as cheaply as one.

It is important, however, that we understand the difference
between the pushmi-pullyu, with which we began our discussion, and the androgynous four-legged creature of myth, meta-
physic, science, and Bible verse. Otherwise, we cannot understand how the pushmi-pullyu manifests that twofoldness
characteristic of the original "whole man"—a twofoldness it
has been allowed to retain (by God's grace) because of its Himalayan habitat—this twofoldness has, ridiculously, been extended even to the matter of heads. This must be a result of
Adam's fall for it is at present a grave cause of sin in the
pushmi-pullyu. For whenever a body has two heads, it cannot
be properly ordered. There will be disagreement, strife, and
even self-contradiction. Hence, if both pushmi-pullyu heads
decide to push at the same time, then it can't go anywhere at

all. "I'll push and you pull," says one; but the other, adamant, says "I've been pulling long enough, and now it's my turn to push." Obviously, a properly ordered and sinless body, a body like that of our original forefather(s), would find two heads to be an imperfection rather than a perfection, since two heads could be the cause of disagreement and self-contradiction. This is why the Apostle (recalling Plato's notion of justice) reminds us that in every marriage, as in every body, there should be but one head, whom all the other members obey. For everything is just or right (even marriage) only as each of its parts does that for which it is best suited and thereby keeps its place within the whole. Hence, the Apostle says,

If the ear shall say, because I am not the eye, I am not of the body; is it therefore not of the body? If the whole body were an eye, where were the hearing? . . . But now hath God set the members every one of them in the body, as it hath pleased him.

In the same way, the mystical body of the Church can have only one head, not many. And the one-flesh union of husband and wife, which is a type of that union which Christ hath with the Church, can have only one head, the husband. The man is to rule his wife with love and the woman is lovingly to obey. In this way the "whole man" of the original creation is restored.

We should understand, against the insinuations of the Friedanists, that such an ordered whole does no dishonor to the woman or to any other member. For is not the wife a member of the body, its very heart? And is it not the case that "those members of the body which we think to be less honorable, upon these we bestow more abundant honor . . . thus God hath tempered the body together, having given more honor to that part which lacked."

Hence God has bestowed his glory upon man, who is a little lower than the angels; while man bestows his glory upon woman who, though she obeys, is shown special honor because of her greater need. Each thing, then, in its place and doing its own work gives greater glory to the whole.

One should not think this insight into the complementary ordering of man and woman within the four-legged beast is the discovery of Christianity and the Apostle. He was simply applying an earlier biblical insight. Even today, Doctor B. B., a well-known clinical psychologist, describes and approves the venerable principle of "each in its own place" as the basis for a satisfactory family life. He speaks of orthodox Jewish groups in which:

. . . the man's unquestioned superiority in the all-important religious sphere permitted both to accept gladly the wife's dominance in running the home and often also the shop. With areas of dominance thus clearly marked out, the wife could be dominant in her sphere without extending it to running her husband's life or her children's. Though such a woman was dominant in the home, no 'momism' resulted. Secure in her sphere, it did not occur to her to challenge the man's.

How marvelous to have discovered the cure for "momism" and the secret of true family harmony. Our problem today, as biblical principles—now corroborated by psychology—make clear, is that women are denatured and disordered by learning to read or by involving themselves in worldly law or politics. When women undertake these male tasks, we have "momism." We should try, then, to educate woman to be secure in her sphere, so that it will not occur to her to challenge man in his. At present we are failing to do this, for, observes Doctor B. B.,

. . . our educational system does not prepare the girl to play the more dominant role in the home sphere or the more surrendering role, either in sex or other areas of experience.

I must confess that, until corrected by this sage advice, I had fallen into the perversion of enjoying my wife's occasional flights into sexual dominance. And I had even affirmed, indeed encouraged, her momistic excursions into the working and the university world. And, also, I had, like some sinful pushmi-pullyus, discussed certain metaphysical issues with her, as if she were also a head. I see, however, that I was moving in the wrong direction. I should have recalled the ancient Germanic sagacity: let the women worry about *Kirche, Kinder,* and *Küche* and let the men worry about *Krieg* and *Aussenpolitik.* My will to repent and adhere to this new course has recently been strengthened by the advertisement for a new cosmetics line, *Khadine.*

The Khadine (my eye leaps, as McLuhan says it should, back and forth from text to image of diaphanous, surrendering sex-slave vaguely clothed in harem veils) was the slave of a wealthy and powerful desert sheik. She fascinated the sheik (the cosmetics work!) so beyond the power of all other women that he spent all his hours with her rather than with the other houris. Finally no one any longer knew whether she was his slave or he was hers! In their separate spheres, the one was dominant while the other surrendered! When the sheik ruled, Khadine surrendered. Where Khadine ruled, the sheik surrendered. It is exactly as Doctor B. B. said, "Though such a woman was dominant in the home, no 'momism' resulted. Secure in her sphere, it did not occur to her to challenge the man's."

You should not think, dear reader, that this interpretation of men and women rests merely on Bible verses, Platonic myths, imaginary animals, cosmetic advertisements, and the nonscientific meanderings of clinical psychologists. This interpretation is also squarely based on fact. If we doubt it, then we must ask whether it is or is not true that men and women are different and yet fit together in order to make a "two-in-one"? Is it not a fact that this is true? Is it not a scientific fact based on the repeated and repeatable experimental observations of bodies and behavior, both in familiar laboratories, and also on nameless islands and in unexplored wastelands? Is it not a fact that men and women are biologically, biochemically, biophysically, psychobiologically, sociobiologically, and therefore logically different? Romantics and humanists have obscured these basic facts recently by disproportionately valuing the ability to read (when only a woman can have a baby), by arguing that men are distinguished from animals by their possessions of thought and speech (when there is nothing like a mother's smile), and even by suggesting that human beings can act purposefully and shape their own future (while you will still be a child of Adam and of Abraham unto the third and fourth generation).

These romantics! These idealists! These humanists! They are always overemphasizing the trivial. Why, given an infinite amount of time and a typewriter any monkey could compose the plays of Shakespeare! And no man can beat a computer at a game of chess! No, if we want to understand man, then we must look at the fact, the basic, undeniable, irreducible, empirical datum that men and women have protuberances and cavities in different, but complementary, places. Pay attention to the important things! The woman does not have, and hence always is seeking, a penis. And the man does not have, and eternally longs for, a womb. This is the empirical foundation of the biblical, the scientific corroboration of the Platonic-mythical, the behavioral basis of the psychoanalytic.

In fact, considered empirically, i.e., in terms of holes and knobs, we now see that there are no such things as human beings. Human beings are not "real entities" at all. The only real entities are knob-things and hole-things. We should not be misled by the fact that because there is the nominative expression *a human* or *a human being* that there also is a real thing that corresponds to this name. If we examine the observ-

able data, discovering only knobs and holes and their fitting together, then we shall understand why Professor K. B. teaches
that *human being* signifies not a thing, but a relation or relating activity between things. The true "is man in relationship
to woman and woman in relation to man." Man is a human
being and woman is a human being only in their sexual relating.

The nominative form of the words *human being* or *a human* obscures our seeing that the real character of humanity is
a relation. It would be more accurate if we were to transpose
this nominative form into a verbal and speak of men and
women *humaning* with each other, just as we speak of hydro-
gen and oxygen atoms *uniting* with each other. Humanity, i.e.,
humaning, is a *transaction* between beings who are essentially
different: male and female, Yang and Yin, dominance and
surrender, yes and no. Since men and women are essentially
different, neither is higher, of greater worth, or more advan-
taged than the other. Each has his unique dignity, and these
unique dignities are not so much "equal" as "incomparable."
For example, which is greater: the apple or the orange, the
bird or the bee, the sheik or the khadine, the rich or the poor?
Each has its unique dignity. Each has its own place in the
whole, its membership in the body. Should the bird entertain
the botanical desire to be a tree? Should the Khadine push
momistically to ride the range with her sheik? Should the poor
be filled with the revolutionary passion to become rich, or the
rich aspire to give all that they have to the poor? Were these
things to come to pass, there could be no justice in the world,
for justice is each thing's doing that for which it is best suited
and refusing to enter into the sphere of other beings for whose
work it is unfit.

What follows from the fact that there is no such thing as a
"human being," but only a humaning, a transactional activity
between males and females? It means that men and women

must not seek an equality of complementaries. Complementary equality is the equality possessed by entities that are essentially different, though related. With respect to the relation between them, they are equally important and equally necessary. For they are equally related and hence they are equal even though their tasks, gifts, rights, and obligations are different. In the family, therefore, the husband, or head, must rule and the wife must obey. But remember, this does not mean that the husband has no obligations. He has the *obligation to rule*. It is his burden, not the burden of his wife. His wife, not burdened by this obligation to rule, is now fully free to obey. In this way we see why Doctor B. B. says that each should surrender dominance to the other in the other's proper sphere.

The principle of separate spheres applies to men as well as to women. Certainly a woman is not to encroach upon her husband's sphere, nor to have a career of her own, nor to seek dominance in activities that are properly man's work. We should remember, however, that this principle also applies to the man. He is not to encroach upon the woman's sphere. And if he is secure in his own sphere, he will not bear children, interfere with the kitchen, or, as Bible verses command, wear his wife's clothes. He should not vie with her in a "papa-istic" way. Observe the lovely order of justice, freedom, and equality that now ensues. For in that transactional *humaning* which constitutes "true man" and "true woman," there is a complementary equality that ensures the essential dignity of each.

The principle of complementary equality not only affects a harmony in marriage, but also in the other institutions of human life. Consider, for example, the justice, equality, and even freedom characteristic of slavery. Of course, many people feel that slavery implies inferiority. However, this is not true. For the slave is the complementary equal of his master, since both the master and his slave are equally essential to the transactional activity that goes on between them. Now in this relationship, a master has the obligation not to work, but to direct one who works. A slave, on the contrary, is freed from the obligation proper to a master's sphere and hence secure in the knowledge that his master will not encroach upon his right to work under the master's direction. Moreover, like the wife in a marriage governed by the principle of complementary equality, the slave knows that his master depends upon him. Without him, the master could not do that for which masters are fitted, for there would be no one to obey commands.

Just as in the relation between the khadine and the sheik, it sometimes happens in the case of particularly hard-working slaves whose labors vastly increase their master's wealth that we cannot be sure whether the slave rules the master or the master rules the slave. Why, just the other day down on the levy, Colonel William Longridge was overheard to say, "I just don't know what I'd do without Ole Jess. He's my favorite, all right, for he does as much work as ten other boys together." My, how good it make an ole darkie feel to know he is dominant in his sphere and that his massa depend on him. What's that science-thing Doctor B. B. said again? Secure in his sphere, it did not occur to him to challenge the massa's. Well, no-sir-ee, Ole Jess'll just leave the headache of all the directing and all that worry about them uppity slaves who don't know their place to Colonel Longridge. And he just smile at them, for he proud to be a darkie and keep a darkie's place!

Item—letter from an alumna to the Editor of the *Radcliffe College Quarterly*:

I love you too, Dr. Blaine.
Your article in the November *Radcliffe Quarterly* reveals a keen understanding of the proper role of women in the Jet Age, and of Cliffies especially.
European women who respect and cherish their femininity smile at the confused American female with her misunderstanding con-

cerning her proper sphere in life. Ladies across the sea have been unable to participate extensively in the business and professional world of men. But these women take a genuine pride in their own greatest role—Wife and Mother. They have not made the error of regarding this role as a mere part-time job . . .

On graduation day a Cliffie should feel, I am pleased that my college taught me what a wonderful thing it is to be a real woman. I can leave here equipped with a sound knowledge of literature, history, science, and psychology. More important still, I am delighted that in my chosen career I will not compete with men, but will use my feminine intuition to supplement their efforts and achievements. In my future role as a Wife, Mother, and Career Woman, I will harmoniously combine solid scholarship and an inquiring mind with feminine charm, the grace that James Barrie calls, "the bloom upon a woman."

Anonymous
Boston, Massachusetts

What's going on here? Where does truth leave off and fantasy begin? The bloom upon a woman . . . The more surrendering role . . . Take a genuine pride . . . Proper Place . . . "His" and "Her" spheres . . . if the whole body were an eye . . . pushmi-pullyu . . . whether she was his slave or he was hers . . . Four-legged beast . . . Humaning, humaning . . . The European woman smiles . . . Complementary equality . . . With areas of dominance thus clearly marked out . . . Anonymous, Boston, Massachusetts.

All these concepts, all these conclusions, all these semi-truths and semi-falsehoods! What's wrong here? What are we missing? It all seems false and yet it all seems true. And it is, indeed.

This is the case. All true and yet all false. It is a caricature. What happens in a caricature is that little truths are given an importance with the best of reality: the nose of Charles de Gaulle, the mustache of Stalin, the breasts of Jayne Mansfield. Given this disproportionate emphasis, an obvious truth made the central focus becomes a great falsehood. We laugh at caricatures because we recognize this disproportion. In the case of the descriptions of men and women presented previously, we are taken in. We fail to see they are contexts of meaning in which these obvious though trivial truths are situated.

Traditional understandings of men and women are, today, all caricatures because they seek to transform a rather primitive biology into a sophisticated psychosexology suitable for guiding the behavior of modern adults.

It was mentioned previously that the key to this primitive biology is its emphasis on the body and its protuberances and cavities. By focusing on the obviously observable differences in the body, a caricature is developed which, making the peripheral of central importance, tries to prove that men are essentially different from women and that both are "human" only in their sexual relatedness.

If we begin in this way, then we can never attain the idea of a humanity fully present in each individual, a "genus" that allows us to say we are all persons first and males and females second. Such a humanity, or personhood, would mean that men and women possess an *equality of identity,* having the same rights and obligations, rather than a complementary equality. If men and women were essentially different so that they must *complement* each other, then it might be just or right for women to be dominant in the home and for wives to obey their husbands. There would then not even be an offense against the *equality* of men and women if they followed a double standard of sexual morality. For even though the sexual behavior of men would be different from that of women, each of them would be acting in accordance with that natural difference which makes males "men" and females "women." Then they would behave differently but equally since each acted in full accord with his "nature." Conversely, if men and women are not essentially different, but fully self-conscious, self-committing persons, then justice requires that neither rule the other. Moreover, this equality of identicals requires a single-standard sexual morality (for now we consider the body and its sexual functions not as biological drives, but as expressions of the thoughtful, free choice of individual persons).

The awareness that man is more than a body did not exist in primitive times, and took much time to evolve. This awareness, the awareness that man has an inner power to transcend his body, to be a spirit, to act in a self-determining way, to commune with an eternal reality, appears in both the oriental and the occidental worlds from about the seventh century to the fifth century B.C. The period when this new awareness evolved has been called the axial period. The new awareness can be traced in the *Bhagavad-Gita,* in the Zoroastrian *Gothas,* in the Hebrew prophets, and in Greek philosophy. Plato, for example, includes the story of the androgyne in his writing not because he believes it, but because he has experienced a spiritual reality, the spiritual reality that transcends the body and the order of nature's time. From this more indecisive vantage point, he can look back upon the myths and stories of the pre-axial age and laugh at them as amusing caricatures and childish exaggerations.

The "axial" development in history can be compared with the transition from childhood toward adulthood in the life of an individual. The child tends to identify himself completely with his body. If he is hungry, he cries; if he wants something, he takes it; if he thinks a thing, he says it. (This is why he is so "spontaneous," and also why he cannot read without moving his lips or subvocalizing.) He has not yet created a distinction between his inner self and his body. He has not learned to reflect before acting, to control his feelings of pain, hunger, and pleasure, or to limit their bodily expression. The child has not yet learned to experience himself as a person who transcends his body and can control it. He is not aware of himself as "soul," as spirit.

I should, however, quickly add that many people, even today, never become adults in this sense—never know themselves as spirit. They lack the internal ability to reflect before acting, to limit the outward expression of their feelings, to "know themselves" by an act of self-awareness. Like children, they depend upon outward restraints and rewards to socialize them. If these restraints were removed altogether (for example, if they had the magic ring of Gyges to make themselves invisible), then they would be the spontaneous servants of their bodily desires. They would be totally unable to say *no* to themselves; they would have no power of self-control. And, too, they would be unable to specify the time and place of *yes*.

There are too many today, of course, who assert that "man is but a body" or that "man is ruled by his sexual drives." We needed, of course, to take them at their word. They themselves might well be self-conscious, reflective, and self-controlled without its having occurred to them that they are. If this is the case, then they really know something that they didn't know they knew. Hence, we see that their "body" explanation of human behavior is inadequate to account for their own behavior. Erik Erikson has provided us with a good example of such a situation: he notes that the sexual theory advanced by Freud to account for all human behavior is inadequate to account for the intellectual curiosity that drove Freud to develop the sexual theory.

I have noted the emergence of "soul" or "spiritual consciousness" in the axial period. I have also tried to suggest its radical implications for the reconstitution of human relations and sexual behavior (e.g., the notions of a human genus, the equality of identity, single-standard morality). Let me now suggest an experiment to help you develop this awareness (or, at least, see what it is). For it may be that you, too, are acting like a soul, or spiritual person, without realizing that this is what you are doing. Here is a vivid description of the soul, or spirit, by Alain, a French philosopher:

The soul is what refuses the body. What, for instance, refuses to flee when the body trembles, what refuses to strike when the body is provoked, what refuses to drink when the body thirsts, what refuses to take when the body desires, what refuses to give up when the body recoils in horror. These refusals are the prerogative of man. Total refusal is sainthood; looking before leaping is wisdom; and this power of refusal is the soul. The madman has no power of refusal; he no longer has a soul. They also say he has no awareness, and that is true . . . One acquires awareness only through opposing self to self.

Opposing self to self. What is this other self that says *No* to the body, that says *No* to another's attempt to define you as a womb or the function of a womb. Do not quibble about the name. Wonder about the reality. What is this other you?

It is your wholeness as opposed to your partness. It is the "whole you," something more than the "partial you" of the body. It is you in your oneness, your completeness, rather than in your one-halfness. It is literally your integrity or virtue, i.e., the strength of soul by which a human being refuses to become a caricature of himself or to behave in a caricaturistic way.

The traditional interpretation of men and women, focusing upon the biological and the corporeal, denies this wholeness, denies that men can be complete in themselves. "Solitary man," our theologian has said, "is not whole man. Man is whole only in his relation to woman and woman is whole only in her relation to man." The wholeness of persons, in his view, is not something that they have in themselves, something that makes them intrinsically complete and hence free from the need to cling parasitically to another in order to be fulfilled. The wholeness of persons, in his view, is not their soul, their spirit, their power to be more than wife, husband, mother, father, khadine, sheik, pushmi-pullyu. The wholeness of persons, in his view, is outside the individuals, e.g., in their sexual relationships and always in someone else. But when this is the case for everyone, then everyone is only the slave of a slave.

Don't now misunderstand the soul by etherealizing it. The soul is not, strictly speaking, one part of you while the body is your other part. Rather, the soul is the whole of you, your power always to be more than you are. Hence it includes the body, the protuberances and cavities, the games we play. It includes them as part of the whole. This is why all the traditional proverbs are true, and it's also why they are not all the truth. If there were absolutely no truth to these proverbs they couldn't be caricatured. So, you see, there's nothing wrong with playing khadine and sheik from time to time. Go ahead. Do it. In fact, you ought to do it, for it's a bit of life and it's a great game. But keep it in proportion, no caricatures. Watch out for *the Khadine*: the one who didn't just play Khadine, but decided to be Khadine. She's mad! Utterly mad! She's making a bit part into the whole of life.

Yes, and Mrs. Anonymous, Wife and Mother: "I'm not making the mistake of regarding this role as a part-time job." You mean you think this part is the whole? You think this role is your life? I grant that there are bigger parts and smaller parts, there are starring roles and walk-ons. But to make any role into your whole life, into you, is mad!

My daughter, Ruth, played Flopsie Rabbit in the second-grade play at Dallin School. It was an exciting thing, *a very big thing*. Imagine her coming home, straight-faced, and announcing, "Daddy, I am not making the mistake of regarding this role as a part-time job. From now on it will be my whole life . . . !" Ruthie, honey, you've got to be kidding. Why even if you were Peter Rabbit, it wouldn't be worth a whole life. But Flopsie Rabbit . . . !

Do not be put off by the stories. I am serious. Men and women, you and I, we are spirits, not bodies. Nothing has defined us to play this or that role, to be this or that part. We are made to be whole, to encompass within ourselves the fullness of life, to play as many roles as we choose. And no one else can tell us to be this or that part. Whatever parts we play, we choose.

To become fully spirit is a hard thing. To refuse the body, to reject the absolute claim of some part, is difficult. And to do this absolutely and always is sainthood, true availability to Life. Not many of us will get this far. We should be growing up. We should be getting soul.

This summer my 6-year-old son, Paul, has finally determined to master swimming. ("He's not afraid to put his head in the water anymore," his sister volunteered.) He's finally got it. Things are coming along. I congratulated him, "Good work, Paul, you are really growing up." "No, Daddy," he replied. "I'm not growing up. I'm getting courage."

Paul's right. It is not a matter of up. It isn't how tall you are in inches, how circumferential you are around the bosom or the biceps. It is a matter of something bigger all right, but of something bigger inside. There is a little more there, something that is making him be a little more, too. Courage, he calls it. And that is exactly what the philosophers of the soul called it: courage, they said, is one of the strengthenings, the virtues, of the soul. Think of that: my son, a philosopher. This biggerness that is inside helps us more than biology, helps us not to be afraid, helps us to try something new. It helped Paul put his head in the water, and it can help you be more than a role. This spirit raises you toward the wholeness, toward the you that you are.

The Generation-Communication Gap 7

WILLIAM M. LAMERS, JR., SHIRLEY STONE,
AND JAMES SEMMENS

Tuesday, 2:00 P.M.

GEORGE CHRISTIE: What constitutes communications? We all communicate daily. We all do it unconsciously, and perhaps one of the few things that has really been reproduced well in the laboratory is the communication cycle. I asked our speakers if it might not be useful to have on hand a diagram of the communication cycle. They said, "Yes," so I have brought with me a diagram which will give you an idea of the scope of the communications process (Fig. 1).

This diagram is an abstract model, but it is absolutely accurate.

Using this model, for example, we have managed to produce the overtone structure of the voice with nothing more than digital numbers. That is how good a model this is. We do not think it is absolute, but it is closer than anything else I

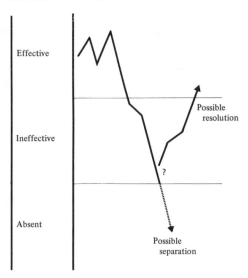

Figure 1. Communication in crisis

know of in modern physics to a really good analogue for a phenomenon as complex as this.

First of all, we start with meaning. I don't think anybody here knows what "meaning" is. We obviously, however, want some kind of meaning in a message. A message is therefore the vehicle for the meaning. Your meaning might be, "I'm going to be late for dinner." So you constitute a message. The transmitter, unlike the receiver, has an option. He can put in a filter. He might want to say, for example, that he's damn sorry that he's going to be late for dinner. He doesn't want to say it directly, but he can introduce a filter that can say that. Then he has to code his message because it obviously has to be put into some form that can be translated into some medium, such as the voice, a radio signal, or whatever is used. Then, of course, it has to be modulated in some way. To transmit we have to have a transmitter. Then we have to be able to generate the noise, the radio signal, to carry the message. On the other side, we have to detect this particular signal. If our perception is elsewhere, we miss it. If we happen to be thinking about what we did last night, the message may come in, may be received, but it will never be detected. Obviously, it has to be modulated.

The poor receiver has a problem. He's got all the filters. Not knowing the intended meaning, he sets up filters to try to separate what he thinks is the significant part of the message. This goes on in a matter of microseconds, milliseconds for human beings. He filters out what he thinks the message probably means and then he decodes it. That is just the beginning. He has to pull out the meaning. He only gets the meaning if he compares it to his intelligence matrix. If this is not done, he can get the right message and the wrong meaning. Even so, this whole cycle can go on its merry way.

It is a great pleasure to introduce Bill Lamers over here, a child psychiatrist from the beautiful Marin County–San Francisco area. Dr. Lamers—who doesn't like to be called Doctor— got his medical degree at Marquette University and did his work in psychiatry at the University of Cincinnati. He's the medical director of a school for disturbed children, and he's going to talk to us about something which I think really embodies what the future is going to mean to us—what's going on today with the kids, and where this all may lead us. I'll resist the temptation to introduce Captain Semmens because I'm a Commander in the Navy myself, and I'd probably overdo it. I'll just leave it in Bill's hands. Take over, please.

WILLIAM LAMERS: Thank you very much, George. We are also going to have a presentation from Shirley Stone, a pediatrician from New York City, who will add in some thoughts on mother-infant communications. A couple of thoughts before we begin. Earlier this morning, I was talking to Kermit Krantz, and gave him an example of something that came up in my practice a year or two ago. A boy related some statements his mother had made to him about himself. Finally, when we involved the family in therapy, I was able to hear for myself the mother saying to her son, "Grow up, and be a man like your mother" (*laughter*).

About two years ago, I was asked to give a talk on sex education at a school in San Francisco. The talk was to be directed to fathers and sons, seventh- and eighth-grade boys and their fathers. The mothers' guild asked if they could provide refreshments. I learned later that the women who brought in cookies and coffee also brought in a tape recorder. When it came time for the talk, two of the women were still standing in the back of the room. One of the men present said, "Hey, the ladies are here. Let's get them out. This is our talk." The ladies asked if they could remain and the men finally decided it would be all right as long as they didn't ask any questions and didn't say anything. Two women sat in the back of the room with a tape recorder so they could play the session back to the rest of the women in the ladies' guild. Following the presentation and a long period of questions and answers, one of the women stood up and broke the taboo by saying, "I've never felt so good about being a woman." She got a message—a message that a woman is something wonderful, that a woman has a role to play above and beyond being a mere chattel, above and beyond giving sexual service. She learned for the first time that she had an intricate, beautiful, dynamic mechanism inside her; that she, too, like the man, was worthwhile.

About fifteen years ago, while studying the history of anatomy, I learned that prior to the time of Vesalius in the fourteenth and fifteenth centuries, anatomists classified women with the lower mammals. They did so because women, like lower mammals, directed their urinary streams backward. I think this gives some idea of the low esteem in which women were held from a biological and perhaps from even a psychological standpoint until recent times. We are experiencing some changes in our culture and our society that will change to a large extent the way we look at women, but, most important of all, as Virginia Johnson pointed out this morning, the way in which women think of themselves.

A recent business research survey of American students pointed to the fact that in the midst of an unprecedented communications flood, we have a misinformation gap between young people and adults. Young people today are faced with the same conflicts and questions their parents faced years ago: Who am I? What am I? What will happen to me? But they are also faced with prolonged periods of emotional and social dependence while acquiring an education which will probably be followed by a period of military service in a war that seems to be without redeeming merit. They're faced with earlier physical maturation than their forebears. They are dissatisfied with the double standards of the adult world. They are fighting the system, as clearly portrayed in Ken Kesey's book *One Flew Over the Cuckoo's Nest*. They're fighting the rat race, the silly little games, and the vagueness they see in the adult world. They have taken up the struggle against the myths of inevitability and status.

An articulate few among the student activists have found a willing audience in the sensation-seeking press. The resultant publicity can easily be distorted by those who are willing to believe the worst about the younger generation. Meanwhile, the inarticulate teenager, the nonactivist student, senses a growing feeling of impersonalization. He searches for meaning, for acceptance, for something to believe in. Can he find what he is seeking, or must he compromise and join the system, the rat race, and learn to play the silly game of the adult world including suburbia, the executive search, and the commute?

Young people of today are essentially no different than they were twenty or forty years ago, except that they were born into a world of transition. They are the children of change. They have seen change all around them, in technology, social customs, religion, and attitudes toward sex and the family. They take change for granted and look upon custom and tradition as things that can be changed. Many have come to see and participate in interracial dating. They have seen the rise in ecumenism and the gradual fall of religious prejudice. They have come to talk about sex more objectively than their parents talk about money. They have been raised in an era that has said goodbye to painful childbirth. They have seen the advent of the pill, the downfall of the puritanical view that sex is a necessary evil to be endured. They strive for sexual freedom, without losing sight of sexual responsibility.

They knowingly poke fun at the laws of over half our states which say sex is illegal except in the superior male position. They poke away at the Harrison narcotics law of 1914, which as interpreted by one Southern state can result in the death penalty for one who supplies a minor with what is now known to be a nonaddictive drug. They no longer look upon menstruation as the curse, but see it as an essential part of being feminine. They know the birds and the bees never enjoyed sex, and they wonder who ever started that ridiculous story about the stork.

Simmons and Winograd in their excellent book *It's Happening* (I recommend it to you very highly) said that young people today see through the tinseled values of America's commercialized eroticism. They see how we have been deluged by movies and advertising into thinking of sex as a sign of adequacy and acceptance.

Couldn't the hippie movement be, in one way, a reaction or overreaction to what young people see and dislike in our world? Could their near fusion of male and female appearances be their way of telling us they do not accept our stereotyped images of what it means to be masculine or feminine?

I think they're trying to tell us something. I think they've seen parents living together without love or happiness or sharing. They say, "If that's what it's like to be married, I want no part of it." And they show that it's possible to live and love and share outside the married state without going through all the hang-ups of the older generation.

Their initial attempts are crude and uncrystallized. But they know what they want and are willing to work at it. They want love without shame, without guilt, without anxieties from an inhibited past, and without promises for the future that cannot be fulfilled. They see sex for what it is, just one of the forms of human activity, a means for procreation, a means for sharing and showing and giving love.

Young people of today are not so much in need of critics as they are in need of good example and guidance. They seek something to believe in, and they are anxious to do something about it. They hope to be taken seriously, to be looked upon as reasonable and responsible.

I'd like to go on for a little while and discuss communication in a more simplified form. George Christie's diagram is technically correct and beautiful—all this coding and decoding and filtering—but I find that in working with patients it helps to get things down to as simple a form as possible. And so I just show them diagrams of people—first person, second person—and describe to them, in the simplest form, communication as the transmission and reception of meaningful signals or messages, and point out to them that communication in humans can take several forms (Fig. 2). It can be verbal or nonverbal. We can have manifest content, that is, that which can be put into print or seen on a video tape or in a film. We can have latent content, that is, that which is implied. People aren't very simple though, and they carry around with them layers: first of all a layer of defenses, and on top of that a layer of anxieties. So they are ready to go off at any minute. I think

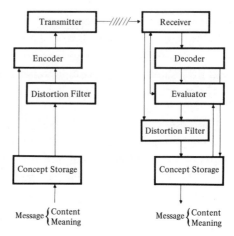

Figure 2. The human communication system
Communication: transmission and reception of meaningful messages. Distortion filter: for emphasis, deemphasis, and subtle shad-
ing of content to meet the expected distortion in the receiver.
Bias: adjustment for emphasis, deemphasis; affects signal perception. Message: final content, reconstructed or rebuilt.

one prime objective as a therapist when I'm working with parents or with children who have problems, or with families who
are having difficulties in establishing standards, regulating behavior, and teaching responsibility and discipline, is to get
them to understand what communication is.

Let me give an example. A while ago I saw a mother, father,
and son in my office. The father had been away from home a
lot on active duty in the Navy. When he came back, the
mother was trying to tell the father about all the difficulties
the son had caused while he was away, and the son said, "It's
because of the way I'm treated in this family. I dislike some of
the things that are going on." He was intimidated, though, by
the presence of his mother and father, from saying what he
actually felt. In order to make him feel more free, I said to

the mother, "Why don't you ask your son what he's objecting to?" So the mother said to the son, "Tell us about it." But she said it with such hostility in her voice, such a provocative attitude, that I put my hand up and said to the son, "Don't answer, because there's only one way you can respond to that, with more provocation." She was speaking to him out of her anxieties, and he would respond in a defensive manner, and pretty soon we'd have a full-blown fight going. I said to the mother, "Try it again." She said, "Tell us about it," but still carrying with it so much hostility and anger that I said, "Don't answer her. Once more, mother." This time she sat. I just had her be quiet for a minute, and I said, "Now, ask him again." She said "Tell us about it" in such a nice manner that the son began to respond without feeling threatened, without coming back and attacking her. I was shocked because the mother started to cry and got up and ran out of the room. I thought, "Oh, gosh, I lost another one" (*laughter*). She came back a little later and said, "I finally see what I've been doing."

She was bouncing messages off him, and he was bouncing them back off her, just from the level of defenses. They weren't really communicating honestly, openly, truthfully. They were being provocative in each and every interchange. They were getting no place. This little vignette, I think, will help to give you some idea of what we're aiming at when we talk about the generations.

I think there is a great generational communications gap. I think there's a glut also. Here we have the adult world, the world of the parent. We want to get certain messages across. We discipline children in a certain way, hoping that they'll internalize a sense of discipline and grow up to be responsible people. It works fairly well for a few years until they reach the teen years. They begin to associate with their peers. They begin to feel a rebelliousness which is natural as they become older, as they have more responsibilities, as more opportunities to do things are given to them. They begin to filter out some of the messages they get from parents and go on to develop a language of their own, a unique set of words temporary in nature, words that are purposeful in describing their feelings, their actions, their fear mores.

It's interesting to note that the language is of value to the teen-ager only so long as the parents don't understand it. As soon as a parent gets to know what it means to be "tough," "cool," "burn," they choose a new word. So it seems to me the name of the game is "keep-away." The teen-agers have the ball (*laughter*). The more we try to keep after them and say, "Come on now. Let's be honest. Tell me about it," the more they're going to say, "Well, how could you understand? You don't even speak my language." And they go on and use more and more words to make us foolish.

How do you approach people like this? I found a very effective way a number of years ago, and I think I now use it to advantage. I do quite a bit of group therapy with teen-agers. Although it's initially difficult to convince them to come into therapy in a group with their peers and with me, a superior, eventually they agree to come in. They find out that within a group setting in which confidentiality is the first byword, in which trust and respect follow naturally, they can begin to talk about themselves, to share feelings with others, to look for reasonable goals and to learn ways—they call them ways—to con their parents. They learn that it is possible to talk to mothers and fathers, to give them a grain of recognition for love; that parents will then open up and allow them to do more; and that parents really aren't such bad people after all. But if parents come storming in, using all the authority and so-called wisdom of their age, children will once again retreat and play "keep-away."

I find it interesting to see teen-agers in a group or see them individually and then, for some reason or the other, to see them in a family conference with mother, father, and teen-ager. I see a great transformation. A child who's been able to function adequately, to think clearly, and to discuss his problems openly, will suddenly become very provocative, making the parents look upon him as totally irresponsible, unable to do anything worthwhile, unable to do any more than provoke adults and become a public nuisance.

I think one of the problems we face now is that teen-agers have become a sensation. Most adults do not understand them. Teen-agers like to perpetuate this image. They need more nonjudgmental parents, educators, and lawmakers who will give them reasonable goals, be firm with them, and yet will hold out for them an ideal, and who will show teen-agers by their behavior that life is worth living, that growing up to be an adult is really not so bad after all.

I deal primarily with children who have problems. It is very gratifying to me to see so many of them do so well. The reason they do well is that they have learned to like their fearfulness of being inadequate, of being young, of being dependent, and they have learned to accept within themselves some of the worthwhile standards and values that they have seen within their parents and within society.

This is a brief introduction to a presentation by Shirley Stone, Jim Semmens, and me. Shirley is going to take this discussion about communications back one step and discuss some of the more primitive aspects of communication as found in the mother-infant relationship. Shirley?

SHIRLEY STONE: I facetiously entitled this presentation "Teaching Young Mothers To Keep Their Cool," but I guess we should not use the word *cool* so long as the teen-agers continue to use it. I might have titled it "It's Not His Fault He's Your First Baby," because it seems more and more apparent that the major direction of emotional and intellectual development is determined by the imprinting that takes place early in infancy and childhood. This effect begins with the very first impact of mother-child handling.

What are the problems, and how can they be handled to help the mother in our urban culture? What does she bring to it in the beginning? Our mass media have so indoctrinated women that, right from the beginning, they expect to see a counterpart of the child they see on the Pablum box or in the Gerber's food picture—the lovely, pink baby with fat cheeks. What did they get?—a little shrivelled, scrawny, unattractive infant. It's quite a revelation if you're in that position. Indeed, the father is in the same position, too. He sees twenty bassinets behind a plate-glass window, and somebody points to one child. He's supposed to have a feeling of overwhelming love, yet he can't. And yet up and down the hallway people are pointing, saying, "Isn't that dear baby lovely? I love him, he's adorable." It's really not true. If a mother goes away with this conception, all she can possibly feel is a sort of rejection and a feeling of surface love.

Even taking care of babies is made difficult in our culture. You almost need a Ph.D. to take care of a baby. Take making a formula. Even the word *formula* is difficult. It sounds like a chemistry professor's job. I can't handle the glass tongs on a hot bottle. It's very difficult. Take the sleeping position. The mother reads *McCall's,* and *McCall's* one month comes out with a whole article saying that you must never let the baby sleep on its belly or he'll suffocate. The next month, *The Ladies' Home Journal* comes out with another article. She must never let the baby sleep on his back because eight children vomited and aspirated. He's dead. The only thing that she can possibly do is hang him from a chandelier and let him sleep upright (*laughter*). But this is the sort of thing that's going on in mass media constantly. It's difficult. She's subjected to sleeping problems and feeding problems, and a normal woman almost has to tear her hair out. It's a twenty-four hour job, seven days a week. It's not very exciting.

Now, about the working mother. Sure, a mother shouldn't feel guilty if there are some times when she doesn't like this child. You don't have to love this baby twenty-four hours a day. It's impossible. He doesn't love you twenty-four hours a day either. If a mother wants to work, there's no reason she shouldn't. But many of the mothers we see in our own practice have a great sense of guilt when they have to leave the baby. We spend most of our time telling them they shouldn't feel guilty. If women want to work, whether out of economic necessity or whether they just prefer to work, if they enjoy working, they should go ahead and work. They should, of course, provide some sort of care during the day and they should also realize that when they come home at night, the quality of care they give that baby should be better.

I think if a woman is out all day, if she's stimulated, if she's happy, she'll come back into the home and give the baby better care than if she were there twenty-four hours a day.

There are conflicts. Suppose the child falls and hurts his knee and runs to the nursemaid. Instead of feeling guilty and terrible, the mother should be overjoyed; that means the lady's been taking care of the baby. The baby likes the nurse. Everything is going well for her, and she should be gratified. I still think the first responsibility of the working woman is to her family, and when she comes home, this has to be understood, so that she does give the child quality care and spends time with him. It's as simple as that, it seems to me. You have to inculcate a respect for individuality, and your baby is an individual, different from the next baby.

It's hard to understand, but there are no books for these things. The last book on baby care was written before your baby was even born, before you became a mother, and just because you've had this baby doesn't automatically make you a mother. It's work. The physician, I feel, should help. He can't lay down laws—do this, do that—because there are no laws for an individual. If he acted this way, he'd spend most of his time on the phone saying, "Yes, do this," "No, don't do that."

We've had people call and say, "Can I take the baby out?" When we look outside and say, "Yes," they say, "Oh good, because I'm outside." The same thing with ice cream. They say, "Can the baby have ice cream?" You say, "Well, how old is the baby?" and they say, "Six months." You say, "Oh yes, he can have some ice cream." They say, "Oh, that's good. He loves it!" (*laughter*).

It gets a little difficult, and if we do nothing more than give these young mothers a feeling of security and confidence, that's important. Right or wrong, they've made a move. They've taken a stand. They've moved out, without this feeling of fear and dependence.

It's almost the same thing when they go on to another authoritative figure when they're a little older. The child goes to school. If the child is ready to read, the mother is afraid. "Should I help him learn to read?" If a child's ready to acquire new skills, there's no fear the teacher won't approve. But, conversely, it's pretty silly to show an infant flash cards; it's not going to help his basic knowledge.

Our obligation, as I see it, is helping children develop to normal maturity and seeing that the entire family moves on to a maturity based on mutual respect. The parent must respect the child's needs. But it's not a one-way street; the child must also respect the parent's needs. Ultimately, the parent is preparing the child to grow up and leave. This is a major accomplishment, and it's very difficult to say to a mother of a one-week-old baby, "This child's going to leave you." She's quite unhappy. She just got her hands on this little baby. Thus, as Mrs. Johnson suggests, the mother must not become so sublimated with her children that she's bereft when they move out. This is a positive factor. This is what she's aiming for and she should be ready for it.

Finally, both as a mother and a physician, it's not too difficult for me to give what I feel is good advice in the problem of living. I'll be the first to confess that putting it into practice is difficult indeed. The average mother yearns for a list of do's and don'ts which will lead to the Holy Grail, but unfortunately these do not exist. Mothers are different, babies are different, and our level of knowledge about emotional growth and development is in the near-natal stage. Many of our friends and patients think that our children are very fortunate to have two all-knowing pediatricians as parents. It's amusing to see a new mother react when I tell her that when my children were infants and awoke screaming at 3:00 in the morning and kept crying, I no more knew what to do than I do now. It's another example of the generation gap (*laughter*).

WILLIAM LAMERS: Thank you, Shirley. To round out the formal part of the presentation, we'd like to switch over to Captain Semmens. Let me tell you a little about Jim. First of all, I met him when I was on active duty in the Navy at the U.S. Naval Hospital in Oakland. One evening I was down at "Happy Hour" in the Officers' Club, and I overheard him saying to someone that he had just received a contract to write a book on teen-age pregnancies. I said, "You don't really think you can pretend to write a book on teen-age pregnancies without having a psychiatrist explaining what it's all about?" He turned to me and said, "Okay, big boy, write it!" so Jim and I are coauthors of a book on teen-age pregnancy.

Since that time he has stimulated me to do many things I probably never would otherwise have done in research and to participate in programs that have proved to be very worthwhile to me. Jim, incidentally, is a graduate of Marquette Medical School. After he went into practice in Wisconsin he went into active duty in the Navy in World War II. When he came out he went into training in obstetrics and gynecology and has developed one of the finest teaching programs in obstetrics and gynecology in the United States at the Naval Hospital in Oakland. He's also director of the Committee for Sex Education for the American College of Obstetrics and Gynecology and has been instrumental in helping some communities develop programs for community sex education in the schools.

Jim's goal, I think, is to help set up teaching programs in sex education from earliest school experiences on. It's of little value to get a student in the fourth year of high school and then say "Okay, now we're going to teach you about sex." Students, by that time, are too far along to be talked down to by a teacher who may be more awkward about it than the student. Jim is going to follow through on the problem of the communications barrier between the generations and explain some of the hang-ups that we've had in our society, and propose a method for untangling some of them.

JAMES SEMMENS: Thanks, Bill. (I really didn't meet him for the first time in a bar.) Actually, I think if we're going to ask ourselves, "What is this particular hang-up in communication and what's to be done about it?" I think maybe we ought to ask ourselves something about our past performance and review some of the concepts of our generation.

For generations, children have been taught by family, church, and community that all things relating to sex are dirty and shameful. Nice people just don't discuss sex. As a matter of fact, in some states today, biology textbooks and the anatomy charts in the classroom are devoid of genitalia. If a child is caught examining his genitals he is chastised and told that he is naughty or bad, or his mother says, "Never let me catch you doing that again."

Exploration of self and masturbation are normal physiological responses in the growth and development of both sexes. Some children confronted by such urges are still told that they are abnormal and perverted, or that these acts will lead to mental illness, affect their offspring, or leave them sterile. The guilt complexes compounded by family and church in this area alone guarantee all the clients that our physicians and marriage counselors can possibly seek.

Is this a hang-up? It must be. Most parents are ashamed to admit to their children that they have sexual relations for purposes other than to generate offspring. They are reluctant to agree with a peer-teen culture that recognizes the physical exchange in human sexual relations as being the ultimate in the human interpersonal relationship.

It is regrettable that these same parents find it difficult to establish avenues of communication with their own children. Instead, they even feel guilty when they have sex. They try to hide it from their children. I think the current modality is to take off to a motel and leave your own home. They avoid all discussions that might lead to the fact that daddy puts his penis in mother and together they share a beautiful, personal, physical experience founded on love and respect for one another.

Perhaps we should examine why most parents and teachers have problems communicating with children. They have found that many of the taboos of sex taught by their own parents were meant to keep them in line by fear—fear of disease, pregnancy, or damnation. They find it difficult to change the approach; namely, to explain how remarkable the human reproductive system really is, to tell the story of fertilization, implantation, and growth, and the birth of a baby. We should tell the story of personal physical growth in the development of adolescents; establish understanding of emotional and physiological changes; and teach that kissing, petting, and masturbation are normal in preparing for heterosexual relationships and need to be controlled by a responsible attitude.

This will mean embarking on a totally honest approach with youth. Although this factual approach has proved itself in selected schools, the hang-up is that it threatens the adult population by exposing their own past inadequacies in teaching their children.

Today's programs, in biology at least, have taught that mammals reproduce their own kind and don't require help from the stork. What we need is the parents' cooperation and permission to help young people better understand the emotional as well as the physiological complexities of life. The development of one's own sexuality, the ability to achieve healthy interpersonal relationships, to project realistic personal images, and to be accepted as a mature individual are all equally important. We must prepare youth for this major area of responsibility in human relationships, as many of them will spend more hours of their lives in the family role than in any other.

To assure them of a meaningful and healthy relationship in marriage, they must be taught positive concepts of moral behavior based on the rights of self and others. Having achieved this for themselves, they will then be able to teach their own offspring the precepts of respect and responsibility by word and example.

Since many clerics continue to be hung up on dogma and interpretations that have been handed down through the ages, and since parents need help and guidance in initiating a responsible approach to the instruction of youth in the behavioral sciences, it is only fitting that the educator who has found comfort in honest communication with the younger generation is the logical teacher. Public and parochial school systems, with their large captive audiences of young people in their formative years, are the fertile ground for responsible, well-planned programs taught by trained people who are close to the daily problems of the growing child and adolescent.

If you'll bear with me, I'd like to go over our concept of the ideal kindergarten-through-twelve program. It may be a little bit physician-oriented. If you'll flip the lights off . . .* This is some material we prepared for the American College of Obstetrics and Gynecology, which has been very interested in working with communities in family-life education simply because we see so many people in adult life or early adult life who are having problems coping not only with their sexuality, but in understanding the physiological responses of everyday living.

Interestingly enough, when this program was started, we worked under the assumption that we were going to make tremendous inroads into promiscuity, venereal disease, illegitimate pregnancy, and such things. I think we are probably recognizing that these are the fringe benefits, because what we are really going to reap, and where we should really concentrate our efforts, is recognizing the fact that 50 percent of married people today exist in this state without fully appreciating its true value, its true meaning, and its reward.

When we talk at PTAs, of course, people are concerned that we're taking something away from the home. So the first thing we want to point out is that, from the moment of birth, a child begins to learn about interpersonal relationships. Maternal acceptance and paternal acceptance are important. The school programs are basic and factual. At home, the individual application goes on day by day. Parental attitudes and parental behavior patterns are observed every moment of the waking day. Parental affection for the child and parental affection as demonstrated between themselves, the way they treat their

* *Editor's Note:* James Semmens showed the group a series of slides as he talked.

neighbors, and how they react to the laws and the workings of the community, are all learned very early in childhood and will be used by the children as they grow and make decisions for themselves as to how to behave. So preschool can be an excellent time for the application in the home.

Many of us miss an opportunity when we are anticipating siblings coming into the family. This may be your own family; it may be relatives; it may be neighbors. When a little boy comes home and says, "Gee, the lady down the street is pregnant," this really shakes the whole family up, and they try to dismiss it. On the other hand, it would be an excellent opportunity to tell the story of human reproduction and the beauty of the reproductive system as a functioning unit. Certainly, if they were to tell the story, and help the child to understand how the male and female seeds unite and how remarkable the uterus is in nurturing and carrying the baby until it is ready for the world, and show the feelings of love and anticipation for the new sibling, the child will develop the same type of love and consideration. At the same time, they have taught basic human reproduction, put it in its proper context, and given it the respectability it needs. It is an opportunity to give at least a basic knowledge of the reproductive organs.

This, of course, helps the siblings welcome new members into the family unit on a less competitive basis. It is much more acceptable, and, from a mental health standpoint, would be a great boon. Sibling acceptance is of the utmost importance and cements the family unit.

It's really kind of interesting that schools today have to pay $25 or $30 to rent a movie to show kids how pigs are born. To those of us who grew up in a rural setting, this seemed to be second nature. I guess we didn't really realize how lucky we were. This is the finest opportunity in the world and many parents kind of drop the ball on it. When Cissie wants to know why Johnny has that handy thing for picnics, this is one time the mother has an opportunity to give a respectful connotation to the sexual capacity of the individual.

There are books and aids that help in teaching, and the list is constantly undergoing change because, interestingly enough, the demand for more sophisticated and better teaching aids has increased greatly.

Certainly, infant acceptance and love between the parents, love of offspring and neighbors, and neighborliness are important. We see this reflected in marriage counseling because a lot of misconceptions of how two individuals should interrelate in marriage are outgrowths of observations from early childhood. If there hasn't been much demonstration of love or affection within the home, it's very difficult for a woman who's not used to this to marry someone who's very demonstrative.

We should teach something about the physiology of sex and put it in its proper context before the age of exploration, before the concepts of obscenity and false modesty develop. At the third- and fourth-grade levels it is not unrealistic to teach human anatomy, and there's no reason we have to limit ourselves to cats. Proper names and terms certainly lend sophistication to the material. In teaching the story about sperm, their vitality, the way the egg is fertilized, in conjunction with the female sex organs, we should apply the proper names and terms. The male penis does deposit the sperm in the vagina; the sperm are mobile and alive. They migrate through the uterus and out into the tube where fertilization does take place. The egg is fertilized. One of our diagrams shows the different periods of gestation for different mammals. Kids often say about the gestation period for elephants that one significant thing is that the reason there are so few Republicans is it takes so long to generate them (*laughter*).

So we can show how the uterus actually nourishes the child

and how it grows. I think one of the things we should stress, especially as a way to give the woman her identity, is to let people know what a remarkable organ system the female has—how it goes through adolescence and begins to cycle, menstruate, ovulate, produce seeds, how it is able actually to conceive a new life, nourish it, increase to 300 times its normal size, return to normal within six weeks, and to function again in a perfectly rhythmic or cyclic manner.

One of the most recent advances, of course, is the little set of slides on how babies are made. These were done with simple tear-outs in a very sophisticated way and have been used in education from the third grade up. The main thing we are teaching is an identity, a personal image, as children are growing up, so that ideally these will be accepted in a very personal way when they have matured.

As Bill has told you, the child with problems in puberty is the child who is devoid of love at home. Explosions at puberty are frequently reflections of the home. At the fifth- and sixth-grade levels we discuss the endocrine system, the different endocrine glands, and tie in the function of the reproductive glands themselves. We're all familiar with the story of menstruation done by Walt Disney and made available through Kimberly-Clark for the past twenty years. It's an excellent film and it is used by most educational programs. We have entered a new area in educational programs, that is, helping children understand growth and development at the time they are actually growing and developing. They learn to respect one another. Girls learn as much about boys' reproductive physiology as boys do about girls'!

We have to remember that in certain communities at the lower socioeconomic levels, the problem of school drop-outs usually occurs in groups of children who mature early and are rapidly becoming capable of reproduction. Here it's necessary to downgrade these educational programs and tailor them to the community. We have to bear in mind that students who terminate their education early have time on their hands and are most likely to get into difficult situations. This is brought out by the Kinsey report. Ninety-five percent of the boys engaging in premarital sex stopped their education at the eighth grade.

One of the most important adjuncts to this program has been teaching growth and development, so students learn, as they reach adult stature, that each one has his own individual time clock of growth and development and thus they develop mutual respect.

In classrooms where these programs are in effect we see very little of the chiding of the student who's too fat or too short or too skinny. Human growth and heredity help carry the explanation one step further. The next area we would like to cover, and one that the children have asked for themselves, is some adult assistance and information on some of the emotional changes that come along with the physical changes at adolescence. There are some good recorded materials that can be used in the home. In fact, the school system that I consult keeps an ample supply of these records in the library. Parents draw them out and take them home, and they're discussed in the home between parents and children.

The American Medical Association and other medical and paramedical interests have covered various aspects of teen-age growth and development. I think the most interesting was the AMA's treatment of alcoholism for teen-agers. Students at the eighth- and ninth-grade levels are interested in social attitudes. They want to know about dating, nicotine, necking, sexual intercourse, alcoholism, narcotics, petting, and homosexuality.

We use a simple diagram to show the difference between male and female arousal and how often the male is apt to misinterpret meaning in the female's dress. She may be dressing to fit the style. The male, on the other hand, who is normally an aggressor, might see some other significance in her dress. By the same token, she's taught to appreciate the fact that he is easily aroused, and that she is the one who's basically responsible for behavior early in the interchange of necking and petting.

We talked today about the double standard. I think there's really a double–double standard. Not only do we have the boy-girl gap, we have a tremendous gap between the adult and the adolescent we are trying to educate responsibly. What we're really trying to teach is a concept of human rights, their own rights and the rights of others. On the other hand, parents continue to fight to establish the "going steady" symbol. Most mothers are guilty of this and, unfortunately, it confronts many young girls with emotional situations they're not prepared to handle. The steady is often two to three years the girl's senior and is interested in more active participation than the girl is ready for. Mothers push maturity. We have training brassieres at eight and nine years old. Physical and emotional problems collide.

In days past, we were threatened with venereal disease and illegitimacy. The one thing students understand is that pregnancy halts their education and decreases their individual potential. This makes sense.

The day of the naive adolescent is a thing of the past. Adults go on with their topless bars, and our courts permit such things. This is very difficult for the teen-ager to perceive. I had as a patient a girl who was caught in a compromising position when her parents came home unexpectedly. She and her fiance were engaged in some breast play. The parents made a big thing out of it. This very family, she pointed out to me, entertained visiting firemen at topless bars in North Beach. They weren't doing what they were saying. On the other hand, without responsible family-life education, adolescents are using terms such as "making out," using Saran Wrap for condoms, and using 7-Up for douches after sexual relations.

My personal feeling is that the teacher is the one to put across the program. All of the disciplines involved should continue their efforts. However, the teacher is closer to the adolescents and is the one to communicate with them. Fifty percent of adult married couples finish their education with high school. They're going to spend much more time married than in any other endeavor. The senior-level high school courses in family life must include in-depth anatomy and physiology, sexual hygiene, nutrition and growth, studies in mental health, and certainly concepts of moral responsibility.

We stress interpersonal relationships as we help students develop their self-image and learn to relate to others. The key is teaching respect and responsibility. Students learn to identify with healthy groups. We use Kirkendahl's outline of moral behavior because it crosses church barriers. The things that are moral are those that bring integrity in relationships: trust of others, broadening of human sympathies, cooperative attitudes, and so forth. Things that tend to break these things down should be considered immoral.

Sex is only a small part of the development of the total individual identity. (I made this slide showing that, when you cut the cake, sex is only a small part of it. One of my students wrote underneath, "Would you believe 99%!") We teach children about divorce rates, the different stages of marriage, the legal implications of marriage, and what the marriage contract actually means. We try to spend as much time teaching them about marriage as we do about driver education.

The main thing is to cover the problems that tend to break down a marriage as well as to go into depth about those things that build it up. We discuss problems of alcoholism, in-laws, premarital sex, budget and finance, and attitudes about sex, marriage, children, and religion.

We certainly have to get a pitch in for obstetrics and gynecology. All family situations are, hopefully, procreative. We teach students how to be discerning about individuals who need care. We teach them about fetal growth and development. Electively they can watch movies on labor and delivery and, because of the number of crib deaths in the first thirty days, we like to stress infant care.

I want to conclude by saying that this type of program is not strictly medically oriented. Ours was a team effort of physicians, educators, clergymen, lawyers, bankers, and marriage counselors. All share their experiences with these young people in a very factual way.

As Kermit Krantz pointed out, when he was over in the Orient and tried to tell dirty stories about sex (not that I think Kermit would tell a dirty story), he failed to arouse the Oriental humor because to them sex is a very important and sophisticated thing. I think we have to look at ourselves in this manner. That's my presentation. I think this is one way to teach young people how to approach and understand their own sexuality, be they male or female. Since this conference is designed for the female, I'll leave it at that.

GEORGE CHRISTIE: By all means. Let's have some questions. We can't rush these people off without working them a little harder. They've had it too easy.

ANNE SHEFFIELD: I think Dr. Lamers started out with an extremely important and valid comment about children nowadays. He said that children have changed. I think children of change have to have a new way of learning about sex and about their personal relationships. I'm terribly sorry to say that I, as a mother coping with a child whom I'm trying to teach in a way she'll understand, consider that a very old-fashioned type of presentation. It's almost as though we've started too late teaching our children about sex, but we're taking our ideas about sex and giving them to children who ought to be having a new kind of sex education, better suited to the totally changed environment they're being born into and growing up in. I think that that is *our* sexual environment, and I don't think that we can impose it on children of change.

WILLIAM LAMERS: You don't want to transmit your hang-ups, whatever they may be, to a child.

ANNE SHEFFIELD: True.

JACQUELINE GRENNAN: I think this is where the communications model has importance for us, for we live in a world that, we hope at least, is continuous, both chronologically and environmentally, with all the people in it. I also think of the vast differences we have: for example, the PTA lady whom Jim's trying to get to, who has absolutely no communication with her own child. I think we haven't said much today about the extraordinary differences we're going to have to deal with, where you have the child who is the product of a very sophisticated home, of somebody who's way ahead, living sometimes in the same school system with a child from what I call South St. Louis. One of the things we've got to do is to help build family integrity. It seems to me that, as an educator, I've got to work for family integrity, for the very ultrapuritan, legalistic parent who has to get the message and maybe won't walk out on this kind of presentation, and also for the child of a parent who has perhaps been in multiple marriages. This is tough for the school. I think your great mandate to give it to the teacher is an awfully hard one. I wouldn't go quite that strong. I would say that the teacher is going to be one of the units. But in lots of cases, I think the sophisticated home is going to be better than the teacher. We've got to come up with what one man called the *educating society*. In a transitional society, your ultraliberals don't condemn the halfway moves, because halfway is a hell of a lot better than zero.

WILLIAM LAMERS: In Marin County where I practice, we have an unusual situation. It's a bedroom society for San Francisco, filled with young children who have an excess of time, a lot of cars, and a lot of money. Fifty to sixty percent in some high schools are either using or have used one of several of the psychedelic drugs. Mothers there call for help after it's a bit too late. To counteract this, the pediatrician Catherine Pike (who was to have been here except her husband is in the hospital) and I set up a program of preventive child psychiatry. In this program, which will begin soon, we will present such a program to groups of mothers, to discuss communication, sex, the development of responsibility, and childhood behavior on an informal basis. We will later involve them in group discussions. So we'll be supplementing at the mother level, and we hope at the mother-father level, the kind of education that children will be getting in the schools. I think you're right that this is not enough, but I think this is much better than anything I was exposed to as a child.

JACQUELINE GRENNAN: It's surely not enough for a lot of kids.

JAMES SEMMENS: The outline I gave is rather skimpy because it covers such a span of years. If we actually work with the junior high school and high school kids in this, in the little round-table type presentation where they can go into depth about anything that bothers them, you can really get somewhere. It's nice to have a program that's taught in a sophisticated home, but there just aren't enough of these homes. I think we're talking about an educational program for the middle people who are not going to provide this. They say they are, but they never do.

CATHERINE CHILMAN: I have a great deal of admiration

for your having developed this very ambitious sex education program. I'd just like to point out that there are many other professions very much involved in family life and sex education, most notably the people in the National Council of Family Relations. I think one of the big difficulties in this field is to get the basic research and know for sure that everything you're teaching is correct. For example, on divorces and interfaith marriages, more recent studies have revealed that earlier findings are no longer so. Interfaith marriages are likely to be very strong marriages. This is just one example. Our marriage textbooks often will quote studies that are as much as thirty years old, based on very tiny samples with biased questionnaires. These get into the books and are quoted from then on.

I believe you were indicating that a cause of marital unhappiness or breakdown was premarital intercourse. Now, while some of the marriage textbooks say this, there are no good studies that would really prove this. For example, it's often said that the reason school dropouts are apt to have illegitimate pregnancies is that they dropped out of school with time on their hands. But studies of illegitimate pregnancies indicate that they are six times as prevalent in the very low income groups as in other groups, and while you might think, "Well, they've dropped out of school," it is more the total situation of poverty and the total life-style of deprivation. I think it's really very, very important to know these things for sure when you're transmitting information to young people, because they can take what you say with a great deal of seriousness and it can be very disturbing to them. Therefore, I would make a plea that people who are going to get into this field really search deeply to find out what knowledge there is about these different subjects.

JESSIE BERNARD: And keep it up-to-date.

CATHERINE CHILMAN: It's a big job. As you say, there are lots of professions involved in this. I think a cross-professional development of material is what's needed, and there will be a book forthcoming. Jessie's one of the editors. Do you want to mention it, Jessie?

JESSIE BERNARD: No, it is just that the Sex Education and Information Council of the United States (SEICUS) had a conference last year, funded by the Office of Education, and Catherine ran it.

CATHERINE CHILMAN: That is a good indictment.

RUTH USEEM: This is all planned.

JESSIE BERNARD: We all agree that the big thing is the teacher; and this is to be a textbook for teachers.

CATHERINE CHILMAN: A number of professions contributed to it: psychologists, gynecologists, sociologists, and psychiatrists. It really is a difficult field. It takes in so many bodies of knowledge.

JAMES SEMMENS: I hope you appreciate that I was just trying to touch the bases and show you all the different things that have to be covered if you're going to make a total and responsible presentation.

CATHERINE CHILMAN: Yes, but I think that someone else raised the point that it is necessary to have an awful lot of different people who come from many different backgrounds involved in the classes, too. When you're talking about human behavior, a statement that such-and-such leads to such-and-such can do an awful lot of damage because of the individual variation. Research findings expressed as group averages don't take translation variation into account. Do you see what I mean? Any finding you get is an average. When you're talking to students you could say, in terms of what we know now, on the average this *seems* to be so; but not this is the way it *is*. You say to a class that so much depends upon maternal love and paternal love. Suppose you came from a home in which there wasn't any? How do you feel sitting there?

JUNE BUTTS: I had some specifics. They may sound like

real criticisms. I hope they're constructive, though, because this is something that I feel very much a part of, too, helping to plan programs for family-life educators. I didn't find that there was any mention of how to develop one's own personal moral code, a study of values, this kind of thing. Maybe I missed it. I was looking for it.

JAMES SEMMENS: It was discussed. That was the Kirkendahl approach. Actually, this was the Hayward United School District I was talking about. They started with a course of marriage and the family twenty years ago, and they've been in operation twenty years, and they were the consultants for the Anaheim program. They're responsible in part for the San Mateo program and some of the others that you are familiar with.

JUNE BUTTS: Excuse me, Doctor. Let me just be more specific. I don't mean what people do. I don't mean the social behavior of groups. I mean how one decides what to do when one is age 14, 15, or 18. I think that it gets back to masculinity and femininity. I didn't think it was stressed enough in your program. Also, it was not a multiracial society. I didn't see any Negroes, Orientals, or any of these other people who must live where these kids go to school, or any allusion to the studies of multiracial or multiple families, for example, an extended family with children who have a mother who's remarried and they're friendly with those children. Since this is about contraceptive culture, where is any open discussion about this?

JAMES SEMMENS: That's very interesting. This is the first year this program has put anything in about contraception. This program was actually requested by the students twenty years ago, and it was through the students' efforts that the PTA and the school board started it. They have a course called Sociology I and it's taught for a whole semester in the senior year in high school. The other courses are for lesser periods of time throughout the whole program, all the way down to the kindergarten level. The things you're asking about are in the program.

JUNE BUTTS: They are?

JAMES SEMMENS: Very definitely. As a matter of fact, I'm the doctor who goes down to the waterfront school and talks to the kids and works with the kids, and I've been down the whole road. It's quite an experience. This thing is just in its infancy, but we thought it was appropriate to this particular type of program because we've been asking ourselves all the time: How are we going to give this woman her identity as a female, as an individual? She projects her image from the time she goes to school, and that image is received by those around her and this is the way she matures. When she finally matures to the point where she's ready for the one-to-one relationship in marriage or out of marriage, where is she going to be? Premarital sex is discussed openly in a forum type of discussion of probably five or six boys and five or six girls at a roundtable with just a counselor. Incidentally, the people who teach this program are the counselors for these kids from their freshman year on, and they teach the big courses at the twelfth grade. They've known these kids for four years, and they know them just like the back of their hand. There are no holds barred. The kids discuss what goes and what doesn't on a date. They set up their own community standards. I think this is very helpful.

JUNE BUTTS: That feedback I was listening for, I didn't hear it.

JAMES SEMMENS: I couldn't go into all those things. It would have taken too much time. In fact, I apologize for the time I took.

JUNE BUTTS: No, it was very good.

GEORGE CHRISTIE: Jim, we have a question from Martha.

MARTHA STUART: I'm divorced. One of the things I keep seeing, as an underlay in all of this discussion and even a kind of a reinforcement in your course, is that divorce is bad. This is a prejudicial thing. Divorce is a very good thing for some people. It's a growing up process sometimes. It's too bad that it is, but it is. It may be a great thing for the children involved; it may be necessary if we want people to have wonderful, happy situations, and men and women with great relationships. But we rarely say that a couple that accepts the fact that they have a hung-up marriage is making a mutually responsible decision, exercising the kind of responsibility and acceptance we're talking about. We're talking about telling our children the truth. You can't then just imply that you keep a hung-up relationship together and pretend that that teaches them more.

JAMES SEMMENS: Nobody's teaching them this.

MARTHA STUART: It's not saying this, but it's implied.

MICHAEL SCRIVEN: I think Martha's point is pretty strong. I don't think graphs about divorce rates connected with whether it's a similar-faith marriage and so on should be in there. Not only because of the point you made, which seemed to me devastating. It just doesn't tell you about Marin County school kids with an IQ of 132 or Marin County school kids with an IQ of 80 from a strong Catholic background and so on. It doesn't give students the data they need. You shouldn't operate on that basis. It's like saying the mean intelligence of Negroes is below that of whites, therefore you shouldn't hire Negroes.

JUNE BUTTS: That's right.

MICHAEL SCRIVEN: It's as bad as that. It seemed to me June picked up a number of these points. The overall reaction I have to that general outline, even if it's taught very well, is this: I have spent years now working to get social sciences in the high schools taught in a better way, and what I've just seen seems to me to be an outline from the days before any of this occurred. It is the outline of somebody telling somebody else what's the right thing to do.

MARTHA STUART: Yes.

MICHAEL SCRIVEN: This isn't how you get them to learn. It's like the idea that you're going to solve the hot rod problem by giving good driving education. In the high school, it doesn't get to it; it doesn't get within miles of the problem. Martha is right about the termination of marriage. It's not interesting that Catholics don't divorce. The question is, what do they hold together? It seems to me this is what you've got to look for, and this is what we have extremely little data on. If they're holding together a killing relationship, which is chopping the kids up along with the marriage partners, there ought to be a divorce. My experience with kids is that at 8 years old they can discuss difficult moral problems better than most of their parents can.

It seems to me this is the point of fact about readiness that one ought to begin with in these programs. This is terribly close to them in almost everything that matters to them. You want to begin by figuring that they're capable of thinking out the hard problems and discussing questions like: What sort of a relationship do you want in the home? What are your expectations from your parents? Are they realistic about themselves? What do you think goals are for? The sex education organ in this country is *Playboy* magazine, and it's not a bad one. Its approach is very different from the sort of approach that you get in even the best of these family-life education programs. The reason is that it is problem oriented. It goes after the things that people really care about, that they fight about, that they argue about, and that are hard to answer. It puts up a particular view, right or wrong. It tries to answer the problems that the kids are talking about all the time, which are not these problems. These are things they have mythologies about and they make mistakes about and we ought to clear up certainly. It seems to me that one really must break away from this very traditional approach. You won't reach the kids with this; they won't listen to it; they'll reject it. It's part of the square deal. It's not going to be something that gets to them. A couple of little sessions from teen group work played back to them from kids who have troubles will excite them much more than fifty of these books and documents, it seems to me. This is not, in a way, treating the materials that the kid has available to him as really useful in sex education.

WILLIAM LAMERS: I think a divorce can at times be the best possible way to solve a marriage problem. I think this program and other programs like it try to help kids ask a question ten years before they have a problem. What about knocking out some of the random mating that goes on for inadequate reasons in our society? What about carefully thinking of yourself as a person, thinking of yourself as a potential member of a family? Let's try and plan for the ideal. If it doesn't work, okay.

MICHAEL SCRIVEN: As long as you're prepared to tell them to go and live in sin that's all right. If you're not prepared to tell them that, if the PTA is not going to buy that, they'd better face having to marry rather than burn and divorce when they grow up.

JUNE BUTTS: May I just say one thing that I think will be an epitome, a capsule, of this. I'm sure that a lot of people here saw the movie *To Sir With Love*. To me that's a great thing in sex education. It wasn't called that. It was dealing with human problems. At first it was facetious. I remember one of the girls said, "Sir, how do you avoid divorce?" Someone said, "Don't get married." Well, that's one way.

GEORGE CHRISTIE: Virginia, do you have a word to add to this?

VIRGINIA JOHNSON: I could have let it pass easily, but I feel I must underwrite the whole trend of comment here. First, let me say I'm totally devoted to the man who presented this, to his motives and the work he does and the way he does it, but I still think that it's apparent he's seeming to present sex education without sex information. I'm in complete agreement that this material is twenty-five years out of date. My 12-year-old daughter uses Ortho's beautiful large pink book on the reproductive system, which is far more sophisticated than any of this. But I'm happy to see that somebody's moving. And I know Jim for his dedication in this work and I know also the formidable blocks he's up against here where people won't even consider talking sex with their children. On the other hand, I think that we have to almost ignore these people and go on over the top because we're losing the ones who are moving.

ANNE SHEFFIELD: I think another thing this presentation does is emphasize and reemphasize the family. Yet so many kids today are violently questioning their own families and think of the family unit as a concept that they're being sold by their parents. You can't stick them back into something that they have already begun to question.

KERMIT KRANTZ: I've seen a thread here and nobody will drag it out. What you're all saying is: the religious and moral values of our society have made the family unit what it is, have set the parameters in which we live. If it is sick, well, then, let's try to get well.

JUNE BUTTS: I'm asking where we get individual values, but it doesn't have to be religion.

KERMIT KRANTZ: There's no question about it, because without it you wouldn't be here. If it weren't for the conflict between the moral values that you hold in a changing society, we wouldn't even have a society, we'd all be out breeding like animals. As you go into the Oriental cultures, you learn that sex has an entirely different connotation.

RUTH USEEM: And they're hung up worse than we are.

LOUIS DUPRÉ: I thought the program was tremendous. I also thought the points some people made were well taken.

Mrs. Johnson said that we shouldn't inflict a particular code of ethics on our students. I agree with that 100 percent. On the other hand, I don't think that religion is really the issue here. Religion is the one thing of which I know something, and I don't see that it has much to do with this at all. Sometimes I find, as Scriven said, *Playboy* may be better than a book on sex education. Usually it isn't. (Incidentally, I don't care for the *Playboy* philosophy.)

I still think that in either case I would like to detach religion from problems of morality. I would like to stress that morality is relevant. I think this is what the Commander was trying to say. Kids should be educated morally. Morality means simply responsibility, but you don't have to have any religion for that. Some of the most immoral people I have known were very religious and some of the most moral people I have ever known were completely irreligious. They had no religion whatsoever. In fact, the person that I morally admire most has no religion whatsoever. He is certainly much more moral than I am and I consider myself a very religious person, but I'm not very moral (*laughter*). So it's very important that you distinguish the categories here. I think that religion has something to do with it. For the religious person, morality is religious; for a nonreligious person, morality is just as good as his own religion. With all respect to your position, I agree with the point Martha was making. I think that in some cases, when a marriage is not working out, a divorce is the best solution for the children and for everybody.

GEORGE CHRISTIE: You know we're going to have another good session coming around, but I want Ruth to get one word in too. But remember, I get the last word.

RUTH USEEM: It's a long point, so I think I better not start it.

GEORGE CHRISTIE: Dr. Liu is looking at me threateningly. You see we're a little bit over.

RUTH USEEM: I speak now as an anthropologist to ask a question because I really don't know the answer. I noticed on your last list that no parents were included in the team effort and frankly I would applaud this. I think there is an intellectual development which does take place when one is relieved from constant sexual intrusion for a woman or constant need to intrude for a man. I think the incest taboos that have been worked out in every society I know of are coterminous with those people whom one can trust not to attack one sexually. I think that parents are getting a lot of abuse for what they feel they should do; that is, not teach. They should perhaps teach reproduction, but they should not teach all of the emotional, sexual feelings because the gender roles of mother-son, father-daughter, uncles, aunts, and cousins are ones in which overt emotional sexuality is taboo, and I think that in this one can develop intellectually. In Philip Barry's *Childhood Through the Ages* there's a great thing. When everything was open, there was no privacy. Children were little people. Everything was open. Remember, they had no intellectual development either. The intellectual development was going on in the monasteries. Albert Ellis used to say he thought that virginity was blatant masochism, and that with constant sexual fulfillment the teen-age girl would at least get her homework done. I think we have to know how to balance the things which are part of our intellectual development and how to feel and care for people that we never see, touch, smell, or anything else. I'm not certain that that isn't a one-to-one relationship, and I think the whole incest taboo is rather too narrow now, rather than too wide. I'm very concerned about all this openness. (I notice, though, you did put a dress on the mother bathing the children together.) One of the problems of a contraceptive culture is that as we have fewer children, we're not so likely to have them of both sexes. I struck out with three boys. How can you have a nice brother-sister relationship,

which is a gender role in which overt sexuality is denied—
how can you have this in a home in which you do not have
a brother-sister relationship? We don't even have the cousins.

JAMES SEMMENS: In school they get the interchange between boys and girls.

RUTH USEEM: That's exactly it, and this is the *kibbutz*
which has developed new kinds of families.

GEORGE CHRISTIE: Ruth, I'm getting real tough signals
from my boss over here . . .

WILLIAM LIU: The most unfortunate task of the conference management is to break up the meeting. In five minutes
we go to the next session in the auditorium right across the
hallway.

How Can Men and Women Work Together? 8

CHARLES P. LECHT, HAROLD J. GIBBONS,
AND JACQUELINE GRENNAN

Tuesday, 4:00 P.M.

RICHARD CORNUELLE: I'm the chairman for the second session this afternoon. I'm in the trade association business, and I talk mainly to businessmen. I always have to begin by telling stories to wake them up. So I'm going to tell two stories. The first is a generation-gap story. A friend of mine, who is a friend of Potter Stewart, told it to me. Justice Stewart was at a party in Washington with a number of other Washington celebrities, including Walter Lippmann, and the conversation turned to the attitudes of the younger generation. The phrase *making out* came up very frequently. At one point, Mr. Lippmann drew Justice Stewart aside and said, "I wouldn't like to expose this ignorance in front of everybody, but I'm not dead sure what that term *making out* means." Potter thought this was kind of unusual, so when he got home and found his 17-year-old daughter was still up, he said, "Cissie, you won't believe this, but Walter Lippmann doesn't know what *making out* means." And she said, "Who is Walter Lippmann?"

The introduction of the panelists this afternoon is a very easy assignment, and that suggests my second story. It's about a blacksmith who was working in his shop. A town loafer was standing in the doorway, chewing a straw and watching. The smith pulled a horseshoe out of the forge, white hot, and put it on the anvil. It changed color very quickly; but it was still hotter than hell. At that point, a little boy wandered off the street into the shop, picked up the horseshoe and then dropped it very quickly. The loafer was amused. He pulled the straw out of his mouth and said, "What's the matter, Sonny? Is that kinda hot?" The boy replied, "No, sir. It just don't take me long to look at horseshoes." So our panelists can be presented very briefly.

Charles Lecht, you'll find, is expert in the field of computer technology, and a kind of hippie capitalist. He believes in such tenets as the idea that work is a bad habit. He hires people mainly because he likes them, and he doesn't do anything he doesn't enjoy. This is a sort of family joke. Those of you who are attending just this session won't see it entirely.* However, Edgar Berman notwithstanding, Mr. Lecht was flown here today by a woman pilot!

I wrote up at least a dozen introductions for Harold Gibbons, because I'm not sure that a vice-president of the National Association of Manufacturers very often has an opportunity to introduce a vice-president of the International Brotherhood of Teamsters. I want to say only that Harold is known nationally as a gifted organizer. Yet, at the same time, I don't know of anyone who has a more urgent sense of the need to protect the individual from being overwhelmed by the organi-

---

* *Editor's note:* This session was held in the auditorium and open to the public and to the Notre Dame students.

zation. I think you'll see the flavor of that commitment in his remarks.

And Jacqueline Grennan, is Jacqueline Grennan!

CHARLES LECHT: Good afternoon. I must say that I enjoyed my flight down here very much. I am very pleased to be here. The title of my talk is "The Personal Impact of Impersonal Automation." Before I start, I would like to state that I intend that my message, its content, be heavily affected by its presentation format. Second, if some of the comments are provocative, they are meant to be, because I want to call attention to something. I've been roaming around as a hippie capitalist —I've never been called that before, but I like the connotation—for years now. One of the things I'm most bothered with is conversations which are out of context, sessions, if you will, and conferences which are out of context. The myth of automation, for instance, is discussed at computer conferences as though everything existed, with total failure back in the user facility—defined by out-of-context considerations. Let's hope that what follows fits into the scheme of things.

THE PERSONAL IMPACT OF IMPERSONAL AUTOMATION

[A radio turned on]

NEWS RELEASE

WHAT WITH THE PROLIFERATION OF MANY AND LARGE AUTOMATION SYSTEMS IT CAN BE PREDICTED WITH A HIGH DEGREE OF CERTAINTY THAT BY THE YEAR 2000, 90 PERCENT OF THE WORK IN THE U.S.A. WILL BE PERFORMED BY 10 PERCENT OF THE POPULATION, LEAVING 90 PERCENT OF THE POPULATION, PRACTICALLY SPEAKING, AT LEISURE.

SOCIOLOGISTS ARE NOW PLANNING A "NEW SOCIETY" BASED ON LEISURE. FOR EXAMPLE, MR. JONES WILL (FIGURATIVELY SPEAKING, OF COURSE) BE ABLE TO SIT ON HIS FRONT STEPS DRINKING A MARTINI AND WAVE TO HIS PERSONAL ROBOT WHO WILL HANDLE CHORES AROUND THE HOUSE WHILE THE MAM-

MOTH STATE-OWNED COMPUTER-DRIVEN INDUSTRIES PRODUCE MORE THAN . . .

[Click]

[A radio turned off]

A LUNCHTIME DISCUSSION NEAR A LARGE PLANT UNDER-GOING TRANSITION TO THE AGE OF AUTOMATION.

Man (*singing voice*):   Home for lunch, darling!

Woman: Again?

Man: By the way, did you do the things I asked you to do this morning?

Woman: No.

Man: Yesterday?

Woman: No.

Man: Last week?

Woman: No. Eat your lunch.

Man (*angry*):   How do you expect . . . ?

Woman: My God! For better or for worse—but not for lunch too!

[Silence]

IF AUTOMATION IS TO RETURN DAD HOME, IS THE HOME READY FOR HIM?

DOES FAMILY PLANNING INCLUDE PLANNING FOR DAD'S RETURN?

I have some reservations about the thought "changing women."

I am suspicious of the *WORDS*.

How can we talk of changing women without talking of changing men, changing education systems, changing society?

The title of this conference implies the words *change* and *family planning*.

Words . . . in a title . . .

Words . . . and their meaning . . .

Where does life's meaning lie? In words? In objects? In our heads? In a mystical union of many media in our . . . and our mind's eye and our intellect?

And, where are the ideas? In words? In our heads? In a mystical union of many media in our . . . and our mind's eye and our intellect.

Questions still debated in the present, in the past too . . . and in the future by all indications . . .

Yet, we do live with our ideas however uncertain we may be, they coming from or having caused words, spoken, written, published, engraved . . .

Define a reality which is quite certain for us if not for anyone else . . . for a time if not for long . . . whether we like it or not.

And while we may argue over *meaning* we may never argue over *ideas* and where ideas come from . . . the fruitless debate.

Are ideas caused by words formed by nonintelligent life? Or

Platonic thought sucked in through the nostrils of the mind? Or divine inspiration? Or what have you? . . . The fruitless debate, and arguing over meaning is itself a fruitless debate unless the idea, its being, will cause action by people, or machines, *or both* or what have you?

Our action: This meeting!

I am afraid that to discuss *the emerging woman and family planning* without discussing society and society-planning, education and education-planning, is perhaps to give respectability to other ideas which will cause action . . . out of context . . .

When ideas . . . their existence . . . cause action, reality or nonreality, still unclear to the most certain of philosophers, becomes a fruitless debate . . . if that action is not perceived . . . things are not moved . . . we are not moved to act one way or another.

I am going to raise an issue, present an idea which I think is in context with our charter. But perhaps . . . Well, let's see.

Work

Now to me, work has a nasty connotation. It implies the necessity to be at a certain place at a certain time to do what you do not want to do. (Notice that "nonwork" is not "inactivity.")

And so, work is *an unhappiness*.

Somehow, long ago we were fouled up. Someone invented work. And we subscribed almost fully to the notion that nothing could change for the better without it.

No activity which produced the symbols of progress could take place without it.

If we were to be happy we *must* be unhappy first.

Toil, labor . . . a code borne by men who were uncertain of their own future and who wanted something to be sure of and who convinced other men that nothing could be done *without force* and that if a man *were to be left to his own devices, doing things he liked to do at a place he liked to do them at a time he chose himself, he would rot!*

And so work was invented. Maybe not exactly that way, but you know we do have much trouble looking at the past through our present-day minds.

If "we look at the future through a rear-view mirror," a highly polished surface honed by God knows how many experiences, environments, people, and what have you,

Is it not just as reasonable to suppose that we look at the

past through a rear-view mirror and we are caught—encapsulated in what we are, mirror reflecting upon mirror, front, side, top, bottom?

Our thoughts about things trapped in what we have been made to be by circumstances—environment. Maybe so. I hope not.

Back to "work." Now, no one has even proved that we could not exist without work . . . as I defined it.

Experiments have been conducted which prove, to me, beyond a doubt that maximum productivity is achieved by men who *like* what they are doing: no force, no penalty, no punishment.

More buildings might be up. More food might be produced. More of what have you, or different happier kinds, but for work. But we discovered work . . . so why don't we quit?

Well, work is a bad habit, and a bad habit is hard to break. And our society, and our schools, and our books, and our rules, and our friends, and our teachers, and our training, and our preachers import, manufacture, write, talk, and on and on and on, feeding our minds, encapsulating our thoughts, molding, polishing, packaging us for a life of work without asking why . . . or if it makes sense, or if it needs to be *that way*, or what else we might do to have what we want in this world without working or suffering?

Blessed be the meek?

Blessed be the poor?

No one ever meant that it was good for the meek to be poor? Empathy turned into desirability . . . pity turned into virtue, despite *Job* whose job it was to prove anything but virtue in work.

Back to work . . . family planning.

Now, family planning implies to many the notion of children, how, when, where to have them so that they don't disrupt the natural order of things in the home, in the city, in the country, and in the woods.

I tell you *that* preoccupation, however meaningful in today's environment where people talk about food depletion . . . air pollution . . .

NEWS RELEASE

IF WE KEEP PROPAGATING OURSELVES AT CURRENT RATES OF INCREASE, THERE WILL BE ONE PERSON STANDING ON EVERY SQUARE FOOT IN 625 YEARS, AND IN 6,250 YEARS THE PERIMETER OF OUR FLESH WILL BE EXPANDING AT THE SPEED OF LIGHT.

. . . and other natural disorders, is itself a hazard if it is thought about *alone,* especially in an age when *the father may be at home frequently, not working.*

The evils of automation finally to catch up with us, returning dad to the wife and kiddies in a world more unprepared for *that* than the promiscuous progenation of children. Family planning should also include plans for dad, the prodigal son, to be returned to a closer relationship with his wife and kiddies.

Perhaps if that occurs, planning the number of kiddies won't be a problem anymore, for most men do not understand today's household, no matter how many kids they may have, since they aren't in it that much; and if they were in today's modern American home, they might quit having kids so quickly.

Who is planning for dad's return? Certainly not the schools, which are chanting the same old liturgy about *work* at a time when our thoughts about work must change. And dad will be returned to the changing woman, still today victim of years of sometimes subtle, sometimes overt degradation.

Notwithstanding our veneration of the female, eulogized in every poetic way, as if possessed of extrahuman qualities, we continue, alas and alack, *to train the minds of children and grownups in the inevitable inferiority of the female* based on man's inability to define masculinity without bringing in the notions of *work-pain-power*.

We live today with a nonsensical heritage of the past, with its codes communicated by word of mouth, venerated books, antiquated thoughts.

A lot of which are based on the fang and the claw.

The concept of power-strength still our God . . . Zeus in his temple—lightning, thunder . . .

Literature, a good deal of which has not changed, written thousands of years ago, binding and packaging minds of men and women so that each knows his place, a place, if not defined by power, interpreted that way all too frequently.

And so it's no wonder that women in today's society are nervous.

And men point to their nervousness and say, "see, it's all correct."

At Treblinka the Nazis starved the Jews and when the time was ripe gathered the townspeople to witness what had been written years before about the scavenger nature of mature Jews by tossing a crust of bread into their lot.

So my friends, the changing woman–family planning must be discussed *in concert* with other ideas.

Automation is putting people out of work.

Now that's not a bad thing because work is a bad habit anyway. But our concept of work mixed with morality and other psychological notions of which we are and are not aware are frustrating men.

And when a man returns to sit out his time not working and believing that he should be or he's worthless, our changing woman may just get her comeuppance, a kind of final *coup-de-grace*.

The explosion just may be orders of magnitude greater than what is purported to be causable by the population explosion —the "pop" explosion!

And all because of a myth on the virtue of work: its continuing propagation at the same time as the propagation of machines to do man's work . . . a good thing, so men can once again take time to evaluate what they are and where they're going.

No one is taking enough time today. A suggestion, a glimpse, a possible solution . . .

A Start in Education

We must stop packaging our children, giving them preconceived and poor notions of the relationship of man to woman in pictures, in words, and in other ways, providing them with notions of good and evil which venerate masculinity and degrade femininity.

Children learn more today by what *we* do not say. There was a time when we could lie to our children and it took so long for them to find us out that they "did the same thing themselves" so they never brought it up again, or they matured so they didn't have to or want to . . . out of hatred or love or fear of either.

Today, mass media, our invention, has turned on us . . . the radio, telephone, television, film, and so forth . . . we get found out quickly by minds too young to know our games. A bitter pill swallowed at a young age . . . creating an incurable disease rather than curing one. Some who preach the fallen, incurable, evil character of man (and at the same time free will and glorification of God's creation) would prevent communications . . . censorship . . . a poor solution . . . while stimulating authorship of communications to be censored . . . piles of water on the tips of flames whose unending source sees not a drop.

We must *stop* preaching about work and suffering and pain . . .

In the schools, as though they were desirable; not that they will not exist, but we have enough unhappiness visited upon us in our lives without being "set up" to choose it.

Yes, yes . . . I know . . . idealism, the difference between the practical and the theoretical. But there never was a practical path to theoretical norms that was not strewn with our true heroes, those whose examples have lived thousands of years.

There are limits to everything, including life.

We must take similar actions in the home, the street, and so forth.

What to do with our fighting boys. Not the ones in Vietnam; I'm talking about the ones who will return home from the "work battle" of life early, unexpected, and to a wife and family who really aren't all that interested in fighting and suffering and beating one's self until it hurts because it feels so good when it stops.

Men will be returned home by machines, so they can, hopefully, get to know their families better and start being fathers and husbands again. I guess we'll need *a retraining program*. But you just don't, with a snap of the fingers, stop hands which are purported to be evil if not busy.

A Curious Saying
Perhaps we may want to use a computer as a contraceptive for a generation or two, until the new bright ones grow up to take over.

A Contraceptive?

A device to prevent the surfacing of primordial drives, learned in our schools, directed at wife and children for lack of a better target?

How?

Work simulation: A large machine centrally located, remote terminals with buttons, gadgets, etc., proliferated in the homes. Men given assignments—work all they like, creating, destroying—linked to a mother processor—rewarded, chastized—and even educated until they pass on or learn the futility of self-punishment.

A bit 1984? Perhaps, but without something, what will Dad do when he returns home?

The machine—automation can be used to send Dad home, and when home, help him overcome the hangover he is bound to have.

Now ladies and gentlemen! I do *not* advocate the use of machines in this way, if for no other reason than because its misuse is too easy. Such thoughts lead legislators (as we heard last summer) to mix theology with technology when the central repository for population statistics was proposed.

A legislator slipped and yelled *blasphemy!*

I wonder what was on his mind? But without something, what will Dad do *when he returns home?*

HAROLD GIBBONS: First let me point out that I come to this conference without the best of credentials or the greatest amount of expertise. At times I think, as I've told some people, that our girl brought me to this conference on family planning as horrible Exhibit A, because I'm the youngest in a family of twenty-three.

In any event, a long background of experience in representing working men and women may have given me some insights into some of the problems we're discussing: how men and women will work together, some of the components necessary for this, and some of the corrections that should or must be made. All I want to do is try to raise some of these problems.

When you take a look at the world we live in and the increasing need for a more effective male-female working relationship, the things that stand out are some of the cultural patterns that bedevil both men and women. The male thinks of himself as the provider, the bread winner, and as occupying the hero status; the female thinks of herself as basically nothing but the child-bearer, the housewife, the consoler, not tough enough to face the give and take of the workaday world. Such ideas obviously must go if real progress in the way men and women work together is to be achieved. I suspect that these are cultural hangovers, in a sense. Statistics certainly indicate that this soft female is doing pretty well at the moment in the workplaces of America. In our country, among women in the 35 to 44 age bracket some 47 percent of them are already in the workplace, as against 29 percent in 1940. If you take women of *all* ages, 36 percent are in the work force today. Unfortunately, an awful lot of them are in the very low wage scales, but, nevertheless, they are in the work force. These women are not necessarily handicapped females. They are not incompetent in any respect. They are doing good jobs in all the areas of traditional male activity. They are competent teachers at every level of education. They are in medicine and in all the other professions. Yes, even despite a previous speaker, they are doing well as pilots of airplanes, as witnessed by the competence of a Jacqueline Cochrane or an Amelia Earhart or the pilot that flew one of our speakers in today!

In any event, to facilitate this trend, and to encourage the female to use her talent—a largely untapped human resource —both men and women must come to a moment of truth on a lot of outmoded beliefs.

I don't know about the women, but I know for the men in our society this is going to be a difficult task. As Marion Sanders, one of the editors of *Harper's,* said, the changing status of women is a much less burning question than the changing status of men. I think this is going to be increasingly the case. *Men* are going to have the difficulty making adjustments.

In my estimation, to have a more desirable, effective working together of men and women we would have to have, at a minimum, these components: we have to change the male's attitude about the capability of females in traditional male areas. During World War II a lot of women moved in, and, while they were accepted largely by the male, they were never very respected. There was always the joke about Rosie the Riveter; and it represented, in large measure, the overall attitude of men toward women trying to do their jobs. As we change the attitude of men toward female capabilities in traditional male domains in industry and the business world, the same erasing of lines must follow regarding men working at jobs that have traditionally belonged to the female. If some of this change in the attitudes of men and women in respect to the job areas in which they should function takes place, the absorption of women into the work forces and the whole business of men and women working together in the business world will be a lot easier.

One of the problems facing women in the workaday world I'll call, for want of a better term, *the predatory syndrome.* In this syndrome, women in the workplace are often looked upon by men as objects of sexual pursuit or seduction—as the easy mark, not as persons or co-workers. This sort of syndrome will have to be erased if we want to arrive at the full acceptance of the female, and if we want to establish the best possible working relationship between men and women as persons. The woman must not just be regarded as a sex symbol. She must become sure of herself and her reputation as a co-worker. Another attitude—which is, perhaps, a reaction to the predatory syndrome—that has to be changed in the working woman's approach to her job is what I suppose you could call a *compensation factor*. It is a kind of defense mechanism which tends to turn a female into a bossy, callous type who is constantly interested in, hour by hour, reproving her competence and abdicating her femininity. I don't think this is at all necessary; but I think it can be found in many a female in the industrial world today.

Of course, the real beliefs a lot of working women bring to the workplace create problems. They feel that they are not fully as capable as men in some of the traditional male work areas. They feel they are different, that they really shouldn't be there. This is a hangover of the idea that the woman's place is in the home, causing an almost apologetic approach that, "Well, I'm only here temporarily, and I'll be getting married soon and get out." Just the other night one of the working girls at this conference was discussing the question of woman's competence and compatibility with men. She said she didn't mind being paid less for her work than a male who might be doing the same job. Of course, when she was checked on it, she soon realized it was kind of an admission which had somehow come to the surface from her subconscious at that particular moment and no one could defend it. She's doing exactly the same work as a male; there's no reason why she should not get the same pay. Some of these hangover attitudes are true of the female and will have to be eradicated if she is to function properly and work well with the male. Of course, I would imagine that the growing use of contraceptives is going to change rapidly women's old fear of the encounter with men in the workplace, the fear of pregnancy with its debilitating effects, which prevailed in the yesteryears. One of the problems, and I've mentioned this before, that must be dealt with, maybe by conferences like this one, is the male's lack of preparation for really coping with the new and emerging woman; for accepting the loss of his superiority, the tough, traditional role he's found necessary to support his ego. Certainly something must be done to prepare him for the female invasion of his little world. Men today are reaching the point where they can say: "Equal pay for women, yes." But they haven't got around to the admission that women can do equally good work.

Finally, a problem I see with the emerging woman which affects the ability of men and women to work closely together is the problem of the "affair," both in terms of the impact on the people involved and the fall-out in terms of their families. I think this is an increasing problem brought out by the broader use of contraceptives. I would say only that it calls for the need to develop some kind of new, meaningful love relationships between people, based on a deep mutual respect for both parties, which will bring neither the lack of respect by men, nor this business of total possession by women.

These, it seems to me, are some of the components that would work to facilitate the entry of the emerging woman and her ability to work better with men in the workplaces of our country. Thank you.

JACQUELINE GRENNAN: I agree with Mr. Lecht in his concern for talking about changing society, instead of simply talking about changing women. However, it seems to me the real significance of a conference like this is that, when you look at any specific in our society, if it indeed poses a fundamental problem, it will of necessity have reverberations on the whole of society. It's in that kind of context that I would like to look at the changing role of woman.

I'm a little appalled by the question in Mr. Lecht's very interesting and intriguing kind of parable: "What do we do with Dad when he comes home?" It's all too reminiscent of the suburban housewife's syndrome of "What do I do with the kids when they come home from school?"

What I really thought he was saying, or what I heard him saying, and he may disagree with this, is that non-mind-occupying work, machinelike work, is disappearing and is being given over to its proper mechanism. Instead, it seems to me that the mental, spiritual communication of social discourse used to build or to make a society is what is really taking over.

That is the new concept of work, and in that sense you and I are working. Whether working on Scotch in Gibbons' suite as we were last night, or working here today in front of a microphone, we *are* working. We are involved in social communion, trying through this communion to build a better society and a better self. I think this kind of working together, if we may keep the verbal imagery, makes personal encounter possible and inevitable.

I think, even further, that the growth of personal encounter and the growth of human communion and communication, whether it's man to man or man to woman, where there are very special problems and possibilities, provide perhaps the most exciting, intriguing, and terrifying possibility that any generation has ever faced.

Gibbons concluded his remarks by saying that we must develop new, meaningful love relationships between man and woman, in which there can be deep mutual respect and no possessiveness by woman. What he's really calling for is an almost complete turning upside down of the page of what so much of previous man-woman relationships have been in our society. We have to, of course, talk about either sexuality or about sex, and there's been a lot of talk in the twenty-four hours that I have been here about sexuality as part of personhood and sex as a commodity.

I really want to ask two kinds of question that intrigue me a great deal and bother me a great deal and frighten me a great deal. I think they are questions that we are not surfacing. I want to ask: how in Heaven's name do we achieve a one-to-one relationship in terms of Gibbons' objective? How do we achieve this *really*—not just in words, whether they be theological words, philosophical words, sociological words, or whatever they may be? How do we achieve a meaningful love relationship with deep mutual respect by both parties and with loss of respect by neither, and, I would say, without possession by either? How do we attempt at all to find even a single, *total* human relationship, where the mind and the spirit and the body and the emotions and everything else are free to investigate and to interpenetrate one another? Is there anybody in this world who really is ready to subject himself to that kind of openness? We are beginning to say, I think, that that's what personal encounter is all about. Maybe those in the younger generation are asking the question early enough that they may have a chance at it. Some of us asked it too late.

If, indeed, we are asking that question, and if we are beginning at least to admit that encounter can be total, that there can be interpenetration on all levels, and that sexuality, and indeed sex, is important if it is interpenetrated with interpenetrations, then how do you handle it in an open world that isn't tribal in the family, that isn't just one to one. If I do make it possible with one person, then how do I keep it from being inevitable with more than one, if indeed man is open, if indeed persons are open, if indeed we are meant to meet each other at the deepest possible level.

I want to make an admission here that I've never made before. I used to teach in secondary school and I was following the party line, which I believed in at the time. I was preaching to my students one day against going steady, out of all the nonexperience of my life! I was preaching against going steady with all my good will and using all the high-blown phrases of: "love and sex are so beautiful"; "it's that jewel box up at the top of the mountain"; "you must not flirt with it unless you're going all the way"; "it's because God meant you to go all the way"; "it's precisely because it's beautiful that you've got to watch out for all the secondary steps." And if you're young and interesting the girls listen to you before they go and do as they please. But then I caught myself a few days later playing the party line with great honesty, at least at the surface level. I was talking to that same group about birth control for the Roman Catholic Church, and I found myself saying that if a man and woman just had the will of God in their hearts and strength in their psyches, that they could sleep in the same bed and practice rhythm. At one point, I came to a kind of disjunction in my own mind, which, in the middle fifties, I could handle only by not talking any more about either love and sex or birth control, simply because I could not come to anything like a resolution on these two seeming contrarities.

I don't know the answer. I don't propose an answer. I don't have an answer, and I doubt if there's anybody in this room who has one. If he tells me he has a simple one, I'll smirk or run away. We say that we want men and women to work together to encounter each other as persons in meaningful activities: in building a nation, in building a future life and helping to direct evolution in the small little time that each has on this planet. But then, bound up in this whole discussion is a terribly important question: What happens, following the Socratic ideal, when we let the argument go where it will?

I think the young students are saying to us, "Tell it like it is." If I really am going to begin to work for a total sharing with someone else, with others, do I let those emotions follow where they will? How do we preserve marriage and the family in a society in which we are going to multiply personal encounters? Much of this conference has been rightly concerned with trying to readmit a real, life-long, total, personal encounter between man and wife, which all kinds of taboos have precluded in the past. Once we have the option of multiple personal encounters, what happens to society? How do we organize our personal lives, both at the level of confronting other individuals directly as well as at the level of confronting the galleries? How do we do this, if every time one is involved in a total kind of affective experience, one is subject to the accusation or to the possibility of robbing another man's wife or another woman's husband? How do we begin to have the open society that we're all espousing and playing with? I espouse it, but I think we must put the cards on the table, and we must ask out loud the questions that all of us are afraid to ask.

It is in this sense, I think, that two seemingly very different revolutions have profound significance. Inside cloistered communities, convent communities of women, the question is being asked: if you take the cloister away, can you be effective? Can you indeed have sexuality? Can you live fully in an open world with true effectiveness, with true personality—which includes sexuality—and at the same time safely? (I personally have a hunch that this revolution has profound significance outside its own evolution in the Chardinian sense of convergence.) Looking at our conventional institution of marriage and the family, many people are asking: can you have one-to-n relationships as well as one-to-one relationships? Or would that mean living schizophrenic kinds of lives?

In my own living room, I said to my students, "Gibbons is suggesting that maybe we could live working lives together and table sex-machine imagery until after 5 o'clock." Some of my naive and not-so-naive young women would be ready to hang him, because they want fully integrated lives from 12 to 12. That's what's at the basis of the hippie revolution, with all its bumbling, fumbling attempts. That's what's under so much of the revolution inside Roman Catholicism today. It seems to me that the theologian, the philosopher, the sociologist, the psychoanalyst, the human being, have to begin to see that's what's under it all.

I went to see *Man of La Mancha,* and in three great scenes in that fantastic play I was terribly bothered. Somehow or other it seemed to me to reflect all the failure of Western Christianity. If you remember, in one scene Don Quixote talks to Dulcinea, who isn't Dulcinea. He talks to her and makes her the virgin on the pedestal. He tells her to go back down into the hold of the ship and to turn the other cheek and to lift the spirits of these men because she is, in his frame, the virgin on the pedestal. She goes down in the hold, and in that fantastic theatrical scene we see the ritual rape dance. Then, as if with no bridges at all (Scene 1: his counsel to her as the virgin on the pedestal; Scene 2: the ritual rape scene), up she comes disheveled and Don Quixote goes back—at least as I heard—to the third scene which is exactly like the first, again extolling from a distance the virgin on the pedestal. It took all I had—knowing that I'm subject to headlines—to keep from getting up in the middle of that theatre and shouting, "Hold her, you fool!"

Somehow or other the incarnational mystery of Christianity was lost in this nonintegrative Manichaean schizophrenia of mind and spirit. The religion which should have produced Freud fought him. We have, therefore, on one level, the sex preoccupation of Hollywood and Madison Avenue and, on the other seeming pole, the sex preoccupation in the Sixth Commandment, in our fifth and sixth grades, and in second-year high school.

What we're really striving for, it seems to me, is the full integration of the human body-spirit. And nobody knows how to find it. And if I told any 19-year-old sitting in this audience that I know a damn thing about how we're going to get there, I would be lying to you and to me. But I think it's the most profound question that faces the human race in the twentieth century.

RICHARD CORNUELLE: I hope the students will feel as free to ask questions as the delegates.

ANNE SHEFFIELD: I'd just like to ask a very practical question, with this brief background. I work in what is considered to be a man's job. I've found that this poses certain problems for me in the way I do my job. I can struggle along with that problem for myself and I can even talk to some of my friends who are in the same position. But this really isn't going to do much good in terms of how men and women are going to work together in a very practical economic sense. I want to ask Harold Gibbons and Dick Cornuelle, as representatives of labor and management, whether they have any ideas as to how you can speed up the process of men and women effectively and constructively working together, other than just trying to cope with it on their own personal plane.

RICHARD CORNUELLE: Harold, I'm the chairman. I'm not allowed to say anything.

HAROLD GIBBONS: When you look around and you see the long, inbred prejudices of the male in our society—I guess basically a product of our culture—it's hard to believe that anything like this is going to happen tomorrow. I suppose the best educational process is going to be the continued flow of women into jobs, and the ability of those women to stand up and command from men the respect they're due and the relationships they're entitled to. I mentioned some of that by saying that women should bring to the workplace a much stronger attitude of their own worth, with less apology and less backing down or giving up to the men, abdicating to the men. Other than this sort of process taking place, there should maybe be more conferences of this nature, or maybe even some conferences to straighten out the thinking of some men on how they relate to women. Finally, I hope the kids coming up in our society will have a lot fewer of the hangovers that the adults today have. Beyond these things, I don't know how you're going to solve this particular problem in the workplace.

RICHARD CORNUELLE: Mr. Lecht, would you like to respond to that question as well?

CHARLES LECHT: I rather agree with Mr. Gibbons except for one minor point: What is the job of the men? Is standing up to the male boss the female's job? I think until we start training people, and giving our young people the right to think, the best way to handle that problem is proper management.

HAROLD GIBBONS: He's turning it right back to you, Dick.

RICHARD CORNUELLE: Well, I've noticed that the only thing more frightening to a male in business than hiring a woman is firing one. I'm beginning to understand that a little better now. I'll give you a report in due course. Some further comment or question?

STUDENT: Something's bothering me! It seems to me that relationships between man and woman are pretty much set by the sexual act itself. Mr. Gibbons says it's part of the culture. Now, I realize that I have to assume this, but if I do assume it and then take into account Mr. Gibbons' point about the woman's abdicating her role in some manner, it seems to me that the sexual act creates a hierarchy or introduces a power. Mr. Gibbons suggests it has to be abdicated or somehow changed. If, on the other hand, you say the sexual act doesn't in any way produce this power element, that it merely complements or enhances this relationship, this integration of life makes it fuller, you think this is the power. What's to chastize a relationship between two men, a homosexual relationship, if it's found purpose and fulfillment? It seems to me that by trying to elevate woman or trying to make woman into a man, you in effect destroy, or change radically, the very device that determines this relationship.

HAROLD GIBBONS: Well, I don't buy the idea that the human sex act necessarily sets up the proper relationship between men and women. It's my feeling that more meaningful relationships between men and women could be achieved, in sex acts and otherwise, if some of what I consider or call *cultural lags* were eradicated from the minds of men and women, because I don't think you can validate ideas such as the male being the strong one, or the tough one, or the more popular one, or the only one who can go out and battle in the world of work. I think this sort of concept simply is not valid. And I think everything in our society tends to show that. There isn't an area of human endeavor that females haven't already invaded with confidence and will continue to invade on an ever-increasing scale. Something's going to have to give, and someone's going to have to make room. I think a large part of the giving is going to be in the superiority concept—the superiority that the male supposedly brings to the man-woman relationship. I think that's what's going to give. I think it's going to give in the nature of the situation. I don't think the present situation is ordained by the sex act at all.

STUDENT: Given that, what's to prevent homosexuality? Or is there anything wrong with it?

HAROLD GIBBONS: Well, I think this is a matter of personal choice, a decision arrived at by individuals, and I'm not in any position to pass judgment on it. I would much rather refer that one to the physicians, the psychoanalysts, and others who are more competent to deal with that particular problem.

JESSIE BERNARD: I must be the dumbest person in the room because I don't see the connection between homosexuality and his first question.

JACQUELINE GRENNAN: No, I see his connection. It worries me a great deal. I think he's saying what has been pointed up here in this room all day: that as the new emphasis on personal encounter (you know the Vatican Council came up with this decision that procreation and total personal enrichment and growth of the partners were the ends of marriage) has been established, and accepted by many people all over the world, a whole battery of young people are beginning to say that the morality of a love relationship *is* the love relationship. I think that's where the whole contraceptive culture we're talking about has ramifications here. For the first time, the consequences of what we thought of as the procreative act can be almost absolutely negated. The moral judgment of almost all our moral authorities is beginning at least to back the notion that sexuality has not this secondary aim but at least this coordinate aim.

I think his question presents the next logical question that will have to have an answer. I don't know the answer, and I agree with Gibbons that insight into this problem is going to have to come from physicians and psychoanalysts and people with a lot more expertise than some of us have. It's going to be the agonizing, anguishing attempt of man to live with this moral integrity, but I don't think we can rule it out. His question has a great deal of internal logic if we've now admitted that that's one of the aims of our sexual lives or affective lives. If personal encounter is to make both people grow, then how can we say only in heterosexual relationships? Why not in relationships between two members of the same sex? The question is at least on the table and verbal and outside, where it's always been down underground. Now the minute you say this (and, God be praised, I'll be in trouble again!), somebody will say that we're now going out for free love and homosexual behavior. That's not so at all. One is opening the question so we can *look* at it. Kids must ask these questions; and we must ask them out loud too. No wonder they think there are generational gaps. We just don't admit to one another that we have those thoughts.

JESSIE BERNARD: Now, are we identifying encounter always as a sexual encounter—I mean a genital sex encounter. I don't think we have the consensus on the nature of the encounter we're talking about.

STUDENT: That is true. It comes to my mind, too. By homosexual I just mean . . . Miss Grennan mentioned, in her remarks on Don Quixote, she wanted to tell Quixote to "Hold her, hold her," and I feel that in a relationship between anybody, between a man and a man, if they get involved enough with each other it's going to be necessary that they hold each other.

JACQUELINE GENNAN: You bet.

STUDENT: This is what we call homosexuality.

RUTH USEEM: I have a feeling I am more on your side, Mr. Gibbons, that you have a role that cannot take the extra freight of that kind of emotion. It's narrower than the total person. If every encounter with a person has to be total, we're in a bad way.

CHARLES LECHT: Well, there's a problem with words.

RUTH USEEM: Yes, because the next step is not homosexuality, but why not fornicate with your mother? I also think that the survival of mankind depends upon large-scale organization; and large-scale organization is never totally encompassing of every person. It's one role of all the persons. To make every personal encounter a total personal encounter is chaos. I think we do need some incest rules outside the fence.

MARTHA STUART: I'm a little concerned about all the fear that we keep expressing. George and I were at a communications conference here not long ago, and someone very excitedly said, "How can we talk about satellites around Latin America when we're the Ugly Americans and we don't know what we'll say to them?" But that isn't the reason that you don't have satellites. The point is, we should listen to those people and what they want to learn. The point is, when we say, "Isn't it dangerous that we might want to have total encounters with everyone?", we're not stating a reason for not having a deep, loving relationship with one person. I don't know about the rest of you, but my feeling is, when I have a loving relationship, when I am loving someone, then I have a different kind of loving overflow, halo effect, with many different kinds of relationships. And I'm not about to go to bed with my father or have affairs with six men at the office, because *I love someone.* Loving someone is a person. As Jacqueline says, my whole involvement with *him* really precludes the kind of experimental context that we all keep getting so nervous about. If you have to ask "Where do you draw the line?" then you do need rules, and no one loves by a rule.

MOTHER GORMAN: I would like to ask a question of Dr. Masters and Mrs. Johnson. It seems to cover the question regarding homosexuality, the question that Jacqueline Grennan brought up. Does every affective relationship necessarily result in profound physiological manifestations?

VIRGINIA JOHNSON: You're very flattering, Sister. I don't know. I'm moved in some way to answer, though. First of all, it requests different things of you. You don't arbitrarily go down the line and say, "I will give you a checklist; I will give you this, this, and this." Different people require different things; they endow themselves and relationships in different ways. So, consequently, does it have to mean sexual encounter? Of course not. I would say of the dilemma that Jacqueline raised that I have shared it many times and I may continue to share it, and I certainly don't have an answer. But I will suggest that in developing the capacity for in-depth human relationships, one must *want* to grow. One must walk before one can run. Only when you evolve to this particular pattern of developing what you want to give and how you want to give it are you able to cope with the dilemma of the type of relationship Mr. Gibbons was suggesting, which I think has a very deep merit, for it is certainly the direction in which we're moving. I don't see it as a frightening dilemma because we do have selectivity.

WILLIAM MASTERS: I think possibly it even goes a little deeper than that, just to carry Gini's concept a little bit further. I think selectivity is the one thing we really want.

VIRGINIA JOHNSON: For the right reason.

WILLIAM MASTERS: Yes, you always say it a little bit better. We haven't had selectivity; we've been too bound with convention and legality and what have you. To answer this young gentlemen's question, certainly he was beyond our scope. That's a question that's unanswerable in terms of current concepts of social patterns. It's certainly not one this conference is going to face in depth. We now know that certainly homosexual relationships, and we've known this for some time, are of an incredible magnitude. It's a one-to-one relationship, particularly on the female side. There's no sense negating the cultural distresses and concerns in this area—the male was forced into the cruising concept. But this is changing and we don't know what will happen because this is an incredible depth relationship.

MICHAEL SCRIVEN: Dick, there is an official complaint that someone is smoking in the back row.

RICHARD CORNUELLE: I was going to announce that later —that we're not allowed to smoke in the auditorium. I was saving that till last! There's a state law that prohibits smoking in an auditorium and this is an auditorium. The room across the hall isn't!

KERMIT KRANZ: In the natural progress of the human being from childhood to adulthood, an individual goes through all the steps that have been described here. Homosexuality is very easily accepted among children. They go through it. They openly have homosexual experiences. We accept this as a part of their natural growth and development. When an individual comes into adulthood, we would like to think he is capable of a transference in these interpersonal relationships to a devotion toward one person. A real question is, is the human being monogamous? If he is not monogamous, then (darn it, I'm blowing what I wanted to say tomorrow) what is morality in his personal relationships? If he then turns and says, "I love you as a woman," that is the art of being in love versus actually loving someone. There's a distinct difference between these two. He may then turn to this man and have a relationship with him which is actually homosexual. They may go out drinking together, put their arms around each other, slap each other on the back. They may have a close personal relationship. That does not necessarily mean they have to get to the point of sex and mutual masturbatory activity. It does in some degree in the female. (I don't know it as much in the male, because I don't deal with males, but I know it in the female.) This is one of their great problems. The real question arises—and I think this is why I can back up what Jacqueline Grennan said so strongly—that when people do begin to find themselves, and look at this whole world, they look back and say, "Where was our ethical background changed and modified?" We may lose everything we want as a civilization. Look back historically and there lie the seeds of the destruction of all our civilizations. The classic case is Greece, or ancient Athens.

JACQUELINE GRENNAN: I really want, on a human person level, to agree completely with you that there would be nothing worse than having multiple encounters. I'm not very comfortable with a lot of "T-group" people I've been with, because they always give me the notion that you can turn on switches and make out at least psychically with seventeen people that you just met. I personally find that very repulsive. Personal encounter of any deep consequence is a very important thing and one doesn't have many. The tragedy is that a lot of people never have any. The thing I'm trying to face is, once you've had one, or once there is one, does that mean that end is one and only one. I certainly don't mean indiscriminate or many or anything like that. I do think the kind of open world that we're building has within it the permissiveness to allow more than one personal encounter and I don't know any ethical system yet to deal with it. We have this all or nothing, this total or not-at-all, complex. Affectivity and full sexuality and the fullness of the sexual act are almost identified in the way we talk about them. I think we're trying to work through all of this, and it's very tough.

STUDENT: I'd like to ask a question. You're talking an awful lot about these deep, full, personal relationships that are so important, that you're not a full person till you meet someone. I think part of your connotation is that everyone should have a sexual relationship. But there's one person we all know who never had one of these. I think he's quite a full person. I think you would agree. That's Christ. When did he ever have this that seems so all-important? It's a nice thing; it's a good thing. But it's not so overpowering that everybody has to go out and do it. The idea that you're bringing across is that we really have to have this.

HAROLD GIBBONS: I was not necessarily saying that everyone has to have this. Look about in our world. People are participating. I'm not saying that makes it right. I think, as a matter of fact, they're participating in a very degrading kind of way, in which neither partner contributes anything to the other. All I said was, given the fact, one of the constructive things that could happen would be if we could build meaningful love relationships instead of the kind of degrading thing which takes place today. I'm not saying it's good to have them as they are. I'm not even saying that the meaningful type I'm talking about are necessarily good, but if we're going to have them, they should be on that level and not on the level which degrades the female, and which only feeds the ego of the male.

STUDENT: But it's not meaningful unless you have marriage.

HAROLD GIBBONS: Well, that doesn't necessarily follow.

STUDENT: The union of two people—you're trying to say you're giving it what you want, but there is an order in the world and God has a plan. I think in some way He sometimes figures that He's going to put purpose in everything in the world. I think He put a purpose into sex. I think that if you search this, you can't say, "Well, I want it to be this, so that's good."

HAROLD GIBBONS: Again, I can only repeat to you, I'm not advocating anything. I'm trying to lift what is a little higher, to a more decent kind of level. It's beyond my competence to pass judgment on whether it is good or bad.

JACQUELINE GRENNAN: I don't know in what frame you ask. It seems to me I would advocate the openness to the possibility. I think I'm willing to say, at any risk, that there has to be in the human being an openness to the possibility. I'm not at all saying that there *has* to be the fullness. In fact, I think it's *that* one that has jeopardized so many lives. I watch my young girls in college grabbing the first guy available, lest they not make it because we've made it so much that and only that. There has to be some other way out of it if, as has been said many times here today, if the marriage *doesn't* make it. Ignace Lepp in one of his books raises, I hope, a good question. He says, if two people have ceased to love each other, whether we call it culpable or nonculpable, if these two individuals continue to exercise the conjugal right, would this not possibly be a subtle kind of prostitution? That's a question I've never gotten out of my mind. Isn't that using somebody in a purely mechanistic, materialistic way, if the love relationship is not there? It's questions like this that have me baffled. I'm all the more where I used to be with my very theoretical, idealistic notion that it ought to be total, and it ought to be as close to total as two human beings can go. But boy, the old form didn't provide much of it; a few people made it. If I get quoted on this, I'll get run out of town for sure!

LOUIS DUPRÉ: I would like to turn myself to the question this young man asked about a preestablished moral order in the world. I don't believe there is such a thing. Let me say first, I agree with him—and this is probably the point he is making—I don't see why every meaningful relationship should result in sex, in the sense of intercourse of some sort or other. I don't see any point to that. In that sense, sex, particularly in this country, is a highly overrated item. On the other hand, I think that every human relationship is somewhat sexually caused. However, if you bring in any kind of preestablished order, I would be very reluctant to accept that.

Man is a developing being. He is also a creative being and he ultimately is the one who creates his own code of moral responsibilities. This is not a God-given thing. I say this as a person who is interested in religion primarily, not morality. This is something that is made by man according to the way he sees human nature. Human nature for the Christian is one thing; for the Jew, it is something else. It doesn't make much difference because, in both cases, we have to work out ways and means of establishing a code of conduct. In both cases there will be morality if it is in accordance with what human nature is progressing toward. There will be immorality when there is a regression. You can't predict this, as Miss Grennan said. We cannot predict today what's going to happen a thousand years from now. This is where we have made mistakes so many times. Time and time again we make the same bloody mistake.

That's why I think this question about homosexuality is very provocative. I have thought about that. I would say that I don't know what it means. Let's assume that researchers think there are people who have homosexual tendencies. I leave whether there is such a thing or not entirely to the specialists. This is a matter of education. If people are made homosexuals by perversion—because I would call it perversion when, for example, youngsters are attacked by adults—this is immoral; this is wrong. But if there is such a thing as people who are genetically homosexual (if such a statement makes sense, I don't know whether it does not not), then I just would drop all moral considerations at that point because I don't see what they have to do with it. I would, for those among us who tend to think in strict terms, refer to the Dutch Catechism and what it has to say about homosexuality. People sit in judgment about someone else and tell him what is right according to human nature. Which human nature? His? The other one's? How can you know?

The same thing applies with the law. This business has the most absurd laws in the world. You get blackmail and more perversion because this is a crime. Why? I think it is a crime to pervert minors, but if two adults are really that way, it's not the law's business, in my opinion. It can only lead to abuse, from a moral point of view. Whether there is such a thing as homosexuality is a hypothetical case. In other words, if people are homosexual, but not by choice, then I would say that we should not make any absolute statements about homosexuals not being able to obtain a meaningful relationship. Usually the ones who say so are the ones who don't know anything about it. So leave these people alone.

RICHARD CORNUELLE: I think this is the kind of dialogue that's necessarily continuous, so any interruption has to seem arbitrary. But we've used as much time as we should. The next meeting of the delegates is a reception at 6:30 over at the Inn. I want to thank the panelists, the delegates, the guests, and particularly the students who got in and pitched today. The next session is in this room at 8:15, and it is public.

Anatomy of a Good Marriage 9

JOSEPH W. BIRD AND LOIS F. BIRD

Tuesday, 8:15 P.M.

WILLIAM D'ANTONIO: I've been authorized by an unnamed priest to announce that a new encyclical has been released—*Pacem in Utero!* Welcome to our continuing discussion on The Emerging Woman. My first encounter with the writing of tonight's speakers, Joseph and Lois Bird, occurred last summer while I was reading the *National Catholic Reporter.* I came across a review by Mrs. Sidney Callahan of their book entitled *The Freedom of Sexual Love.* This title just casually caught my eye, and, curious to know what it might be about, I decided to read the review. I discovered I could ignore the theology and still enjoy the book. The first thing I observed when the copy I had ordered arrived was that there was an imprimatur on it. Those who know me well know that I have long felt this was an outdated practice. I was put out, and thought I had invested my money poorly. Nevertheless, I decided to go on with the reading. The following day, I placed an order with the bookstore, thinking the book would be very useful in my family course as corollary reading to the regular sociology text we were going to use.

As it happened, *The Freedom of Sexual Love* arrived before the textbook and, by the second day, the students had nothing else to read. They had already finished the book—the first time I didn't have to give an assignment! It has been a popular best-seller on campus, and I presume that in the months ahead it will compete well with the Dutch Catechism.

A few months later, I gave a talk—my own feeble effort to define the changing relationships between men and women in our society—and I casually mentioned the Birds' book as appropriate reading for the audience. Afterward someone came up to me and said, "We've heard them speak. They shook up our part of California for three months. That was quite a period!"

With that amount of information, and with the knowledge that this conference was forthcoming, I encouraged the powers that be to find a way to add the Birds to the program. I'm not sure what they'll say. I find that whatever they say is fascinating and interesting. I will ask Dr. Joseph Bird to begin his lecture on the anatomy of a good marriage, with the assurance to my students that they will have every opportunity to join with the rest of the audience in a question and answer period following the formal presentation.

JOSEPH BIRD: Talk about being wiped out in an introduction! One difference between us and the Dutch Catechism is that we seem to have gotten our imprimatur a little bit more easily than they did! However, I do think I have to explain something about the whole business—the cop-out—of getting an imprimatur. The imprimatur *is* nonsense but that is neither here nor there. We are attempting to reach a certain group of people.

I feel we can go at the whole discussion of freedom and sexual love kind of roughshod and iconoclastically, and say, "The hell with you, we're going to beat you over the head with it." On the other hand, we can attempt to reach people where they are right then. There are still, and perhaps unfortunately, an awful lot of very good, physically mature children within the Church who would not buy a book that didn't have some bishop's plus mark on it. We are trying to reach this group. We didn't actually get the imprimatur; our publisher did. We are glad he did because it helps us reach certain people, and we feel they need to be reached.

First of all, one should never begin an address with an apology. However, since several here have started by saying "I am not an expert," I think we will perhaps be in a little safer territory by beginning with a similar introduction. Lois and I were asked to speak on the anatomy of a good marriage. We don't really feel that we can, at least not in the sense that most so-called authorities would speak on such a subject: bringing out data, making generalizations, talking in terms of abstractions, theories, and so on. We're not sociologists, so empirical data, although available, are not our thing. The sociologists are doing a beautiful job of compiling this. However, if we were to speak in that vein, we would only be borrowing from them.

Furthermore, it seems that in my own particular discipline, psychology, we have long played a game in the area of psychotherapy. We have said this theory is more or less correct than that theory; this methodology is more or less effective than that methodology. Seldom do we admit that the psychotherapy we do is really a projective technique. It's "me." I could not be a nondirective therapist, not because I do not feel that nondirective therapy is effective, but because Joseph Bird doesn't happen to be nondirective. When we come down to talking about the anatomy of a good marriage, I'm afraid we have to take the only possible honest approach and talk about the anatomy or the physiology or just the existence of one particular damn good marriage—our own.

What we will attempt to do, then, is to take, as a sort of structure, the variables that are most often talked about in pre-marriage courses or in marital books as being important to a marriage—as being the requisites for a good marriage—and attempt to examine what meaning they've had for us, or whether they have just been irrelevant to us. In doing so, we're not in any respect holding out our own marriage as any sort of model. It's our marriage, nothing more. Any value that might be found in what we say for any individual would, of course, have to be through identification, through some sort of generalized, shared experience, and perhaps through whatever insights, if any, we may have had that might lead someone else to make a reevaluation of his own values and assumptions.

We've been married fifteen years and have nine children: six girls, three boys. We live in a suburban, rather quaint community, with all that that implies, in Northern California. I'm engaged in full-time practice of psychotherapy. We do our writing together, but aside from that, Lois is not now, nor has she been during the course of our marriage, engaged in any occupation outside the home.

We are not active in any organizational work, other than in a consulting capacity. We do accept several speaking engagements each month. We are neither partygoers nor party givers. We have a number of friends, many of whom are members of the clergy; and we do a very informal type of entertaining, usually late-night, wine-and-cheese sort of thing.

We date very frequently, but almost never double date. We could probably count the number of times we have gone out socially with another couple in the years we've been married on less than the fingers of one hand. We're very jealous of our time together—luncheons, strolling through bookstores, the theater, picnics for two. (We have some beautiful redwoods in our part of the country.) Other than the hours we spend with our children, we very much like "hand-holding," if you will. We prefer it to be just the two of us.

With seven children in school, and a rather active professional life, we find it necessary to structure the existence of our time together. We both find very great satisfaction in sharing our thoughts and feelings, and discussing what we are and who we are and what we feel. Hence, we almost never run out of conversation.

This, of course, is an expression of our life at this point in time. It differs very greatly, in many respects, from what our life was five years ago or even one year ago. The one thing we can say with sureness is that our life has been marked by constant and rather dramatic change. If we were to make any statement, we could say that yesterday was very different from today; and we are awfully sure that tomorrow is going to be different again. Fortunately, in most instances, the important changes have been marked by growth or have stimulated growth.

We would like to look now, if we may, at these variables that I mentioned: first, the question, so often raised, of family background. A lot of emphasis, as we all know, is always given to this. Very often I talk with couples in therapy who say, "Well, that's all well and good, but if you came from the sort of background I come from . . ." They then use this to excuse who and what they are and what they're doing. We knew, or were told at least, at the time we married, that family background was important. We therefore went into marriage with a certain amount of concern in this respect. I came from a broken home. My father, an alcoholic, had deserted my mother before I was born. Lois came from an intact marriage, but one which, in all honesty, lacked the closeness, the integratedness that we wanted to exist in our marriage.

From family, from friends, from older couples—I suppose from all that we call society—we had been given a concept of marriage which, unfortunately, was a very unhealthy and cynical one. We heard the usual predictions that the honeymoon would come to an end; that marriage was no bed of roses—wait until you've been married one year or two years, or five years or seven years. There is some sort of crazy numerology that I find gets played with this: wait until you have had two children or four children or whatever. Everything was then supposed to come crashing to a rather dull and apathetic end.

We had no appropriate model at the time we entered marriage. I didn't really know what marriage was, or what it would be to be a husband; nor did Lois know what it would be to be a wife, or what it should be. Certainly the ideal of love, the concept of commitment and growth, had not been presented to us. Even those authorities who wrote on Christian marriage more often wrote on the concepts of compromise and getting along together; or else they wrote pietistic essays and gave meaningless abstractions—nothing that we could hold onto or apply.

We entered marriage running scared. We wanted a marriage unlike any we had seen before, unlike any that our friends had, and one, furthermore, that everyone told us was unrealistic. Perhaps, in one way, this was an advantage. At least we knew what we didn't want, and we didn't take an inappropriate model. Perhaps our stubbornness before the challenge of being told that it couldn't be done provided the motivation for us to cling to some sort of an ideal and to each other.

Alan Watts has said, and I think very rightly, that people claim that the honeymoon comes to an end when the couple comes up against reality, but that, in fact, the honeymoon ends when the couple kills reality, the only true reality, love. We fully subscribe to this thought, but at the time of our marriage we couldn't have been aware of it. Our awareness has made very gradual, and at times painfully slow, progress. We went into marriage with a popular view of love. Love was some sort of feeling, an emotion. It was not something you could choose or control or give; you felt it, nothing more.

Certainly we didn't go into marriage with any true understanding that a deep, mature emotion *grows* out of the choices of giving; it doesn't motivate them. More than a few times we found ourselves, of course, in stalemates which grew primarily out of the fact that we had confused, as I feel so many couples do, giving in or giving up with *giving*. Despite the fact that our views reflected our total background, we do not feel in any direct way, in the sense of using a model, that they have been important in determining what we have become within our marriage.

Another background variable is the matter of religious values. This, as we all know, is given a great deal of importance when we talk about "mixed" marriages. For us, this variable is one of the most difficult to assess, since, in one very real sense, we entered a mixed marriage. We are both Roman Catholics and were both raised in Catholicism. However, we cannot say that we shared the same faith at the time of our marriage, or that we share today a faith similar to the one taught us in childhood. In fact, if my Church's faith were actually what I was taught in childhood, I would have long since run from it.

When we married, our religious convictions formed little more than a habit pattern. They gave us little more than a set of rules and clichés. God didn't exist for us. He wasn't real. Now He is, but we have found Him in and through each other. As our love has deepened, the meaning of Christianity has emerged, and Christ is no longer a picture on a holy card. We have learned the truth in the words "God is love." In our marriage, we have learned even more profoundly that God is sexual love. He is very much *our* God, however.

We'd like to be able to say we found Him in and through our Church. We know others have. We have not. We've found no theology of marriage. We've found no theology of sexuality which helped us discover the meaning of this union. We were taught through childhood, through high school, that marriage was procreative. We wanted our marriage to be creative, not procreative. We were not sure who or where God was. Now we know Him. We find Him in our livingroom, in our kitchen, in our bedroom; particularly in our bedroom.

Our life together, then, has not been centered in our Church, except in the respect that we very deeply and sincerely believe we *are* the Church. Our faith has not been found in the institutional Church, but rather in our search for a oneness in our marriage. We have found Christ in this search.

A third variable in marriage, one that is very often brought up for us, has to do with children. The number of children you have is supposed to have something to do with the quality of your marriage. We do not, in any way, subscribe to the view that marriages are helped or hurt in some sort of direct relationship to the number of children. We both came from two-child families. When we married we both hoped to have a large family; and we feel we are very fortunate in having the size family we have. Our children have given us a great deal of joy and many satisfactions.

The conception, the birth, and the rearing of each child have provided us with a specific opportunity for sharing, have given us an individual experience through which we could grow. Our sharing of each experience in marriage has provided growth. Had we, however, been unable to have any children, we feel there would have been opportunities of a different sort which would have provided the growth.

During the past three years, we have used anovulants for contraception. This has meant a certain measure of frustration in no longer anticipating the conception and birth of another child. We feel, however, that having more children at this time would not be a responsible choice, not due to financial problems or the burden of caring for more children, or anything of this nature, but due to the conditions existing in our society today. Hence, we have been and are still exploring the possibility of adoption.

Speaking of finances, a fourth variable, many people will tell you that the one problem marriages run up against harder than almost any other is money. Here we'd have to say that we have not experienced this problem, so we really can't relate to it. We have no real conflict over money, nor has it ever caused us to suffer such extreme anxiety that we could call it a relevant variable in the growth of our marriage. Our income has varied greatly over the last fifteen years. At one point, when I was just completing my doctoral studies, we lived on $220 a month. At that time we had six children. However, we feel that finances, the handling of a budget, and the decision on purchases can become a problem, with both constantly on guard against being taken advantage of, if one or both of them has placed emotional security within a framework of money.

We had four children when I returned to school, and a very limited budget. In fact, at that time we really stepped off a cliff financially. During the school years the necessities demanded all our income so we couldn't dispute purchases. We knew where the money had to go. What seems more significant, in terms of the relationship between money matters and the growth of our marriage, is the fact that our emotional attachment to money and things was always loose enough to prevent any build-up of anxiety. Now this, we feel, isn't a virtue at all.

It isn't a matter of being nonmaterialistic. It is merely a matter of individual security. If both husband and wife are secure enough, they won't need to bind up their marriage or themselves with material things.

The next variable, one which will probably touch most of you students more than any other single thing at the time you marry, if you're like the average couple we counsel, is the matter of relatives, of in-laws. During the first year or two of our marriage, many, and perhaps most, of the arguments we had directly or indirectly involved parents on both sides. Rivalries, jealousies, requests, and demands of parents versus those of spouse, the role-playing expected of a child by parents, and all the other conflicts which usually arise in the establishment of any autonomous family showed up. Had we not been able to work through this area of conflict, we feel sure that our marriage would have virtually atrophied.

Our views on this have been reinforced by countless couples whom we have counseled. Making the in-law problem so much a topic of humor seems to us somewhat like laughing while walking through a graveyard; these problems are simply no laughing matter. We have not yet seen the marriage which was helped by the actions of the parents of either spouse. Parents simply do not make good marriage counselors for their own children. It took time and often a great deal of pain before we could recognize the totality of our commitment to each other. We had to learn to say no, to be able to make choices regarding our own parents. We also had to learn to resolve questions, requests, and demands within the framework of the essential question of where our responsibilities lay.

We had to come to the painfully difficult recognition that we owed no obligation to our parents, that our lives were not owing to them, and that our commitment was to each other. Only when we recognized the primacy of this commitment could we be free to love our parents, because any action based on the binding of an obligation cannot be love. In this area of relatives, as in all other areas of our life together, we have found answers, a growth and a oneness, only by looking at problems always within the context of our commitment, a sort of first-things-first view.

One question which this whole conference has been concerned with and which perhaps gets more play in marriage articles than any other single thing, almost ad nauseam at times, is the whole question of roles and identities. It has been so discussed and defined and dissected that some would have us believe that everyone lies awake nights in the throes of some sort of identity crisis, caught up with the so-called existential questions of "Who am I?" and "What am I?" "Where in the heck am I going?" "What reason do I find for my own existence?" "What is it to be a man?" "What is it to be a woman?" and so on. I'm very sure that, at one time or another, we were also caught up in some of this, although I don't remember that we were verbalizing the questions. If we look back, I'm sure a lot of the defensiveness we expressed was related to a great deal of insecurity in our sexual roles and our sexual identities.

We went into marriage, of course, with the usual number of stereotyped specifications as to what a husband, as a man, was supposed to be and do, and how a wife, as a woman, was supposed to function. In attempting to cling to these role expectancies, we stepped on each others' toes more than a few times. Lois has a father who is very scrupulous in the care of his automobile. If I get the car serviced every six months, I'm doing well. A car to me is a means of transportation, nothing more. At first, Lois interpreted this as a lack of responsibility and a sort of lack of manhood. There were many times when I looked at her and thought, "What would a woman do in this position? She isn't acting like a wife should." It was only when we could recognize that our sexual identities are simply not established by sexual roles that we could learn to live together.

Perhaps a few decades ago, the roles and identities of the spouses were very highly correlated. After all, the man went out and chopped down the trees and tilled the soil, and built his log cabin and shot Indians and the whole schtick. The wife, of course, stayed in and tended the house and the vegetable garden, collected eggs, and, of course, particularly gave him sons who could then go out in the fields and work with him. This was the contract. How happy were these marriages? I don't see how we can assume they were anything other than happy, since the contract really defined roles. This was what she was to do, and this was what he was to do. There wasn't much question about it, so there wasn't any of the conflict about how she could find herself as a woman. I can't imagine that many of the problems presently discussed between spouses even came up.

However, there are now very few functions, as we all know, that can be performed by the members of only one sex—child-bearing, of course, being a notable exception, and sometimes rather a frustration to men, I might add. (As long as we are all hung up on this business of women feeling penis envy, what about men feeling an envy of woman? Because I think it's there!) At first, Lois and I, like so very many couples, divided our functions into the chores of a husband and chores of a wife. We made demands, asked to be loved and considered, and we asked, particularly that the other one behave as the stereotype should. We threw away an awful lot of time, I'm afraid, muddling around with these rules, until we finally recognized that I don't leave my manhood if I diaper the baby, and Lois doesn't lose her womanhood if she carries out the trash barrel or even mows the lawn.

This, of course, raises (if I don't mention it I'm afraid I'm going to be shot by one of the students, if by no one else) the concept of headship of a family. We very much subscribe to this concept. However, we find that we need to give the word *headship* our own operational definition. It has been so battered about that nobody really recognizes what we mean when we use it. Usually the concept of headship has been defined in terms of who makes the decisions. Then the husband comes out looking like a nineteenth-century patriarch, pounding his fist on the table. The wife is kind of servile, and the children bow to daddy. It has sometimes been viewed as a kind of masculine divine right. St. Paul made an unfortunate choice of words when he talked about women being "subject" to their husbands. Ever since then, feminists have been railing about this and interpreting it as meaning "subjugated" by their husbands.

Within our own definition, the concept of "headship" has meant an assumption of certain responsibilities. Any decisions, therefore, that I have made have been a natural outgrowth of assuming these responsibilities. They have not been a product of any kind of masculine right. In my particular role as head of my family, the responsibilities include the material and emotional support of my family and the education and moral and spiritual guidance of my children. This is not a role demanded of me, or demanded by me. It is not something that I extracted from my wife. It is something which she freely gave, and I freely accepted.

Furthermore, I would say I have not yet met the woman who has convinced me that she wants to be the head of a family. My wife is every bit as capable of assuming any and all of these functions as I am. Of that I am absolutely certain. In fact, I think it is specifically because she is capable of assuming any and all of these responsibilities that she doesn't feel threatened, and that I don't feel she is hanging onto me. Therefore, we can freely structure our life and the headship of the family as we prefer to structure it.

While she hasn't been employed outside of the home, we do

not believe that a wife working is *per se* either a help or a hindrance to the attainment of a good marriage. We would say that, in and of itself, the question of work is pretty irrelevant. We are never going to contend that if a wife goes out and works that somehow she loses her womanhood, or if the husband stays home that he loses his manhood. The motivations, however, for the wife working or not working may be very relevant to what happens to the marriage—her motivations or his motivations. They may reflect role stereotyping, a battle of the sexes, insecurity on the part of either the wife or the husband. They may reflect social pressures which dictate that she should stay at home or that she should get out and "fulfill herself" selling real estate or driving a bulldozer. The work itself isn't the important thing.

One aspect of marriage stressed as most important by many authorities is this whole business of sexual compatibility. Some would make it the essential ingredient. Prior to marriage, I was sexually experienced; Lois was not. We did not have sexual relations—sexual intercourse, that is—before being married, although we did engage in considerable petting and lovemaking. We had been taught, and we both believed, that premarital intercourse was wrong; but neither of us questioned why this might be nor did we question anything in terms of meaning to ourselves. The guilt we felt was very minimal.

Today, we have found a great deal of meaning in our sexual experience. Looking back, we can see many reasons why there might be emotional damage to a relationship through premarital sexual intercourse, but we find it very difficult to discuss this as a moral issue. We do not feel that any of these variables in terms of our sexual experiences before marriage were relevant to either the subsequent growth in our sexual love or to our marriage as a whole. We feel sure our marriage has been no better because we didn't have premarital sexual intercourse.

Initial intercourse was mutually satisfying. However, complete sexual fulfillment was attained only with the growth of the marriage. Our lovemaking has been varied, imaginative, and, in all respects, it has been continually exciting for both of us. We have been able to discard any of the inhibitions which would restrict the free and full expression of our love for each other; and we have used as our criteria for any sexual acts together the question of whether or not this is mutually desired and whether or not it is loving—nothing else.

We almost never have a sexual experience together now which is not deeply fulfilling. In most cases, for Lois, it is a multiorgasmic experience. We have, through the growth of our marriage, reached a point where we no longer feel it necessary to look at sexuality in a way that so many seem to write of it, as if this thing is of deadly seriousness and simply cannot be fun because you have to approach it in terms of very profound questions. If it isn't fun at the same time, forget it.

As for sexual compatibility, we'd say that we are in all respects compatible, but I dislike the word. It doesn't seem at all sufficient. We have found that sexual union meets many varied needs, and it has several dimensions—physical, psychological, and spiritual. It provides solace for us in sorrow, a catalyst when we have felt apart, meaning in our total life together, and, of course, it has climaxed joy in our life together. It has provided a bridge, a very human bridge, through which we have found God.

We do not subscribe, however, to the notion that sexual compatibility brings about a good marriage. It is one of the rewards of a good marriage. That would seem somewhat obvious, but I'm not sure, since I find so many articles discussing sexual compatibility as if it were merely a matter of computer matching. If you find the right sort of couple, and they just happen to fit, then you're going to have mutual fulfillment sexually. We've found that the growth of our sexual love has at all times paralleled the total growth of our marriage and the extent to which we have made a commitment to each other.

We've also discovered something else: that our marriage is sexual in its entirety. I was interested this afternoon when Jacqueline Grennan mentioned the approach that we have taken so long, a Manichaeanism that has been stamped on all of us, that we were raised with a dichotomy of body and soul.

When we had completed our book, it was submitted to one Catholic book club, and the editor of the book club liked the book. He wanted it as a book club selection, but he objected to the title *The Freedom of Sexual Love*. It scared him to death, I guess. One of the three words that most petrify people is the word *freedom*. In any case, he came through with three alternate titles and said, "Why don't you adopt one of these?" I can't recall all of them, but they were about the same. One of them was *Christian Marriage, in Body and Soul;* another, *The Sacrament of Matrimony, Physical and Spiritual*. Here we go right back to the tendency to *slice people in half*.

One of the things we find in our marriage is that the total relationship is in every respect sexual. I am a man. That means I am sexual. Everything that I am as a man, as a male, is going to be represented in my marital relationship. When my wife pours a cup of coffee for me, that's a woman pouring a cup of coffee. My response to that cup of coffee is the response of a man. This is true of every relationship. You simply cannot keep what you are out of the relationship. I wonder in absolute awe at people who say, "I have to become a person first, before I can be a woman or before I can be a man." I assume what they are talking about is going through some sort of a neuter stage, after which, at age 35, the individual who has been trying to become a person suddenly develops his genital organs. I was born male. This can't be changed, and this isn't merely true in terms of marriage.

I get right up to here (and I don't know what the rest of you do) reading so much about this whole nonsense. I just don't dig it, man. If I am relating to someone, I don't care whether that person is a 15-year-old high school girl or an 8-year-old. She is still female. I'm simply not going to have the same relationship with her that I would have with a man. We somehow always keep wanting to get down to a genital thing. Then we're not talking about sexuality, we're talking about genitalism.

We freely admit that in talking about sexuality and sexual relations in our marriage, we are very much romantics. Sister Jean today leaned over to me and said, "Stop holding hands." She wasn't serious. This much I know. My answer was, "No, we're not going to quit holding hands. I happen to like holding hands with my wife." We have at all times had a great deal of romance in our lovemaking. Holding hands in Church (which we once got called down for, incidentally) or making love on a deserted beach, as far as we're concerned, are one and the same thing, since they are both part of striving to make our life together an actual *making* of love. I become very bothered when I hear people talk about making love. They aren't talking about making love. They're talking about going home and screwing their wives, nothing more. If it isn't a making of love, if it isn't the growth of love, then it becomes a sick and a very sad business.

We can't get away from the one further, very important area of marriage. In recent discussions this has replaced the business of sex and finances as the paramount value. Everybody is talking about communication, and worrying about the failure to communicate. Nearly every couple that we have counseled has expressed some inability to communicate. However, in most cases, it has seemed to us it isn't actually frustration of communication they're talking about as much as frustration of conversation. They want to chat together, or one of them wants to make a point, or somebody wants to have a good argument.

Suppose we come down to the matter of defining communication. With all the talk about it, it's like Will Rogers and the weather: nobody's doing much about it. Nobody is really defining what they mean by it. Communication seems to us to be a skill, one which can be learned. I have often found myself wondering why, since this is a skill which can be taught and learned, and one which everybody is claiming is important, why the schools have almost totally ignored any responsibility in this area.

For our own definition, we think of communication in our marriage as a striving to enter the world of the other person: to understand, to empathize, to give oneself fully. This comes very close to what Miss Grennan was saying this afternoon. It is essential to a good marriage. I simply cannot love a person unless and until I am able to see her world, to see her needs and her desires.

Two things, we have found, slowed down and got in the way of our communication at times. First of all, difficulties in the use of language; and second, the threat that we each experienced so very often and in so many ways when we attempted to understand or to make ourselves understood. We gradually discovered that our association to words and our emotional reaction to them differed so very frequently that we were often hurt by not adequately exploring and expanding upon what we were trying to say to one another. We would express a view or opinion and then merely go on to something else, not really seeming to care about what the other person was hearing, assuming always that our frames of reference were exactly the same, and that words had the same meanings for both of us and elicited the same reactions from both of us. Consequently, we spent an awful lot of our time saying, "Yes, but that isn't at all what I meant."

Also, of course, both of us interjected a considerable amount of verbal meditation into conversation. We mentally added phrases onto what the other one said, then we very righteously claimed to know what the other really meant. "You said this, but I know what you meant." Worse yet, we even claimed to be able to interpret voice inflections and facial expressions, something which we later found almost never works. Our ability to communicate grew with our marriage; and without it the marriage would have remained a very superficial relationship, which would undoubtedly have been very frustrating to both of us. However, the development of communication, like the growth of our sexual love, has not been just one factor in making our marriage. It has *been* our marriage, since it has been both a means of loving and an end of loving.

This brings us, then, to what we feel are really the essential qualities in our marriage, the ones that have enabled its growth, as well as the growth of all good marriages, at least the ones we have had the opportunity to observe: motivation and freedom. These two elements, we feel certain, lie at the nucleus of any good marriage, now or in the future. Certainly, if there is any one thing that has become apparent at this conference, it is that marriage in the future will, of necessity, change.

Let's look at motivation first. We talk with very few couples who do not claim to *want* a good marriage. At the same time, we counsel many who we believe are unwilling to put forth the effort to achieve it. They are willing to go just so far, to give to each other, but always to put a limit on the giving. If there's one all-important lesson we've learned during these fifteen years, it is that marriages are not made in heaven. You make your own marriage, and you create your own heaven.

Then what supplies the motivation? Well, I suppose there could be very many sources of motivation—social, religious, economic—but I think they are seldom sufficient to do much more than keep the couple living together. In order to spur us to work toward a good marriage, the motivation is going to have to come from internalized values, very strong ones at that. There is going to have to be some combination of a fear of punishment and an expectancy of reward, used in its broadest definitional sense. Many couples we have seen lack the motivation which is so often cited as essential to success just in therapy alone. They simply are not hurting enough. They may be hurting initially, particularly married couples who come in to us facing the imminent break-up of their marriage, or a husband or wife who has just discovered an unfaithful spouse. But in a very short time, the relationship improves just enough to reach, as one of my patients once called it, "the comfort zone." They are comfortable again. Now in order to continue growing, they would have to make themselves uncomfortable, and this they're unwilling to do.

As far as expectance of reward is concerned, many couples can accurately assess their marriage as certainly being as good as the marriages of all their friends. So the reward is not going to be, "I hope if I really get in and work on my marriage, it will be as good as Mr. and Mrs. Jones' next door. They already have a marriage as good as Mr. and Mrs. Jones' next door. Unfortunately, they've been taught, as most of us were, to expect little more than the marriage that Mr. and Mrs. Jones have, which is probably pretty lousy. There are simply not that many good marriages around.

Of course, we are frequently tempted to scream in frustration at those who are painting this "the honeymoon will come to an end" picture of marriage, those who are force-feeding our teen-agers with the bile of their own cynicism, their own marital failures. It's been an interesting thing for us to see, working with adolescent groups, the beauty of the idealism that they are trying so desperately to cling to, despite the fact that they are surrounded by parents who are cynics. Perhaps one of the finest things that we have going today is the communication gap. This will at least help some teen-agers not to listen to their parents. It seems that nearly every institution touching on marriage is guilty. Our Churches are certainly guilty. Our schools, our universities and, as we all must be aware, the mass media, are very guilty. They are reinforcing this marital iconoclasm of embittered parents.

I certainly cannot say, nor can Lois, what provided our motivation initially. As I mentioned, it may have been a sort of stubborn resistance. I don't know. There's been a gradual deepening of awareness of the intensiveness and the extensiveness of our commitment, with the realization that a truly good marriage is not a fifty-fifty proposition, but rather the total and free giving of self on both sides. This awareness has led us to rewards which have then provided even further motivation. Our marriage has been our life. It has become our life. We feel deeply that we have but one vocation, and that is our marriage. Our goal must be a perfect marriage. We'll never attain it, but only if we aim for a perfect marriage do I feel that we have a chance of attaining a good one.

Freedom is a word that has much meaning for us. It touches on all that we feel is our life together. We use the word *freedom*, of course, in the title of our book on sex. We found it an extremely threatening word, something that shouldn't have surprised us. Erich Fromm pointed out that the concept of freedom is something which threatens people and from which they flee. Fifteen years ago, we both lacked a great deal of freedom, in almost every area of our marriage. We were seeking to meet many emotional needs in each other. We were insecure, uncertain, consequently very easily threatened. The opinions of others were given far too much weight. Our self-images were fragile, and we managed as a result to bruise each other painfully many times.

Each of us felt strongly dependent upon the other. I felt Lois needed me, that she needed a man to look up to, to follow, and to sever the relationship with her parents. I needed her recognition of me as a lover, a provider, as a source of strength. In too many ways I needed a parent role and needed her to be a child. In my insecurity, I handed my entire emotional existence to her. I said, "Here, you take charge of it, you nurture it, you protect it. Above all, remember it's a very fragile ego. Handle it with care." Of course, she didn't always. She couldn't. There were too many ways in which I could be threatened. A word that was said or unsaid, a look, a gesture, and I'd react. My defenses would go up. I wasn't able to identify it as a threat to my masculinity. No! I'd turn it into some real, existing problem. I'd given her the power, then, virtually to destroy me emotionally.

Lois did much the same thing. She felt sure she needed me. She needed my acceptance, my support, my reassurance. She needed me to be strong and, particularly, she needed me to need her. She feared my reactions without knowing them. But dependency breeds resentment and hostility. As long as we stayed convinced that we needed each other, in order to feel secure or fulfilled or whatever, there were the ever-present dangers of threat and resentment and defensiveness. Our marriage, as long as we viewed it in terms of a need structure, remained a symbiotic relationship.

One thing now seems very apparent. It has not been our marriage that has grown, but rather each of us individually. We have each become more secure. No longer do we feel inadequate, at least in the areas which are meaningful to us individually. Hence, the probability of expressing feelings of threat has greatly lessened or vanished.

Living, we have discovered, is very much like dying. You do it alone. Lois has had to find her answers and her security herself. I have had to find my own. Security, peace, meaning, happiness—these are not gifts that can be given by another. Lois cannot make me happy. My happiness can come only through ridding myself of egocentricity and neurotic needs. We have learned that a good marriage comes only when we can say, "I choose to spend my life with you, to give my life to you, to find satisfaction through you, but I do not need you. I don't need you to make me feel I'm a man, or to give me emotional support, or to fulfill me, or to provide my answers." Only as we have become free of each other, of the demands which arise from insecurity, have we been able to make a commitment to each other and to our marriage which is truly loving, truly a free gift of self.

During the last two days we have heard so much discussion of what it is to be a woman or a man. I don't think we're going to provide answers to these questions. I'm not sure there can be meaningful answers. It reminds me a little bit of the man who asked Louis Armstrong, "What is jazz?" He said, "Man, if you've got to ask, you'll never know." I think that becoming a woman or becoming a man is something which, like living, like dying, must be done alone. You may look to others for certain insights. You may ponder. You may relate to others of both sexes. Ultimately you're going to find the answer in some sort of dark night of your own probing.

We cannot say at what point in the fifteen years of our marriage we became married. Certainly, it wasn't when we went through the wedding ceremony. It was only when we found that we were able to make a free choice of marriage to each other that we could say, "We are now married." And our marriage is very good.

STUDENT: Why doesn't your wife say anything?

JOSEPH BIRD: We live in a feminist culture, and there's always somebody waving a banner at some parade. Because I'm doing the talking, people want to know what about my wife? All I can say is that Lois doesn't particularly care to talk before a microphone. Hence, the way I feel I can best love my wife is to talk for the two of us. Yes, Mr. Lecht.

CHARLES LECHT: My! I was very impressed with the very smooth and well-organized description of your marriage. Even the words *threat, frustration,* and *difficulty* had the same tone as the words *good, beautiful,* and *love.* Don't you think that a small amount of your success in marriage is dependent upon your psychological training? What do the common folk do who really do have difficulties overcoming problems? Some of them can't make it without help. There's a very young audience here from the university, and this question should be answered. It reminded me of a picture I once saw outside a school. "Tough? Join the Marines!" And they'd line up.

JOSEPH BIRD: Let me answer in some sort of order here. First, if I gave the impression that this is a fait accompli, I'd like to change that right now. Our marriage is better today than it was last year, and I feel certain if it is not better tomorrow than it is today, it will collapse. Marriage, if it is anything, is a dynamic process. If at any time it stops moving forward (it can't stand still) it is going to go backward, and fast. We feel right now we have a very good marriage, that it has become better each year. We would not want the marriage we had during the so-called honeymoon first year, or the second year or the third. We want the marriage we have today, because it's better than it was last year. It's a dynamic process, a growth process. Yes, we can each still be threatened, and threaten the other, but fortunately both of us have become more secure, at least in the areas which are meaningful to us, so that we cannot as easily be threatened.

Second, and obviously, we have learned enough about one another, about the areas in which the other one may feel threatened, so that, in loving one another, we are not going to hit these areas as often through inadvertence or deliberation. You made another point to which I would like to say flatly no. I do not feel that my professional training has much to do with my marriage. I'm afraid that headshrinkers, as a total population, don't have the greatest batting averages in their marriages. I honestly don't think that there is anything in my own training or in my discipline as a whole that has given my marriage much of anything to go by. Your third question, "How do couples find their answers?"—well, obviously we can't suggest that everybody be admitted into therapy. This would be no answer. I think what you're still going to be stuck with is, How badly do they want a good marriage, and how much are they willing to go ahead and get banged up in the process? Learning how to communicate involves getting a few scars. It involves getting hurt. It isn't just a nice coffee table process.

CHARLES LECHT: Yes, but I'm sure that you, as a psychologist, know that the difference between what a man or a woman wants to do and what he or she is capable of doing is frequently very wide.

JOSEPH BIRD: I'm not sure, but I think this has been a kind of cop-out that we've all used for too long. You know, we've talked about, "I can't do this" or "I can't bring myself to do that." I can tell myself all sorts of things. This is why I mentioned the business of family background. I have people coming in all week long telling me, "That's all well and good, but, gee, you know mother did so-and-so to me when I was five, and . . ." My feelings are very often that we should start out with the basic premise that we all came from lousy backgrounds and the whole society is a mess. But what do we do right now? I think there are a lot of things we can do, and I get awfully weary hearing people say, "Well, I just simply can't," or "I'm in a bind," or "I'm in a box," or "I'm hung up," or what have you. I'd have to say that the majority of people here, if given the motivation to go through the pain and some of the flowing of blood that's necessary, could have a good marriage if they desired it. Yes, Dr. Liu.

WILLIAM LIU: Although I left the room for a few minutes, I heard every word of your lecture through the public speaker.

JOSEPH BIRD: I thought I was projecting better than usual!

WILLIAM LIU: I was really moved by your lecture. At the same time I was struck by the statement that if your marriage doesn't improve every day then it will collapse. You place so much emphasis in your married life on being together, on complete identification, on supporting each other, on being secure. You have little else to divert you. I worry about the balance in such a relationship, the exclusive pursuit of a desirable married state.

JOSEPH BIRD: Let me distinguish something. First of all, I do not feel that it's essential to our marriage that we be together, that it be this "togetherness" à la *McCall's* magazine sort of concept. A great deal of the time we are of necessity not physically together, nor do I feel that this is essential to the growth of our marriage. This is why I said I don't think the matter of working wives is really an issue here. What is important is the total relationship and how secure you feel within it. We happen to choose to be together when we can be. This is something in which we make a choice. I haven't found anybody whose conversation I enjoy as much as Lois'. That's the beginning and the end of it. If I can be with her, I'd rather be with her than somebody else. It isn't that I feel we have to be together, or that I'm going to be insecure if I'm not with her, or that she's going to be insecure if she's not with me. It's a matter strictly and simply of choice.

WINFIELD BEST: I like the initial premise that the anatomy of a marriage must be the anatomy of your own marriage. It's a very courageous thing to do and the only honest thing, because that's the one you know something about. I think we all admire the fact that not only do you speak to it, but that you obviously have a good thing going here. It swings, right?

JOSEPH BIRD: Right. I think that's the word I like more than any other. It swings!

WINFIELD BEST: You've described your own role in some detail as a breadwinner—the hunter, or spiritual arbiter or whatever words you chose, which were better than that. Among the other things you do is that you speak for your wife. I speak for mine, too. She just does my thinking for me. You said just now that you like no other conversation better than your wife's. I accept the fact that you speak for her, and I would like you to tell me a little more about what her role is in the context of the emerging woman.

JOSEPH BIRD: This is exactly what we always seem to get hung up on, "What are the specific roles?" I don't think I could attempt to define what my total role is.

WINFIELD BEST: I didn't ask you about yours. I asked about hers.

JOSEPH BIRD: I couldn't define hers any more than I could define mine.

LOIS BIRD: I make a lot of decisions every day about what is going to be done where, when, and how, in a household with often about twenty people existing in it. If I were going to say what I do the most of, that would be it.

JOSEPH BIRD: Actually, it would be impossible for us. Could you really try to describe what your role is, or what mine is?

WINFIELD BEST: The word *role* is probably the big nuisance here.

JOSEPH BIRD: I think it is.

WINFIELD BEST: I'd just like to have you tell more about

what she does. What is the importance of her relationship to you?

JOSEPH BIRD: Her importance to me! I'm tempted (I suppose it may sound like a cop-out) but the only thing I can really come out and say with real honesty is, "She is my wife." She is the woman I choose to share my life with. She gives me a great deal of satisfaction in countless ways—intellectually, emotionally, spiritually. How can we define areas, really? She *is,* even before the fact that she is my wife. I'd have to boil it down to one thing: she is Lois. This isn't a role. It isn't an identity or anything else. She is this person. That's the only thing I could say with real honesty.

LOUIS DUPRÉ: Dr. Bird, what you told us tonight is the most impressive and enlightening thing I have heard about marriage in my entire life. A couple of years ago, I covered the country talking about marriage. I wasn't married, but I was talking about the religious meaning of marriage, the human meaning of marriage. Well, now I know what it is. I think if more people could listen to your witness (because that's what it is), many problems would disappear. Something which came to my mind as I listened to you, and kept coming back to me, were the words of the Gospel, "If your eye is pure, your entire body is clean." Thank you very much for the courage of what you have just said. Thank you, and also Mrs. Bird, for the courage of telling us.

JOSEPH BIRD: Thank you, Dr. Dupré. I must personally thank you too, because some time ago my wife and I discovered a book you had authored which we mentioned to you earlier in the conference. We enjoyed the book immensely. It had a great deal in it, we felt. We also enjoyed the locale and the setting in which we read it, which was up in the redwoods, far away from everybody else, lying on a blanket one afternoon. It was a tremendous place to read a book.

UNIDENTIFIED OBSERVER: I have two questions, perhaps

a little on the negative side. These aren't questions, but things you said (I don't mean that I'm a negativist) about the decisions that you made and your role. First, you made the decision as to how you would educate your children. It seemed to me that you made this decision all on your own, that this was in your pigeonhole and not a joint decision. Second, you spoke of your marriage as a growing thing which has been better year after year, and said that if it didn't grow, it would collapse. My experience, not only in marriage but in many things, has been two steps forward and one back, and then two forward and one back. Are you indicating that if you don't grow in a certain period of time, your marriage will collapse? Is it that weak, or what do you mean by collapse?

JOSEPH BIRD: All right. Let me take both questions in the order in which you posed them. First, I was *not* saying that this is my pigeonhole, my domain, sort of thing. When I said that, in my role as the head of my family as we have structured it and as Lois and I have lived it, one of my responsibilities includes such things as the education of my children, this does not mean that my wife does not have a very important role in the education of our children. It does mean, however, that the buck stops here, that I'd better not be an absentee father. Certainly, since Lois spends more time with the children than I do, she is going to play a more important role, in terms of the actual time spent with them, with their education, than perhaps I will. But *I* am going to have to say, "Okay, Buster, it's up to you now," if something's going wrong with that child in school. Or even as to where they are in school, I simply cannot pass the buck to my wife, to the school teacher, to a Sunday school teacher, or anyone else. It's going to have to come back to me. I am sure there are other couples who may structure their relationship differently. The wife may take over the whole ball of wax—educating the children, their emotional development, their spiritual growth, and so on. We would not find this particularly comfortable. I would have to say, parenthetically, that this is one of the things I hear wives complain about all the time, that all the man sees is his role as a breadwinner, nothing else.

As to the second question, concerning growth, certainly there are going to be times when by being apart (here I'm talking about being emotionally distant from one another) you hurt one another. I would reiterate first of all that marriage is a growth process. It better be getting better. Certainly the graph may be somewhat like this. It may be jagged. There may be a day, there may be a couple of days in which it's down, but if the total marital relationship is not one of growth, it's not going to take too long before it does collapse into what we would consider to be a poor marriage. That isn't to say divorce. It isn't to say one of us is going to be stabbing the other, or anything else. It's going to collapse into the sort of relationship that we want no part of. What happens, I feel, is that as we grow closer to one another, as our love deepens, if you will, the periods in which we are emotionally distant, emotionally apart from one another, grow shorter and shorter, primarily for one reason. We find the pain involved in being apart from one another becomes increasingly intense. When we were first married, we may have been able to take for a day or two, even a week or two, this business of being kind of cool to one another, the kind of overly polite "Would you care for another cup of coffee" business. You know the sort of thing. Now if it goes on for twenty minutes, one or the other of us is going to say, "Aw, look, let's sit down and talk. Let's hash this thing out, with tears and the rest that may go with it, but let's not stay apart and go through this silliness."

JESSIE BERNARD: Is your office at home?

JOSEPH BIRD: No. It used to be. Until about a year and a half ago I directed research at a hospital. I had a private practice part time. At that time I had an office right off the entrance to our home. Now my office is about five minutes away, which I find very convenient. We do our writing at our office at home, and I have my private practice outside in an office. Having it only five minutes away means I can come home for lunch and so forth.

STUDENT: Describe your communication thing.

JOSEPH BIRD: There are two dimensions of it. One is the skill with which we can learn to define and redefine what we are saying, our attempt to at least understand the way this person is using language—what we do in writing when we state something and restate it, reiterate it, rephrase it, and so on. You can say at some point, "Okay, I think my reader will get what I'm trying to say." Even then we find there are breakdowns. The second part of it, of course, is only going to come through exposing yourself and going through the pain of being exposed. That's saying, "Okay, I want to know you and I'm willing to go ahead and get pretty banged up at times trying to know you. I'm willing to have you threaten me, have you say things that are going to leave me a little bit scared and a little bit bloodied."

STUDENT: Do you both do psychotherapy?

JOSEPH BIRD: Only in one area. Some time ago, we found it to be very effective for the two of us to work together in group therapy with married couples. In group therapy with married couples, we are co-therapists.

STUDENT: How much influence should, let's say, younger couples let their parents have over them in later life? And—I'm sure you're coming to this now—how much influence do you expect to have on your children?

JOSEPH BIRD: In answer to the first question, none. In answer to the second question, hopefully none. No, I sincerely hope, really, that we will stay the heck out of our children's, our adult children's, lives. They're going to have to make their own mistakes, just as we made our own mistakes.

STUDENT: I wonder if you would say a word to several of us in the audience who are students of theology in terms of what you would recommend, either in or outside the institutional Church, toward a better theology of marriage. You, or Miss Grennan, or anyone else here.

JOSEPH BIRD: Theology has been given, it seems to me, a sort of a framework, an aura, that has prevented its growth in many areas, and particularly in marriage. We have thought of theology in terms of its being a very exact discipline that's up here and is written and discussed and carried on by people who only talk to other theologians, who always have to have fifty different references from other theologians whom they may disagree with, but never admit it in their writing. They say, "I agree with what Schlangfeister said. However, I think we could make a distinction . . ." The game kind of goes on and on. As a consequence, we never have had a meaningful theology of marriage. The ones I would blame for this are not the theologians doing the writing. They don't know what they are talking about, but how could they? We've been stuck with an Augustinian orientation of this thing for two thousand years. The ones who *could* form and will eventually have to come up with the theology of marriage, if it's going to make any sense at all, are those who are *living* this vocation. The married laity, the ones who are attempting to live the vocation of Christian marriage, have just totally turned their backs on the responsibility. They've said, "After all, marriage is a private affair. We won't talk about it. We'll let Father so-and-so tell us about it. He will tell us what our theology is. He'll tell me what I feel when I'm making love to my wife. We can look to him and he'll tell Lois what she experiences sexually." The laity, those who are living the vocation of marriage, have got to grab the responsibility, because theology, unless it is experiential, comes out absurd. This much I'm convinced of.

STUDENT: I'm concerned with the question of compatibility of interest in marriage, being an unmarried student. I don't think you brought it up. Obviously it's true you and your wife have a tremendous compatibility and mutuality of interest. I was wondering what you would say about the similar interests and similar types of occupations and preoccupations that the two of you share? What is the importance of this sameness of interest?

JOSEPH BIRD: I think this has been thought of as a requisite prior to marriage. I think this has been very misunderstood and overrated. We talk about it as if it's a matter of matching. This is the whole computer dating technique, in which you find out that Mary's interests are such-and-so, and that John's interests are such-and-so. Therefore, you just pair them up and if the correlation is over a certain point, say point seven, then you should have a pretty good marriage. It's also assuming, of course, that their interests are going to stay there, and that all they have in their lives are just those particular variables. What leads to the interest, really, is the same sort of thing as with sexual love. It's a growth process. We shared very few of the many interests we share now at the time we married. Neither one of us had and were interested in many of them at the time we married. Either we have discovered new interests together, or it's been a matter of one or the other of us sharing an old interest with the other. When we married, I'd never been to a professional baseball game. I had no interest in it. Lois had a kid brother who was a star pitcher in high school. We were living at that time in Southern California. I decided Lois would probably, since she'd always gone to games, enjoy going to a baseball game. I took her to a minor league game out there, and then to several more. I found out much later that Lois actually had no real interest in baseball; she'd gone to the games because her kid brother pitched. I think we'd be hard pressed to say which of us is the greater Giant fan, even though they never end above second place. These are things which really *grow,* and part of it's a matter of having a kind of looseness. Are you willing to try things? Or are you just hung up with this? I won't try this because I don't like so-and-so.

STUDENT: I'm sure you would not allow your children to go to school and be taught religion any more than you would allow your wife to go and be taught how she feels about marriage. How do you prepare your children for marriage? How do you try to teach them religion before they can experience religion through marriage? I know you're Catholic, and I want to know whether or not you do bring them up Catholic? I would appreciate, if it's not too personal a question, your comments on that area of your children's education.

JOSEPH BIRD: Since I've pretty well taken off my clothes in every other area, I don't think that is too personal. First of all, we do not have our children in parochial schools or in CCD* programs. We feel, however, the responsibility is not one of *teaching* our children religion, but one of sharing our particular faith in Christ, as we find Him, with our children. This is a *lived* experience. If they don't find God sitting around our dinner table together with us as a family, we're going to waste our time talking to them about religion. We're going to waste our time trying to shove some sort of catechism down their throats. Yes, God is discussed. Christ is discussed, not in the sense of, "All right, we'll now sit down with our children and cover *this* with them or *that* with them," but it's talked about as we'd talk about any other meaningful area of our own life. There are a lot of shared religious experiences with our children within our family. We're great ones for parties. Our whole family digs parties, and Lois and I dig parties. Following the liturgical year of our Church gives us many opportunities for parties. I think an awful lot of it is just a mat-

---

* *Editor's note:* Dr. Bird is referring to Confraternity of Christian Doctrine, a Catholic religious instruction program similar to Protestant Sunday school.

ter of living, talking with your children, and sharing what you have and what you feel. The only reason we do not have our children in CCD or in parochial schools or religious education programs is not that we feel these programs are poor or failures or anything else. It comes down to one thing. The only thing we can really give our children in terms of religion is to share our own particular faith with them. Therefore, if we're going to send them to some sort of program, we would have to be certain that whoever is teaching that program—and here I'm not talking about the formal structure of it or what the book says or whatever—happens to see God in the way we see God. If we cannot be certain of that, I feel we have an obligation to get our children out of such a program. I don't think that constitutes making a judgment of the program, however.

STUDENT: How do you reconcile the demands of your large family with the commitment of giving to one another?

LOIS BIRD: They're part of it.

JOSEPH BIRD: They're part of it, that's all. They're part of it. First of all, anything we're going to be able to give our children that's really going to contribute to their emotional health is going to have to start with our marriage. The security and the love that a child feels between husband and wife in a marriage is going to be, for the most part, a reflection of the love between the husband and wife. They're really part of the total marriage, as it were. It's not the marriage and the children. They're an outgrowth of the total marriage. There doesn't have to be any conflict.

MOTHER MARGARET GORMAN: My question is directly related to that. I was struck by the statement you made that marriage is your one vocation. When you ask a girl, a student in college, what she's going to do, she'll say, "I'm going to get married." You ask a boy, and he'll say, "I'll be a lawyer, a doctor, an engineer." I wonder whether the answer of the boy may be somewhat the cause of the trouble?

JOSEPH BIRD: I think there's a corollary in an answer that girls often give. A hell of a lot of girls are saying, "You know, I'm going to be a mother." You know. Good grief! I'm first of all a husband. Lois is a wife. Ultimately, out of our marriage, we became father and mother. Part of my total vocation is to earn a living for my family. I happen to do this as a psychologist. I could do it in a number of other ways perhaps, but that happens to be part of the total responsibility I feel to my vocation. But unless I am seeing it within the context of my vocation, I'm going to run into trouble eventually.

STUDENT: You mentioned that you weren't in any clubs or organizations except as an advisor. Do you think such activity can be disruptive to a marriage?

JOSEPH BIRD: It certainly can be. A lot of things can be. I don't think they necessarily have to be. We just don't happen to dig clubs. What this really comes down to is that we're not club people or organization people, as it were. I find a heck of a lot more fun walking on the beach somewhere at night with my wife than sitting in a meeting. So we're really not involved in organizations.

UNIDENTIFIED OBSERVER: You discuss your marriage as a growth process. One would assume that your relationship before you were married was this way, and that you predicted maybe this or that would work after you were married. Can you say something about your premarriage experience?

JOSEPH BIRD: It's awfully hard to assess, really. Up until the time we got married, I can be sure of only one thing. I certainly hadn't grown to the extent I would have liked. Had I grown more, I think we wouldn't have had as much skin peeled off. We had an awful lot of information about marriage before we married. It's remarkable now when I think back over all the books we read. I don't mean to say we read a dozen or two dozen volumes. We probably read half a dozen good

Christian books on marriage. Fortunately we have been able to overcome them. If we hadn't, our marriage would be in a heck of a mess now. We've tried to analyze it. Everything I've said up until this point has represented the thinking of both Lois and myself. Lois would not subscribe to this view I feel sure, but my own personal view is that the primary and almost overwhelming motivational force responsible for the success of our marriage has been the woman I married.

STUDENT: Do you think premarital intercourse may be emotionally crippling? Second, what is to keep you from sexual love with all women?

JOSEPH BIRD: Let me answer that in inverse order. I think we get hung up on this business of eros agape: as a Christian, I have an obligation to love everyone else. If you say or infer, and many people do, that if I love someone, this is going to lead in a direct line to an overt sexual expression of that love, I'd have to deny this flatly. This would almost imply that I couldn't love any woman other than my wife without at some point making a choice of an overt sexual expression. This is simply not true. Yes, I can love this person and our relationship is sexual, because she is a woman and I am a man. But at some point I could still make a choice as to whether or not to have intercourse with her.

As to your second question, I couldn't possibly presume to say how one individual is going to find his or her answers about premarital intercourse. I think we have too long played a paternalistic role and attempted to give young unmarried people clichés, pat, secure little rules to go by. Often they're asking questions for which we never found answers. They're going to have to find their own answers. I believe some people are getting emotionally scarred by this. This is all too evident. Depending upon the totality of the relationship, what the relationship is, whether or not it is exploitative, how much guilt is experienced in it, some people are being emotionally banged up. As to what answer you find for yourself, I couldn't possibly presume to try to answer that.

WILLIAM D'ANTONIO: Thank you very much, Doctor and Mrs. Bird.

Education for Real Living 10

MICHAEL SCRIVEN AND MOTHER MARGARET GORMAN

Wednesday, 9:00 A.M.

WILLIAM LIU: I first met Professor Michael Scriven early in September in his very beautiful apartment in California. I was really taken both by the magnificent view and by the work that he has done there. I learned for the first time that a real philosopher is working with computer technology; and I saw the fascinating statistical work he is doing. I developed the highest respect for his work. I think it is a real honor to have him here.

Mother Gorman's name was referred to me by Dr. Shuster when I asked him if we could have someone who is totally dedicated to women's education. He told me that Mother Gorman is one of the most outstanding educators of women today. Michael Scriven has something very specific to say and he wanted to say it earlier, so he will be the first speaker.

MICHAEL SCRIVEN: I don't know about something specific, but I wanted to say it earlier because if it doesn't snow too hard I have to get a plane out of here rather shortly. But I hate to hit and run so perhaps if the snow stops that'll be a blessing in disguise.

I have called this "Putting the Sex Back into Sex Education." It seems like a good title. I doubt if anyone talks very much about that. I want to begin by summarizing the general themes of the conference as I believe they would have appeared to an intelligent lay listener like, say, Martha Stuart. Laymen aren't afraid of a few value judgments, unlike the nervous professionals. After all, it is the layman that we ultimately have to address; I think this is how Martha sees the whole affair.

The human female is an essentially retrograde and indeed unnatural sex. Moreover, the human female is practically the only one in the animal kingdom not to have accepted its obvious inferiority with good grace. (One doesn't see cows in the bull ring, hens at cockfights.) It is clear they are sexually inferior, as Mrs. Johnson and Dr. Masters pointed out so clearly yesterday, in that they characteristically require multiorgasmic experiences in order to achieve full satisfaction, unlike the more efficient male (*laughter*). One must think of them, I suppose, as suffering from a kind of congenital repetition-compulsion in this dimension, a sort of sexual *stuttering*, so to speak (*laughter*). Despite this and other handicaps, they persist in the attempt to subvert the natural superiority of the male.

Given the blatancy of the counterevidence—for example the fact that even in their own domain of housewifely activities, the true masters of cooking or of dressmaking are *male* chefs and couturiers—one must regard this persistence as at least perverse and perhaps symptomatic of a deeper psychopathology, a syndrome we might tentatively identify as the Venus complex, the concept of the female as part of the pantheon of gods. Associated with the failure to achieve this status is the morbid pathology of this megalomaniac syndrome, which must be regarded as a kind of inherited sex-linked paranoia. Not content with this long-standing attack on the natural order, women have recently even taken over the role, or attempted to take over the role, of the *decorative* sex, a role which throughout the animal kingdom is naturally that of the male. It's the cock pheasant, the male Siamese, the fighting fish, and the male mandrill that are the standards of beauty, not the female. This defiance of natural law must surely lead to disaster. I am sure that in the Great Plan these roles were not meant to be exchanged.

There is no niche in the life-space that is secure against these invasions. There was a time when the meaning of the male rallying cry, "I'll show *her* who wears the pants in this family," was entirely clear. In this century, however, one of the typically unfortunate results of education for women was their recognition of the importance of the adage, "If you can't lick 'em, join 'em," for their grand strategy. Thus we find ourselves moving toward a new sexual role-switching—or rather role-filching—where the female has simply stolen the man's pants or pants suit, literally as well as symbolically.

At any rate, male supremacy is gone from our land, and even the purse strings of corporations and foundations are now controlled by women more often than by men. It behooves us poor males, in these declining days, to attend such gatherings as this, arranged by female powers, in order to discuss what might be called *the intellectual rationalizations for the official surrender of power.*

As a conservative, I wouldn't quite agree with this point of view of Martha's, but I do think it deserves to be considered *seriously*. At a conference like this, after all, a good case can be made that *everything* is considered seriously. If it's going to be considered seriously anywhere *else*, I guess the place for that would be the educational system, about which I want to talk today.

Sex education so far has mainly meant education about the physiology of reproduction. In the Army and in very enlightened school systems they toss in something about contraceptives and venereal diseases, in college something about Freud, and at home something about cooking. Attempts have been made to develop marriage courses which go beyond this, but they have so far not had a large effect. For general ineffectiveness, I'd say they were on a par with nice citizenship training programs. I think we can do better than this, and I have some suggestions about what we can do.

In the first place, two general points have emerged at this conference which have impressed me as particularly important. The first is that most of the apparent solutions to the problem of the life-style, or role, or identity of women are very incomplete. I think Edgar Berman, among others, was right when he stressed that the contraceptive is not a magic wand that breaks the iron bands on women. Contraception provides the opportunity for women to liberate themselves from one kind of restraint that impedes the development of one kind of life. On the other hand, having children is not a restraint but rather the goal of another life-style. Indeed, within one woman's life, it can change from being a goal to being an impediment, as her family size becomes adequate to her needs.

There's no way of escaping basic questions about purpose in life; the aims of man; the extent of his responsibility for his fate; the foundations for moral imperatives; in short, philosophy. (There's nothing quite so reassuring as discovering that one's profession is indispensable to the salvation of mankind, or even womankind! I think everyone else here has already made the same discovery about their profession.) The search for the female role or identity is not separable from the search for our place in the universe.

But we can be more helpful than that. We can exhibit in three dimensions, not just in abstract terms, a full range of alternative actual life-styles for women. We can present, not just in profusely illustrated guidance manuals, but on video-tape, film, and sound tape, the traumas and stresses of the woman's role and the many ways these can, by some people, be handled. I'm talking about a specific educational procedure that I'm calling *the traumas approach*. I suggest approaching the solution of the problem of the woman's role in this way, rather than in an auxiliary process which leads to a description of ideal arrangements, and of the factual background that one requires to understand the details of reproduction. Why?

It's very simple. You can be a child of a happy marriage and be happy in that situation but absolutely helpless when confronted with catastrophe in your own personal relations. It is an extraordinary defect in educational thinking to imagine that setting a good example in any way provides the solution for the problems that the individual will later face. It's very charming to have a happy family. It inevitably leads to a personality which in that situation is happier and more balanced, but it does not in any way whatsoever convey to the child anything about how he or she is going to handle the enormous difficulties that have to be solved in the earlier pre-child days of that same happy marriage. It's possible that during the course of everyday life in that marriage there will be enough difficulties arising so that something can be learned about how to handle them. It's not obvious. In many cases it's clearly absent. Living on a boat doesn't teach you how to swim. It's nice if you can put your children on a boat. It keeps them out of the water and they don't have to swim, but, after all, they're probably going to have to learn sooner or later and it's not good training for their lives to avoid teaching them how to swim. Hence, the traumas approach.

Exactly the same thing comes up in citizenship education. The traditional approach is to spout a lot of stuff about the lives of great American folk heroes—allegedly political and historical figures but, in fact, just mythological ones. Of course, this is splendid stuff as a substitute for fairy stories, but it has no value whatsoever. We are attempting to put people in a position to be able to face the stresses of public issues in which they themselves might have to play a role. The first point I'm making is that, in talking about education for the woman's role or for sex education in general, we can't get away from philosophy. The second point I'm making is that we can't get away from the traumas approach, the problem-oriented approach. I'm going to expand on both a little bit.

Regarding the relevance of philosophy, take the concept of equality which has frequently plagued us at this conference. Charles Lecht castigated those of us who've been talking about equality between the sexes. He said there is no equality between the sexes. One constantly hears political commentators, usually, curiously enough, from the right wing, producing as a brilliant insight the fact of individual differences in denying the validity of equalitarianism. Both attacks reflect the staggering deficiency in our philosophical education and, indeed, our political education—indeed, in our education for citizenship. No one arguing for the equality of the sexes is attempting to deny the physiological and possible psychological differences between them. They're arguing for equality of rights, for equality of opportunity, for equality in the eyes of the law and in the hands of those whose choice affects them. This is not asking for something contraindicated by the facts. It is simply asking that only the *relevant* considerations, which *may* include prejudice, whether racial or sexual, be applied.

I can go on about the difference between legitimate and illegitimate uses of information about intersex or interracial differences. There is a legitimate use of these differences, but it's very limited and practically never applies to job selection. In general, in fact, one can say that, excluding the exceptional cases such as choosing male fashion models, washroom attendants, or topless waitresses, where the physiology is presumed to be a definitive requirement, all jobs should be open on a merit basis. That means some women would lose jobs they presently hold as nurses and secretaries, and many more men would lose their jobs as cab drivers, airline pilots, union leaders, and politicians. There are some difficult cases, such as receptionists and airline hostesses, which need further discussion about the nature of the job itself, but the general condition is clear. Equality of opportunity does not require assuming universal equality of skill.

We might talk of three kinds of marriage, which I call preliminary marriage, personal marriage, and parental marriage. Preliminary marriage is a quasicontractual arrangement for cohabitation which explicitly excludes any other implicit or written commitment to the support of the other person, let alone support of the children. Preliminary marriage is essentially cohabitation made more official by giving it a title.

The second stage of marriage, which might very well be thought of as something one rationally enters into only after a period of some time in the previous stage, would be personal marriage. Personal marriage involves the guarantee, through the marriage contract, of mutual support and welfare to whatever date a termination occurs because of death or divorce. Again, this does not include in any way provision for the support of children. It does not constitute an endorsement by either party for having children. It seems probable to me that in society, either now or later, where explicit attempts are made through taxation devices to encourage limitation of family more directly, it will be necessary to have a distinction made between marriage in the personal sense and marriage in the third or parental sense.

The parental sense, of course, might require a license of some kind. A person is committed to undertaking the support of the children of the marriage. Now, naturally, the present situation, with contraception, means that the woman is entirely responsible for the matter of conception, responsible in the sense that she can prevent it if she desires to do so. In such situations little remains of the man's obligation. The man, if he has not in fact agreed to parental marriage, has no obligations to the children whatsoever, unless vasectomy is agreed on.

A number of natural questions arise if one starts an analytical approach to the nature of marriage. Some suggested practical implications of the reconstruction of the arrangements I've suggested are, for example: What about three-party marriages at some of these levels? Should it, must it, be the case that marriages be monogamous? Maybe they should also be polygamous or polyandrous or with more than just two or three parties? (This is an arrangement that has frequently been entirely successful over long periods of time in civilizations that have attained a degree of culture not distinguishable from our own, although the number of electric can openers was fewer!) It doesn't seem obvious that we should abandon the discussion of that sort of alternative. What about homosexual marriage, at both the preliminary and personal stage? It seems there's no obvious reason to avoid it.

What about reevaluating the incest taboos? These are sorely in need of explicit discussion. The most liberal people thus far are talking about divorces but are shattered at the thought that it might not be such a bad thing to allow marriage between siblings. It's not clear why it should not be a good thing. As far as the genetic problems go, these exist and, of course, make parental marriage more of a risk. They do not, of course, absolutely preclude it. Cleopatra was the result of six generations of close intermarriages, so this is apparently not beyond our concept of the possible.

Why not discuss these alternatives as part of the procedure for trying to get people to understand the nature of marriage? Won't this kind of discussion put people off marriage? No, we can always tell them great tales of folk heroes—marriage sagas of, for example, the Birds. I think that saga is a great one. It deserves to be told and it serves as a source of inspiration. I'll always remember the first time a highly religious man, who was also a professor of the philosophy of religion, told me that he didn't think it mattered a bit whether Jesus lived or died. This seemed to me to be a shattering and improper suggestion. He then went on to explain. The point was this: The life of Jesus, as it's being passed on to us, creates a possibility in our minds. The only important thing about it for the individual is the fact that it presents realistically to him a way of life that he should think about. He should consider its own meaning to him in exactly the same way that the stories of the great folk heroes serve educational purposes.

Certainly pictures of ideal marriages of any kind and the pictures of nonmarriages of another type should be painted in full and should be made real. They should be created in the minds of students as real possibilities. It's true that the law lags far behind the suggestions that I'm making. That doesn't matter. There are lots of ways in which one can, in fact, follow these suggestions perfectly simply. In the city cultures at the moment, it's the case that cohabitation is more common and less frowned upon than ever before. Personal marriages can now be arranged legally, if by unduly complicated procedures. The stigma attached to them should be removed. One should work on the process of sorting out these independent considerations about the relationship between two people, their capacity to look after children properly, their interest in doing so, and their interest in supporting each other. It might be the case that we would get fewer instances of people committing themselves to a personal contract for children when, in fact, what they want is a personal relationship alone.

There are many other things I would like to talk about. I have just tried to mention a couple of these specific things, as

Bill said. Also, I want to say that if we are going to take this matter of educating for marriage or sex seriously, then we simply have to go about handling a great many of the very difficult and unattractive problems that we continue to sweep under the rug, that we continue to say should not appear in the official curriculum because the PTA won't like it. We may have to knuckle down to the PTA, but we ought to do everything we can to face them out on this point and to educate people seriously for this kind of a problem. I do have a few minutes if you want to give people a chance at these ideas.

JESSIE BERNARD: I feel guilty. I am always imposing data on these discussions, which takes away the glamour and excitement, but I've had occasion to review some of the statistical data on this and it's true. I went through the 1960 and 1966 data studying households of unrelated individuals, i.e., one-person, two-person, three-or-more-person households, and, indeed, we do have these kinds of marriages—relationships, excuse me—and they're growing at a fantastic rate. Relationships of unrelated individuals grew at a rate seven times faster than marriages per se between 1960 and 1966. So we are having these noncontractual marriages. I was studying only people under 25, but a large number of older people also live together without commitment. The social security law was changed to make it possible for women to marry and not lose their annuities. Three-party marriages, sometimes called hippie pads, are also increasing. These trends are taking place. The thing that's so interesting is they aren't hurting marriage at all. As I've said before, marriage is doing very well along with these alternative relationships.

JACQUELINE GRENNAN: Dr. Scriven, could you make the distinction once more between the first and second stage of marriage?

MICHAEL SCRIVEN: Preliminary marriage involves no commitment to support the other person at all. It involves no economic commitment particularly (but not solely). It doesn't require divorce for termination.

RUTH USEEM: Did you intimate that your family marriage in the third stage could exist without the second one?

MICHAEL SCRIVEN: Well, it seems to me inappropriate for it to do so. Technically, it could. You might want to undertake to support children of another person. That would just be as legally possible now as an adoption form without being personally married to the mother, but guaranteeing the children's support. I do think it would be improbable that this arrangement would be mutually satisfactory.

MARTHA STUART: Michael, I hope that I'm correct in saying something about your views, as correct as you were in talking about mine! "Equal rights is the only morality" is a Michael Scriven quote, right? I think that's very healthy. There has to be something in it for each person or each country or anything. I mean, anything is unhealthy without an equal something. What happens, then, in tripartite marriage? Doesn't that almost immediately handicap things? What do you think about it?

MICHAEL SCRIVEN: It doesn't strike me that a three-way marriage involves loss of rights for anybody.

MARTHA STUART: Equal rights, I said.

MICHAEL SCRIVEN: Equal rights doesn't mean numerical equality of the sexes.

MARTHA STUART: You're implying one person of one sex. You can't have complete equality among three people. You will have one who is in more demand than the others, it seems to me.

MICHAEL SCRIVEN: Maybe. Maybe not. For example, one of the forms in which this has occurred anthropologically is when the mother function is separated from the sex-partner function. This is not a case where either suffers extremely from deprivation. Remember that one of the important things here is the enormous individual differences in sex appetite; for example, a male who is highly sexed and two females who are not so highly sexed, or the alternative symmetrical arrangement, in which nobody is shortchanged as far as sex goes.

MARTHA STUART: Suppose both of those women just love to cook.

MICHAEL SCRIVEN: It is the same situation where both husband and wife love to cook; they have to make a decision.

MARTHA STUART: Yes, but if they both love to cook for that man, then what? The other thing I want to know is why you think this three-part process has to be set up legally. Isn't this in a sense what anybody who goes into a marriage responsibly does?

MICHAEL SCRIVEN: Has three partners?

MARTHA STUART: No, three stages.

MICHAEL SCRIVEN: Three stages? Yes, but the point is that sophisticated people like us, we hope, can get away with it. Ninety percent of the population can't. Their jobs would go. The peer-group pressure would be fantastic. They couldn't possibly handle the preliminary cohabitation thing. Cohabitation is at an all-time high in the intellectual group and perhaps in the lowest economic group, but it's certainly not something which is a socially acceptable procedure.

JUNE BUTTS: Isn't the breakup rate greatest with the most intellectual and most severely deprived economic groups, so that the experiments and the breakups are going on in the extremes and not among the "proletariat"?

MICHAEL SCRIVEN: Yes, the rigidity of this middle group is much greater than it should be with respect to this kind of arrangement.

MARTHA STUART: Instead of helping them become less rigid, we're just feeding their rigidity by these boxes of types of marriage, aren't we?

WILLIAM D'ANTONIO: We're also making value judgments on their rigidity.

MICHAEL SCRIVEN: It doesn't seem to me that by introducing very diverse arrangements you're increasing rigidity. Giving people a choice between alternatives and an explicit arrangement seems to be an improvement, a flexibility.

MARTHA STUART: It can be, I know, but do you know what I mean?

MICHAEL SCRIVEN: No (*laughter*).

MARTHA STUART: No?

MICHAEL SCRIVEN: No, I usually do, but not this time.

VIRGINIA JOHNSON: I wonder if you'd clarify for us the enormous differences in sexual appetite.

MICHAEL SCRIVEN: You're being naughty, Virginia. That's a terrible thing for you to say to me after you so carefully defended yourselves yesterday from our misinterpreting you about these things.

VIRGINIA JOHNSON: No, I'm very serious. That wasn't a nasty question.

MICHAEL SCRIVEN: What I said was not that there are enormous differences in sexual appetites, but in a case where there are . . .

VIRGINIA JOHNSON: This presumes that you can create or will this naturally.

MICHAEL SCRIVEN: Not at all. It presumes you cannot avoid the fact that these differences exist. Do you wish to argue that they don't?

VIRGINIA JOHNSON: No. Your term *enormous* is the only thing that triggered me to respond to that. If you want to be technical, that was the trigger point.

MICHAEL SCRIVEN: Do you doubt that there are any cases where one man can service two women's sexual appetites satisfactorily or vice versa?

VIRGINIA JOHNSON: Oh, I think vice versa is by far the more realistic.

MICHAEL SCRIVEN: That's all we need.

VIRGINIA JOHNSON: I was really interested because you were predicating a so-called constellation here, based on the possible existence of that. I wouldn't count on it as the only thing. I'm with you that it can exist.

MICHAEL SCRIVEN: Look, take a man and woman who marry in the ordinary situation. First of all, they characteristically have to make adjustments in this demand fulfillment. Second, they change themselves and at different rates. Further adjustment is necessary. Sometimes it's impossible and divorce results. The situation is not going to be crucially different in this case, provided that common sense is used in adjusting the initial requirements and trying to extrapolate these into the future.

VIRGINIA JOHNSON: It can be the crucial difference if we're dealing with three people instead of two, certainly.

MICHAEL SCRIVEN: I can't see any reason why it should be more crucial than in the other case. A lot of women, really, for hung-up reasons of various kinds, just like a lot of men, have little interest in sustained sex.

VIRGINIA JOHNSON: They like to play the game, however. It takes a long while, in my estimation, to adjust and develop the rationale for living with this.

JESSIE BERNARD: In the age bracket where men are so scarce, I'm all for that. You know, I'd like to see the women who have husbands share them with other women.

WILLIAM D'ANTONIO: You're talking about a very real problem, the surplus of women in the older-age group.

JESSIE BERNARD: The women aren't at all interested in sharing their husbands.

MOTHER GORMAN: I'm only concerned about one side that hasn't been brought up, and I guess I'm not only concerned with girls from upper economic levels in my educational work. I go down to the inner city in Boston and I have to help mothers. One woman was 34 with seven children: her oldest son was 20; the next son 18; and the little boy was 6, and he was, they think, by a white father. Nobody knew the fathers of any of them. The mother I was not so worried about. I was worried very much about these children. Maybe it's going to be taken care of by contraceptives. When I speak to the mothers, they say they feel guilty about having these children and being so unable to help them. I say, "Are you going to have some more children?" "Yes." "Why?" "I want to show that I'm a woman." All right. So this is happening and we are just inbreeding this thing over and over again. We can talk about having marital satisfaction, but there's another side to it. There are children evolving from this, and where does this fit in?

MICHAEL SCRIVEN: I think that's an excellent point, but part of the procedure, of course, for education must surely be to get across the idea that the role of the woman does not demand having children. That's a terribly important part of any decent process in discussing marriage fulfillment.

MOTHER GORMAN: I know it does not demand it, but they're doing it and, from what I gathered, even though I were to educate them in some way, this was happening and the children were suffering.

JACQUELINE GRENNAN: I think that's why Dr. Scriven's suggestions are terribly important. I don't think that one is necessarily making a value judgment about the rigidity of the middle group if you offer alternatives. What he really seems to say, to me, is that you've got to offer people all kinds of alternatives. You can't say they don't exist by denying them, either overtly or covertly. I find the tripartite marriage kind of distasteful, probably because, among other things, my whole education and background don't bring me that way, and I'm sort of glad they don't. I still don't see how the opportunity psychically makes anybody go that way. I think so much of education has gone the other way. We tell people ahead of time what their judgments ought to be. We preclude, and exclude, and include by a prior judgment and we're always afraid that our own value judgment is suspect if somebody else has another one, if there's another one that's called orthodox.

MOTHER GORMAN: Yes, I heartily agree with Dr. Scriven's statement that we must explore these possibilities. I would say that we must explore all their consequences also. I wouldn't say what passes judgment on the consequences. I want to see them in their ultimate results on the whole society as well. I'm not saying that they are right or wrong.

JESSIE BERNARD: I'll pass the judgment on it and give you evidence for it. I won't take the time now, but I think we can pass judgment on this.

KERMIT KRANTZ: All the aspects we spoke of are in outright existence now. I know a woman who had twenty-three children with eighteen different fathers. I don't know how it happened, but some of them came back. Actually, there were two sets of twins. The real question that comes to my mind is, how much can there be of this overtly within society, because a society must have a certain structure to it to exist. The minute you make this overt, you take the large group of people who want an inward security in order to hold themselves together and find a real purpose in life. If you beat them too much with this, then you may have an internal explosion, the whole society may go to pieces. How far can we go on this? I don't know, but it's there and I wouldn't deny it.

MICHAEL SCRIVEN: The answer is to try and see.

KERMIT KRANTZ: Yes, that's right, but not at the expense of destroying the very thing that you want.

MICHAEL SCRIVEN: Until you do try it's a question of keeping an outmoded institution going when it shouldn't be here.

WILLIAM LIU: The next speaker is Mother Gorman.

MOTHER GORMAN: I'm very glad, though in a way reluctant, to follow Dr. Scriven, because I think he posed some very good problems. I also want to say that I cannot claim an exclusive relationship with girls as an educator. I go at least once a month to the Army. In discussing the problem of communication and the communication of values, in December I am going down to Fort Lee to talk with forty chaplains on the problem of speaking to 18-year-old boys. I believe that this does help me in working with the problems of women. Recently I was at the National Institutes of Health, planning a conference in May for the scientific study of the basis of moral development. We worked out a conference of psychologists, sociologists, philosophers, theologians, and priests. One man said, "We have said nothing about sex, and that is what everyone says is the subject of morality." At that point, a man who is working on the study of moral development in children raised a very good point. He felt the basis of moral development lies in a respect for the human person, and that when you put it on the larger basis, sex would come under that. For that reason, we need not confine it to one element. Therefore, I'm speaking from the point of view of scientific psychology, education, and philosophy. I have an identity crisis in that area, plus the fact that my very basic black and white garb indicates another identity crisis!

I would like to sum up what I feel are two questions that came up repeatedly in these talks. They were questions that are based on fear. Now that we have been able to control the whole of nature, what are we going to do with people? How are we going to relate to them? We're free now of trying to control nature, relatively free. Are we going to act in the same way that we do toward *things*? Are we going to control people? You saw that yesterday, as they said "What is the relationship of man to woman going to be?" Can one relate to the other without either submerging the other? The second question was not a fear from outside, a fear of being exploited by another, but a fear of our own inner freedom as all these external conformity matters are being lifted. If I will be open, will I then be open to everyone, and is this not a very dangerous thing?

So there is a fear, both of our own inner impulses and a fear of what we will do to the other, and what the other will do to us, as many of the "thing" functions are being taken care of by machines. I think that it really is a question of how to handle freedom within and without. Last night it was fairly evident that you don't *handle* freedom, you *achieve* it. I feel that this is the great function of education.

What I propose to do is this: to present the scientific *mode* of knowledge as a model for all education, and to present the very great danger of adopting the scientific model as a goal. In other words, I would say let us choose education's scientific model in its methodology and its attitude of mind, but let us carefully question the scientific goal as one that we would want for education.

First, I would say that education cannot give content, it can only give a mode of acting. This is terribly necessary because, with all this information, it's far better for us to show our students how to retrieve information by computer systems than it is to memorize information. To my mind, the scientific method and attitude is one of openness, constant reevaluation, constant tentativeness. George Kelly, a psychologist who recently died, wrote a book called *The Theory of Personal Con-*

structs, and I was very struck by it. He said that one afternoon at 2:00 a student came in to talk about his research project. Kelly told him first to set up the problem, formulate a hypothesis, work out a project for testing it, then come back and change his hypothesis and go back and test again. He said at 3:00 P.M. a boy came in with a personal problem. Kelly told him to formulate the problem, to set up a hypothesis, to go out and test it, to come back and reevaluate it, and to change and try another way. In other words, what the scientific attitude does is to state all the options and formulate the problem clearly. This is why I was so emphatic just before this. State the consequences. What are the consequences if I choose this method? What are the consequences if I choose that method? Systems analysis and decision-making by computers are terribly important methods of approach that we should definitely use. The old, classic decision-making was "Which is the best one?" With the new method we must also reckon with the losses and the gains from each option.

I do not say that Dr. Scriven's proposal is right or wrong. But I say that, if we wish to change society, we must, as far as possible, list all the options, list all the losses and gains for every party concerned, go out, formulate a tentative plan, come back and revise, and go back again, always in line with the goal, which I feel is a little different from that of science. This I will go into later. We must develop this openness, this tentativeness in our students, that is, the scientific attitude. It need not be at all confined to scientists. Any great philosopher does it; any great artist does it.

The second point with regard to the scientific attitude is the way it views failure. I don't think as educators we have at all faced it. When we burned up three astronauts, they didn't say "Scrap the Apollo project." Never once, in any scientific project that I've heard of, did they expect instant success immediately, but we are living in a society in which there is instant everything, and we demand of our students instant perfect scores on the next tests. Instead, what does science do? Science uses pilot projects in which we do not expect success, but we expect feedback to see if we're off course. It seems to me that failure must be viewed as feedback, a way of saying we're off course, the way radar points the way. It must always be an ongoing thing. Last night we saw that in the saga of the Birds. When they did have conflicts, failures, so to speak, they said, "Where were we wrong?" not "It can't work."

I can't resist one aside because I have such great respect for the work they're doing at Cape Kennedy as a scientific endeavor. I'm not going into the goals. When Russia made the first soft landing on the moon, the head of Cape Kennedy said, "Now I know how Avis feels." I feel that this is a terribly good point about the scientific attitude. I don't mean that we're number two or one-and-a-half, but rather, we try harder. We must keep trying. I feel that whatever we do do, it is to so set the environment that it will liberate the natural problem-solving tendency in our students. I am studying very thoroughly how education stifles creativity. It has done this, but not in the scientific sense. It is always looking and saying, let's go on, on, on.

Let us look at the goals of science, and I think we come to the crux of the problem. As I understand science, its goal is to predict and control, to manipulate for the good of man. I would say that the goal of education, on the other hand, is to liberate. Therefore, we must look more carefully. If I were to take the problem of communication from a scientific and then from an educational point of view, it might clarify this. The aim of scientific communication is really to develop a superb mechanical method of transmitting information. One of the most interesting things that has happened to me was once when I was in the Army they said that they were launching Telstar and that it was stationary. I said, "Stationary? I thought it was moving at 25,000 miles an hour." They said, "Yes, it's stationary." I said, "I thought stationary meant immovable." They said, "No, stationary means moving at the same rate of speed in relationship to another object." I feel that education is like this; it must move or it's going backward. This is what we must do with our students. We must make them, as it were, stationary, remaining always in the same relationship to the world. This means above it, rather than under it. Science investigates things to control them. Communication in science is when you input something into a machine, and it outputs. You do it, and it gives it back. Sometimes the machine combines it in a new way, but you have given the direction.

Human communication is not mere input and output. At the end of scientific communication, the machine is still here and you're still there. At the end of communication between human beings, you're up there in a community, both of you, and I think that this is where our goal is. It is not in manipulating or merely putting things in. We cannot see the goal of education if it only resides in each person. This is what worries me. This is what worried me this morning when we said, "What is the relationship of marriage?" It was always the husband and the wife; there was no larger consideration. We mustn't say that the goal of communication between human beings will never be anything unless it is beyond each human being for some ultimate, transcendent goal. I do not necessarily mean a vertical one, because no one knows whether it's horizontal or vertical. But I do mean it has to be outside the individual.

We know in psychology that a person cannot become a person without another person. Yet the other person can very well destroy the person. We are aiming at a goal which is beyond each person. No man can be wholly for the other person, nor wholly for himself, nor wholly for the state. There is something beyond that, and somehow maybe this is what we have to show them: there is something beyond this, larger than the individual little community. It is a community of man. We haven't explored this. We've kept it on the pragmatic level, but we are all members of the human family and whether or not any of us will be alive in the year 2000, we must have contributed to the ongoing process of that human family as well as to our own personal fulfillment.

In this sense, we must also give something to the students. I say to them the same thing Kenneth Keniston has said: that young people want unfinished goals. They don't want us to say, "Here's the way you set up a marriage, do it." They don't want anything finished. I once said to my students, "We've united the world by mechanical communications, and we've set up barriers that are unbelievable between human persons. This is your unfinished goal." That is how I would come to these educational methods. We have to look for the goal.

There's another point about science I wanted to bring up. Science throws away obsolescent models. In the year 2000, not only is the woman going to be very old, but the man is, too. That is one problem we have to look at. We cannot treat the old models by destroying them and putting them in a junk heap, because machines are not men, and men are not machines. We must, in some way, show them how to grow from within. Therefore, where science would throw away old models, we have to show man how to create himself anew always. It's something science doesn't do. It is something deeper.

Each man creates his own relationship in marriage. Each man and woman create their own model, always in view of the larger context of the family of man. I'm not giving any positive solutions or any definitive ones. I'm just saying, let this attitude of mine be here. Let us explore the consequences.

When I went into the subject of freedom, I said that the scientific attitude says, "Keep on asking; keep on asking." This is a freeing attitude. We evaluate the attitudes of society and keep on going. The other aspects of freedom introduce a far more difficult process. Science can give us phenomena to work with. Science can tell us the "what" and the "how," but not the "why" and the "what for." We have here a problem of how to develop people who are free to make the choices they wish.

The aim of psychotherapy is not to cure the person of his neurosis. It is to enable him to choose whether or not he still wants the neurosis. In other words, the aim of psychotherapy and the aim of education are to enable the person to be relatively free of his own uncontrolled impulses so that he can make the choice and say, "I can do it," independently of what society says, independently of anything but what he freely chooses. When we discuss the levels of moral development, it is interesting to note two things that happen as the child grows older. He changes in his view of the value of the human person, and he changes in his motivation for conformity. In the beginning, the child values the person for what he could give or, eventually, for what he had or what he did. That's a pure external evaluation. Then he moves to value the person as a member of society, and then to the highest level of valuing him as a person, not because of his function in society or the fact that he has equal rights, but because he is a person.

The motive for conformity is even more interesting. Before age 6, the child acts for pleasure, pure pleasure. When he's a little older, he acts to avoid pain. At the third big level he acts because "other people do it"—external conformity. It's either in the Church; it's in *Glamour* or *Playboy*; or it's in something else outside. The fourth level is law—authority. At the fifth level, he becomes aware of the fact that what is legal can be immoral. There is a conflict. At the sixth level, he has resolved the conflict and says, "It is not because it's legal that I do this, but because of the value of the person." In other words, he has freed himself of the first two levels, of his impulses for pleasure and pain, so that, although he wants them, he can still say, "I might give them up for something higher."

Mrs. Johnson spoke about Abraham Maslow, and he is one whom I would highly recommend to you. Maslow's latest article (he sends them to me before they are published) is on the theory of metamotivation. I think you know the person's basic needs (physiological needs), order, then love (really belongingness), and then esteem. Those are the needs that we have to free ourselves from in order to have self-actualizing needs. They are never destroyed. They never can be destroyed. They are hierarchized and we deliberately choose the hierarchy we wish. This is what I wondered about. If a child or an adult chooses to make physiological needs dominant, I just want him to do it because he can choose it, not because he is bound by it.

Just let me give you a couple of Maslow's premises.

Self-actualizing individuals are, by definition, motivated in higher ways. All such people are devoted to some task, some beloved work, outside themselves. That is what I meant—the ongoing process of the human family. In the ideal instance, inner requiredness coincides with external requiredness. The task to which they are dedicated seems to be interpreted as an embodiment or incarnation of intrinsic values.

He then lists the values that he feels self-actualizing people would choose. He says that when a society does not give these values, we have metapathologies. I'll give you only two or three of them. A value, a being value, is truth. If there is a pathogenic deprivation of honesty, the metapathologies (and I'm using Maslow's terminology deliberately) are disbelief, mistrust, cynicism, skepticism, suspicion. In other words, if these relatively self-actualized people are deprived of truth— and he goes on to add goodness, beauty, unity, wholeness—

certain metapathologies arise: utter selfishness, hatred, revulsion.

The metapathologies of the affluent and indulged young come partly from the deprivation of intrinsic values. Frustrated idealism, disillusionment with society they see, mistakenly, as motivated only by lower, or animal, or material means. Here I think it's true that they misinterpret the behavior of their elders. They want to be free, to know, to love, to create. They feel that their elders are bound down by the needs of esteem, belongingness, physiological requirements, security. They do not want this. They want to be free of them so that if they choose them it's not because they have to, it's because they wish to.

One other aspect of freedom that was brought up: if I go out to a person, he might hurt me. If I go out to a person, how do I know there will be no bounds whatsoever? I might have to go out to all, and this would be catastrophic. It seems to me that education must help students to recognize this very real problem. Although we cannot give them answers, we must give them situations in which they learn how to handle this problem. The function of education is no longer just to tell us how to exercise our roles in society, but how to open up to each other without submerging each other. We are already doing this in education, through group counseling.

I would take issue with the criticism of the T-groups yesterday. The function of the T-group is not to have a personal encounter. The function of a T-group, for two solid weeks, is to make me aware of the screens I have put up so I cannot be open to others, to be very much aware of these so that I can relate afterward and also be aware of how my behavior affects others. The T-group is a learning situation about ourselves. It is not an encounter at the deepest level. It is merely to enable the person to have this encounter, by working at it. It's a long, hard, painful process. This is what the T-group is trying to do. It is trying to pull down the protective screens we have set up for each other.

I would say that if we were to look at the changes in society and, therefore, the changes in the way we look at men and women, I could list them and show what educational process I would recommend on the other side. There's going to be a lessening of the work week, and consequently an increase in leisure. Yes, dad is going to come home, and it appears that people are panicked. Do we have to see work as just a task in the sense of something to do, or is it, as we work with people on some positive ongoing project, really our life?

Maslow says this over and over again. Self-activating people are devoted to some task, some beloved work. Less evolved persons seem to use their work to gratify lower basic needs or neurotic needs—a means to an end, a habit, or a response to cultural expectations. Maslow is saying that the person doesn't say, "I have a world of work and a world of being related to persons." They are one, for a larger goal. The second thing is that there will be such an explosion of knowledge that we will advocate showing students how to retrieve information, not how to memorize it. The third thing would be that there may be breakdowns as the roles and functions that seem to make up the lives of people are no longer necessary.

Poor Willie Loman, in *The Death of A Salesman*, every once in a while said, "I kind of feel temporary about myself." Because, his son would say, he never knew who he was. He was a salesman; he was only that function. You can't find out what he was selling. He was selling himself at the price that was given.

We're going to have breakdowns of people whose whole lives are absorbed in their roles and functions, unless we can show them how to go out and explore, how to experience fail-ure, how to tentatively relate to the other person, come back, reevaluate, and feel themselves. Modern education is much more how to get along with people than it is how to manipulate and control things. That kind of education will not be needed as much. We'll have much more time to make the family of man mutually growing. There will be greater emphasis on teamwork. Therefore, education must enable people to see both sides.

There also will be another thing that I have not yet spoken about. Mass media will break down local symbols to a certain extent. We can then gradually set up new systems of symbols to express our deepest needs. Symbols express the mystery of life, which cannot be fully expressed in scientific terms. The new symbols must be organically related to the culture out of which they grow. Our present symbols have broken down and we are now witnessing the death of one culture and the birth of another.

Woman's role has always been to conceive and give birth in the biological sense. It seems to me that today both men and women have the greater task of conceptualizing, giving birth to, a new culture. It is the task of education not to inculcate techniques or content. It is the task of education to liberate the potential in the child by setting the environment so that the child can meet other persons and create the new culture.

WILLIAM LIU: Thank you, Mother Gorman. That was full of ideas for us to digest. I just don't know where to begin. I used to think that there were certain psychological constants, but I'm not so sure anymore. It seems that everything is changing. Maybe Professor Chilman can tell us from the psychologist's viewpoint whether or not we still have psychological constants.

CATHERINE CHILMAN: I want to say that I have been very much moved by what you have said. I've been struggling with a lot of the same ideas myself. In our discussion recently on liberating ourselves from the old ideas and constraints and taking a fresh, new look, I have really been disturbed by hedonism. Then I say to myself, "Be careful, Catherine, you came from a very puritanical background, you probably are very constrained." On the other hand, it does seem to me that a very central part of what it means to be human is to have an aspiration. It seems to me that all cultures have always had central objects of aspiration which people never really achieved. The need to aspire and to feel lifted above ourselves is central to being civilized. I think there's a need for this aspiration. Simply freeing oneself to express one's needs, such as sex, tends to make relationships shallow. We live in a shallow society. People fly around very fast. We are in huge groups, and yet it seems to me that all of us need deep commitments of intense intimacy, grown-up loyalties to people for whom we feel responsible and whom we feel are responsible to us, and with whom we share this aspiration you have been talking about.

From my own point of view as a mother, these are some of the deep things that marriage and motherhood mean to me: to make ourselves available to others as the impulse takes us, not to feel, "This is all too heavy a burden, and I am not getting enough out of it." I know this sounds very puritanical, but I think really by some discipline and some boundaries and some units there is an intensification of commitment and feeling. I struggle with these things, but they are some of the thoughts that have become central to me.

MOTHER GORMAN: I did not really bring out that each choice we make always entails losing something that we really wanted. However, we do it for a higher goal, and somehow we have to show this to the younger people. They go into a supermarket and they can get everything. We have to show them that if you take this, you cannot take that.

There's a song by Simon and Garfunkle—or is it by the Beatles?—that talks about the space between us that could be closed up and the way we hold onto our illusions and don't see the truth until it's too late; the idea that love can save the world but we go after other things instead. Do you know the song? I think it's called "Within You, Without You," and it talks about how life goes on inside you and outside you, and if everyone could get into this feeling, we would all be one.

This is what the young people are really talking and loving and quoting, a kind of expression of what I was trying to aim at. It does sound idealistic. I deliberately brought it in because I felt that it was necessary.

DONALD BARRETT: Much of the literature that's come out in the last couple of years, including the report of the President's Commission on the Status of Women, has indicated that much of the education that women receive in our society today is irrelevant in the second half of the twentieth century. First of all, do you agree with this? Second, are there any specific recommendations that you would want to make?

MOTHER GORMAN: There's a marvelous article by Bruno Bettelheim called "Growing Up Female." He says that in high school a girl is told to compete with boys: "Your mind is just as good as a boy's." By the time she is a sophomore, she realizes that if she shows the boy that she's just as good as he is, she is going to lose a husband. In her sophomore year, she has to make a choice. Either I go on and develop my mind (I'm grossly oversimplifying this) and lose a husband, or I do not go on and develop my mind and gain a husband. Usually she makes no decision and drifts out of college or through college.

You asked me how we ever justify a college education for women in the lower economic levels. I would say that maybe this doesn't apply just to women, but also to men. The thing they need is much more psychology (of course, I *would* think this), an understanding of human relationships both intellectually, cognitively, and dynamically all through experience.

Both men and women need to understand what is going on in a generation gap. In a sense there has been a generation gap all the time. I wish education could be geared to what is happening in society. We no longer need to spend so much time on content or on skills. They can be learned. We need to teach how to relate to people. The goal should be more clarified and unified, so that specific subjects would be geared to this goal. I cannot see really that the education of men and women should be different.

They ought to know that woman is naturally biologically different, and, therefore, she is going to approach things differently. She experiences her body differently. At the same time, a boy must know what's going on. There should be much more study of that.

Science seems to be dealing with little picayune things. Science is excellent, but there needs to be some kind of subject that would take the tremendous research that Dr. Masters and Mrs. Johnson and the psychologists are doing and put it into a science of the person. I don't know if this is going to be interdisciplinary. I feel it is. At this meeting for the study of moral development, we realized that it had to be interdisciplinary with cross-pollenization.

KERMIT KRANTZ: Were there reproduction people at that meeting?

MOTHER GORMAN: There were ten people there, and we had nothing to do with the make-up of the group. We were simply asked if we could come. One of the things we brought up was that the biological sciences were not represented. I feel that medical ethics is important. Medical and psychological consequences should be stated. That's only why I wondered about intermarriage of brother and sister. I don't know enough about the biological facts of it. I would go to a biologist or a geneticist on this.

SISTER MARY ALOYSIUS SCHALDENBRAND: This is probably taking us down a little bit different track. It's a request for some clarifications, really. You were suggesting that we needed models of men and women. You quoted Rahner's idea of autocreation. I have a problem with the notion of model and autocreation. It seems to me that these cancel each other out. I wonder if we ought not to get rid of the language of models and roles.

MOTHER GORMAN: I'd like to clarify that I said a model not of a person but a model for education, and I implied that one thing science does is throw out old models. Rahner's language is notoriously difficult. He uses the term *self-transcendence* and this is equally difficult. Maslow also coins terms. We are constantly growing and going beyond ourselves in what we are doing. In other words, I am not satisfied with the model of marriage that my parents had. I would go on and make my own thing, but it needn't be a model in that sense. It is the goal I would choose and for which I would work. What it means is that I create myself through the goals I look toward and through my choices.

SISTER MARY ALOYSIUS: Yes, I would be completely in accord. I was just anxious to have the model language clarified. You spoke of the need for freeing ourselves from esteem. I know there is a pathology of self-esteem, but I wonder if we can do this. A person becomes a person thanks to the esteem of others in the request for recognition.

MOTHER GORMAN: This is very true and this is what Maslow says. You cannot get esteem unless you get it from others. Then, he says, when you have sufficiently been satisfied in that, you can freely say, "I do not need it," or "I do need it." I would take Thomas More as an example. Bolt chose More for his play as a person with an adamantine sense of self. He knew when he could lose esteem and when he had to hold onto it. There is a marvelous place, not in the film, but in the play, when his wife is chastising him for not giving in to the king because he is losing esteem. More says, "I would never rule my king but there is a little part of me that no man can rule, no larger in my kingdom than a tennis court." What he can do is be so rooted in an esteem that is really there that he can afford to give up all the other esteem.

SISTER MARY ALOYSIUS: Yes, I would certainly agree, but I think then the term *esteem* has to be qualified if one says freedom from esteem, which is okay.

MOTHER GORMAN: Maslow is saying hierarchize it, and when you hierarchize, you include it, and you can freely choose. I think to understand this you would have to read carefully what Maslow is saying. Freedom doesn't mean that I don't have a thing. It means my option to have it, to choose it, if I wish it. It is much more the power of choice than the power of not having it or getting it.

WILLIAM LIU: I feel I have to cut in. Having lived on an island for the last two months where we didn't have any newspapers or telephones and I had the only watch in the family (my wife's watch does not work), I didn't hear about time at all. Nothing worldly really bothered me. Right now I am terribly concerned about time. So we have to cut this off. Since this is probably my last chance to have an audience I want to say one terribly important word. This conference was triggered by a letter Jessie Bernard sent to our last meeting, saying that the Notre Dame conferences on population had always missed 50 percent of the human race, namely, the female. It was then that Martha Stuart suggested we have a conference totally concerning women. Martha has been so marvelous in putting together a group of excellent people. Without her help, we could not possibly have met together—a team that was not only interdisciplinary but even included the Executive Vice President of the National Association of Manufacturers!

That is really marvelous. And then I skipped to the Philippines and Bill D'Antonio did all the dirty work at this end. So I wanted to make sure that the credits go to people who deserve them.

Martha Stuart and Bill D'Antonio, thank you very much. And, thank you all. I really mean that.

Where Are We Going Together? 11

KERMIT KRANTZ, RICHARD C. CORNUELLE,
SISTER MARY A. SCHALDENBRAND, AND LOUIS K. DUPRÉ

Wednesday, 11 A.M.

Louis Dupré: I am happy to be at this very interesting symposium and I am pleased to be on the panel with people I so highly respect. Two of them I've known from many other occasions. Let me give a short general introduction before each person presents his paper. There will be no discussion in between the papers.

First is Dick Cornuelle, whom I have known now for quite a while. I would say that what characterizes him is that he thinks big and solidly. If there is any kind of mind that I, as a philosopher, envy sometimes, it's the executive mind. Many philosophers nowadays are hung up on the scientific mind. I can see their point, but I am not that way. What I like is the mind that sees the importance of ideas in terms of their realization. These are the people who implement freedom. You know from the program what Dick's work is, but all of you may not know, or remember, that three years ago he became famous for the ideas of a new conservatism in his book *Reclaiming the American Dream*.

Further to the right (*laughter*) is Dr. Kermit Krantz. I have never been with him on a panel, but I have heard enough about him to know that he will be very interesting.

I have also known Sister Mary Aloysius Schaldenbrand for a very long time. She has what I would call a subtle mind. She gave a paper about a month and a half ago at a symposium in Rochester which, I think, was one of the best expositions I've ever heard on the relation between man and woman from a philosophical point of view. Her paper had all the subtlety the subject requires, and which it usually doesn't get. Time and again such an analysis is done by men who have neither her kind of mind nor her eye for nuances. So we're going to start right away. I would like to ask that the speakers all limit themselves to fifteen minutes and I'll try to do the same thing. The first speaker will be Dr. Kermit Krantz.

KERMIT KRANTZ: I feel like the parrot in the story. The old Vermonter's chickens weren't laying eggs, so he sent away for some new information. At the end of the instructions it said, "How about getting this parrot for another ten bucks?" So, he invested in it. One November evening the parrot came, and he put it out in the hen house. Then he went in to eat and said, "Laura, put the vittles on, everything's going for us. We'll have eggs coming out our ears." (You see I stuck to reproduction.) Then, by golly, he heard the most awful ruckus you ever did hear, and he went out to the hen house and opened the door. He saw all the hens over on one side, and all the roosters were over on the other side, and just then he heard, the parrot say from the rafters, "Honest gents, I'm here for educational purposes, that's all."

I think we can often understand you folks better than you can understand us. I don't say this in any arrogant or derogatory manner. What I'm trying to say is that we have become, in the basics of reproduction, somewhat sophisticated, and have not had adequate communication from the basic biological law to the highly cerebral activity—that means up there in the front of the brains of the rest of society. I have noticed one thing at this conference during the three days we have spent here. A great deal of time has been spent speaking about a small percentage of our society. Nobody has talked about the other 98 percent, and I don't think that we should forget them. They're mighty important, because only at their pleasure do we exist. We are a privileged group, but we can be destroyed very quickly, as other civilizations have been.

I'd like to pick up where Dr. Richardson finished and try to trace the woman today as I see her. She is *not* the same as a man. I think this ought to be clear from the beginning. If anybody wants to use the term *equal,* I think they must really redefine equality. Biologically, she is very different. She reacts completely differently under stress. She's bound to, since she has a different makeup, a cyclic behavior that no man has. Let's not ignore the real fact that a man is not a woman, and a woman is not a man. Let me just give you an example. During the menstrual cycle, a vasal dilation and constriction of the blood vessels show up in a woman's eye, something you just will not see in a man. This can have a tremendous effect upon her depth perception, as has been shown in landing of airplanes, for example. Not only are men and women biologically different, but in the evolutionary scale she is one step ahead. I'll make the assumption right from the beginning that you women are better than we are, and I'm not ever going to knock it down.

Woman began to be emancipated from the chattel state when she first found a way that she could identify with things about her. I think the industrial revolution, the steps that men like Eli Whitney made, allowed this nation to start to develop and gave women a chance to identify. I wonder, as I read history, whether or not the woman was after freedom for the slaves, or whether she was really after freedom for herself, because she identified with slaves.

One of the classics tells how Sara Grimke and her sister left South Carolina and came North to New England and caused a tremendous fomentation in 1838. In her own writing Sara Grimke said, "I believe that a woman will only find a way out through her identification with those who are equally oppressed." Maybe there's some clue here to a genetic pattern inherent in a woman. She did achieve this, fortunately for the progress of our society.

Woman's second chance and opportunity to free herself intellectually was when Congress provided, in the Morrill Land Grant College Act, the right of equal education for all people, and, at Morrill's insistence, left out the words "for males only." Education previously had been completely directed to the male. A Pandora's box opened—Thank God! Woman was able to show, not an equality, but the fact that she did have intelligence. Until that point, she was basically a chattel. She had been freed in part but not enough, and as she began to develop, she was able to show her influence. "Woman, you are capable within yourself of being a woman. You are not dependent on a man." With this attitude came a real threat to the whole Judeo-Christian tradition, which was matriarchal, but patriarchal on the surface of the society.

Even within our structured churches, what did they do to the woman? They oppressed her, right down to the bottom. She had no word, had no ability to speak forth. She stayed in perpetual mourning for the sins not of woman, but of man. The male has a certain guilt perhaps, sociologically, in this whole picture.

The woman was trapped until Margaret Sanger came along. Maybe Margaret Sanger thought of the oppressed children. I don't doubt that. But the few times I happened to meet her, I was sure of only one thing. She wanted to release woman from her last burden of dependency she had upon the male. That's the real difference, I think, between the woman and the man. She has the right and privilege of immortality. No man has it. She gives life, and with this she holds a tremendous power that no man can have. We men are ego-driven creatures, and we have to be handled tenderly, girls. Man has had to create some monument to say, "Look, I've been on this earth." He fights as an artist, as a poet perhaps, or as a scientist; and he always uses accomplishments as an ego satisfaction. He said, "Woman, you are a chattel. You are incapable of this." We now realize that her sexual capacity is even greater than the male's. We really begin to wonder where we are going. *Quo vadis feminus?* Where goest thou, woman? (I have tried to go over these things very quickly. If I drop some points, it is not because I wish to, but because of a lack of time.)

In this, woman has now brought herself to the point of shaking the very thing that she wanted most—security. She wanted security for her offspring, so that immortality could live. At the same time she is saddened. She wonders if there isn't a certain futility in life itself. She has challenged her security. That is why I've tried to provoke here another avenue of thought, that we cannot discuss social issues without a structured philosophy. What gives us that embodiment that holds us together and gives us a reason for living? What says to the large mass of our society, "I can go this way because it is the dear God's will."

Woman has now really begun to ask questions. "Where are my offspring going?" "I'm beginning to grope; I'm ambivalent in my behavior." We see women from one extreme to the other. A woman comes in and wants artificial insemination. She doesn't want a man at all. Should she not fulfill this immortality? She tells us, "No" without any question. At the other extreme, some just become brood mares. We have the whole spectrum now in front of us.

It's very interesting if we look at the sex symbols of our society. I'm a consultant to several corporations, including one which makes girdles. They make no bones about the fact that the girdle is one of the greatest substitute security agencies on the market today. She feels held; she feels wanted. It gives her a sense of security.

What I'm really trying to say, and I'm using an obtuse example, is that a woman in her passive-aggressive personality controls her destiny, but she has to do it in an oblique manner because this is inherent in her personality. She'll get at her man negatively or positively. You never find a wife saying, "Will you go to bed with me? I want intercourse as of now." She will beat all the way around the bush, and if the guy hasn't got enough sense to know what she's doing she'll say, "Wake up, Daddy-O" and go off in some other direction.

The male, in his psychosexual drive, is an aggressor, and we cannot forget that. This has to be channeled. How is a woman going to handle this? Is she going to be like the black widow spider and gobble him up? She is now so powerful and controlling of the total destiny that she now puts all her efforts into the children, and we have a matriarchal society. She wants so much to control the child that he's rebelling almost beyond comprehension, with the teen-ager being thrown out of the family as soon as possible. I don't know why, but this is what is happening.

Woman has pushed out the male. Yet she wants him; she needs him. I think the beautiful biological studies that have been done have shown it.

I'd like to go on, but I have only one moment. I'd like to pass this on to the women. A lot of things I've heard said here as if they were new ideas aren't new at all. They've been said throughout history and they'll be said again. I don't think a new idea has entered on this earth in the last thousand years, only elaborations of known concepts.

John Donne wrote something I'd like to pass on to the women:

No man is an island, entire of itself. Every man is a piece of the continent, a part of the main. If a clod be washed away by the sea, Europe is the less, as well as if a promontory were . . . Any man's death diminishes me, because I am involved in mankind; and therefore never send to know for whom the bell tolls: it tolls for thee.

Womankind has a tremendous responsibility on her back. The only difference between the past and now is that she is becoming aware of it. Use your responsibility carefully, because we poor men are fragile. We may soon have to depend upon parthenogenesis for the existence of any human entity. It is happening in the lower ends of the biological scale. It may happen to us, too. I'll quit at that point.

RICHARD CORNUELLE: Bill expressed some alarm that an executive of the National Association of Manufacturers is on this program. I assure you he's not nearly as alarmed as is the National Association of Manufacturers.

The layman is always a little frightened of a scholarly audience, and so he usually teases the academics about their jargon. I'm going to get that out of the way by telling one jargon story. One of our companies is working with paroled prisoners, helping with their difficult reentry problem. We find, as we do so often, that the best people to help them are former parolees who have already been through it. Men who have successfully reentered civilian life from prison naturally turn out to be most skilled at showing others how to do it. One such man was talking to a group of men who were about to get out of jail and describing some of the problems. "Now the first problem you're going to run into," he said, "is the problem of destigmatization. I want to be sure you all know what that word means. Charlie, do you know what destigmatization means?" Charlie said, "Sure, that means you're a name and not a number."

I'm a good deal more comfortable now than I was at the beginning of the conference because I found that the work of many of the scholars cited here is familiar to me; for example, Abraham Maslow and W. C. Fields. I read many of the same journals that scholars do: *The National Observer, Playboy*. So I'm not as scared as I pretend to be.

I got into the business of trying to work out some new approaches to American polity because I got so damn discouraged about the growing evidence that a nation of nice people were doing very cruel things to each other; that a people unique for their directness were building a society that was more than anything pretentious; that a people I have found to be uniquely concerned about the problems of their fellow men seemed to be collectively indifferent.

I found everywhere discouraging expressions of despair. I read the conclusion of a famous national columnist, after Watts, that "the race problem is basically insolvable. And we shall simply have to learn to live with it in pain all the days of our lives." I watched Dick Goodwin leave an enormously influential position in the White House and listened to his pained valedictory. He didn't see the wisdom to solve America's problems in Washington and he didn't see the resources to solve them in the communities that had the problems. He didn't know what to do. (Since that time he's taken a more optimistic view and has published some upbeat stuff.)

I tried to provide some answers in the little book Louis referred to. It turned out to be partly successful and partly a failure. The only thing that was very original in it turned out to be wrong, so I had to do some more thinking. In that process, in that search for some ways to rebuild our institutional structure so it will express the best that is in our people rather than the worst, I think I found the key while I was looking for something else.

In the process of trying to learn how to love and be loved by a woman, I think I found the key to building a polity through which people can express their best rather than their worst.

We have discovered, Martha and I, that the key to building a good relationship is to find a relationship that doesn't corrupt the dominant party and doesn't diminish the subordinate party. (Here the language lets down. We have to talk about "dominance" and "submission" because we don't have any better words. I think we need some new ones.) To do that—it's a good deal easier to say than to do—I think you need to comprehend and to respect your own identity fully and accurately, and you have to comprehend and respect the identity of the other person fully and accurately. When that's accomplished, a lot of other things seem to happen automatically. The kind of spontaneous mutuality Bill Liu spoke about so well the other day just happens.

This is pretty important as a possible key to building great relationships between men and women. I think it is also the key to building great new institutional arrangements that will bring out the best in the people, arrangements where human potential can be expressed more and more fully and accurately.

I'm enormously encouraged to see signs that this is happening. I see it happening in business. You'd be astonished to go with me to management conferences and hear more talk about love than double-entry bookkeeping. You may be astonished to know that the intellectual whose work many businessmen most often cite is not Adam Smith, but Abraham Maslow. You find companies adopting forms of organization where it's damn hard to tell who's boss, where a whole new kind of leadership is being expressed. This is its quality. The subordinate party, that is, the employee, is not diminished by the relationship and the dominant party, that is, the employer, is not corrupted by it.

Time is too short today to do anything but jump around. I've seen signs of this new spirit in education. We worked with some boys from Harlem. Everyone else had given up on them. We wanted to see how fast we could teach them to read and write and do arithmetic. We took some very sophisticated educational hardware and went to work. We finally found that we could move these young fellows as much as four years in achievement of basic skills in seven weeks. (They were achieving at about a fourth-grade level when we found them.) We went up some blind alleys because we thought for a time that the magic was in the hardware. It turned out that their success had very little to do with the teaching machines and that jazz. It had to do with the character of the teacher of the class and her attitude toward her students. She understood them; she respected them; and, literally, she loved them. The kind of spontaneous mutuality that developed led to those stunning educational results.

We've built so many organizations in this country. I serve one in which the leadership doesn't really respect the membership, the subordinates, if you will. You often hear expressions of contempt for them. You find professional association executives who say, in effect, "The membership is dumb, stupid." They say, "We're gonna have meetings and keep the members drunk and we'll give them a 'sense of involvement,' but the guys on top will make all the crucial decisions." I don't want to speak for the labor movement because Harold is bigger than I am, but I know he sees some of the same dangers in the kind of organization he leads.

Take poverty programs. When you're trying to help people move up from poverty, and you start to build the organizational machinery that's necessary to help them, you've got to know what these people are like. You've got to respect their identity or you can't accomplish anything. There was talk in the early organization of the federal poverty program about "maximum feasible participation of the poor." They took people who had an understandable difficulty, because they had moved from the rural South to urban centers, who were puzzled when they had to transfer from one bus to another, and put them on the boards of corporations that were planning the immensely complex economic structures that are necessary for slum rehabilitation. This is outrageous miscalculation, or misunderstanding, of these people and a violation of their identity. A leader is asking them to do something they're not suited to do. We find, however, that proper leadership, leadership that understands and respects the character and the identity of these people, can work with them so that a kind of spontaneous mutuality develops with dramatic results.

The authors of the "maximum feasible participation" phrase have backed away from it. We're building programs in which the poor contribute 98 percent of the energy. They are almost totally involved in the solution of their problems, but in ways that are consistent with what they *can* do. They are working toward aspirations they have for themselves, not toward aspirations we try to impose on them. (We don't try, for instance, to get them to sleep in pajamas.)

Look at political parties. Party leaders most often express contempt for their constituents. I think the clearest, cleanest expression of that was in an article in the *Saturday Evening Post* about a political organizer in California who said that if you would put up the amount of money he specified and promise to keep your mouths shut, he could get you elected to any office you wanted to name. This means he thinks the constituency is stupid, subject to manipulation. I think we are seeing a new kind of political leadership emerging, one that respects the constituents, one that listens, and one that honestly involves people in political action.

Here's another illustration from an entirely different field. A professional football team that is getting remarkable results is the Green Bay Packers. Someone asked the coach why in a public interview the other day. He scratched his head, and said he guessed it was because the guys on the team loved each other.

Well, I just want to restate my principal thesis. It's going to take us a long, long time to figure out exactly how it applies to some fields, for instance, to state-federal relations. If you have a federal government that misunderstands the identity and potential of subordinate political units, you're going to have a polity that diminishes the municipality and corrupts the federal establishment.

The exciting thing to me is that we're beginning to find the keys to building the kind of world we want as we begin to understand the right relationship between men and women. I was the child of the manse in a fundamentalist Presbyterian household not far from South Bend. They told me that I should love my neighbor as myself, and that seemed like a good idea. They failed to tell me that that was a very difficult thing to do, and they failed to tell me how to do it. I am terribly excited that a lot of people are beginning to recognize that need and to give us guidance in so many different ways.

SISTER MARY ALOYSIUS: I was already resigned to being the last speaker before dinner and the follower of several brilliant speakers, which seems to be my lot.

To restrict somewhat my wandering thoughts, I will impose a sort of tripartite structure and attempt to give some response to the question, "Where are we going together?"

First of all, I would suggest hopefully it's toward a creative society, a society creative of persons. I am very suspicious of those key terms and will try to explain them. Second, I would like to take up the obstacles or ambiguities of our situation—those things which presently stand in the way of developing this kind of society. Third, I would like to suggest what things are going for us as we move toward a society creative of persons.

What is the meaning of *person* as I use it here, as we've been using it at this meeting? It seems to me to be referring to the individual, the self. I would like to suggest perhaps a broader meaning. A person really is not so much an "is" as an "is to be." It is better perhaps to say "to be accomplished" or "to be achieved."

Gabriel Marcel, the French philosopher, likes to say "a person is not a sum, but a sursum." I would suggest that the person is a complex unity. On the one hand, the person is singular and unique. No two of us are alike, in spite of all our talk about woman as woman, and man as man. Certainly no two women are alike. I've been terrified here, before one-tenth of one percent of the world's elite. Will I look like a woman? Will I be feminine? Those are tremendously threatening questions. The point here is that every person is unique and his hereditary capital different.

In any case, our individual style is different, and here I would like to locate the sexual difference. I couldn't agree more that men and women are differently constituted; that's obvious. It seems to me that to speak of a woman as "woman," to speak of "woman's role," is very dangerous. It seems that every time we use the category, every time we define the role, we put people in some kind of box. We say women must respond in this style; they must limit their activities within this scope.

If we locate the sexual differentiation on the side of the hereditary capital, we must list it as simply one aspect of the person. The person is a unique, but a unique who, we may say, looks out on the whole field of human motivations. There are no human meanings and no human values that I can't respond to as a person. So we may say that the person is "unique universal," or "unique infinite." Perhaps this would be of some help to us in trying to free women for the full play of their human responsibilities. This is not to say that if you are a woman you *must* be passive; you must be a feeling person, for every person should be a feeling person. Every person should be effective, passive and active. These are the rhythms of life. Why divide us up between sexes? I suppose maybe that is like beating a dead horse, and yet here at this conference we have had a lot of discussion along the lines of whether women are feminine or not.

First, this matter of a person is very tricky, but then how do you create a person? How did society create a person? Very simply, I suspect. You become a person when somebody else recognizes you as a person. We feel respected as persons, and then we discover that we are capable of who knows what—capable of all human meanings and values. What is more unique, we appreciate our uniqueness when others appreciate it.

It's others in back who tell us who we are. This is one reason why some of the statements made have been a bit difficult for me to put into this framework; for example, the notion that we live alone, in a sense, and we must change ourselves by ourselves. I don't really think that's true. I think we receive from the other person. It's not that we are absorbed or we are destroyed in this kind of communication. This, I think, is the test of the communication. Does it free me to respond, or does it strike me with sterility? I become myself *in responding*. I do not become myself and then go out and relate, but I become myself *in relation*. It's the relation that gives me my identification—various relations, all kinds of things. I don't achieve an identity and then go out and relate, it seems to me. Maybe these are very obvious points.

Second, I don't want to be sanguine about our possibilities for moving toward this society of creative persons. We have all kinds of problems. The greater number of people in the world today are miserable. They can hardly express their uniqueness. They don't have the material base upon which to inscribe their personal signatures. We have a tremendous task here. The stereotypes that we've been talking about just now are very much with us. We do put people in boxes, in categories, and limit their responses and their scope.

I think John Dewey, the great American philosopher, was so to the point here. He said the recognition can short-circuit the perception. If I recognize a woman as a woman I don't have to perceive her in her uniqueness; she's already boxed. The task of living so that I perceive you, without short-cutting or short-circuiting, is a great point in life which could be developed, but time marches.

Certainly a great negativism toward the body exists. I think Jacqueline yesterday was right in questioning our unwillingness to accept the totality that we are. Even the language of "lower" drives, and "higher" drives is already prejudicial to this integral unity which I am. We're not comfortable about being body beings. One of the reasons why I'm veiled here is that I think that this is one of the questions the sisters must ask, "Do we speak of a certain negativism toward the body, my body, itself?"

It seems to me that here we enter into the third point: what we have going for us. It's precisely this debate that we're beginning to see as overt. We have today discovered, I think (and here Professor Krantz and I may argue), that there is something new, that time does bring some new things, and what we have today is a kind of awareness of what it means to be embodied. That's all positive and different—my body as a condition and being present to you. It's quite a different thing than we are accustomed to thinking about—about my body.

This really revolutionizes our concept of sex. This would seem to me to be the first existential meaning of the body in human sex; that my body itself is the place, or really is the meeting place. We become flesh for each other, and give ourselves to each other in flesh as flesh. We don't have to be ashamed or sorry about that. That's the greatest thing. My whole being is sexual, so that I give my body as an opening to you.

This raises all kinds of questions, as Jacqueline rightly pointed out yesterday. We might call another conference to discuss those things. The point is, we have also a critical consciousness. This spontaneous living of the body as openness is great, but we're also cool about it in our happiness.

The critical consciousness, I think, is very important. The demythologizing of femininity as a nature, as a prescribed way of response, is very important. The whole question of gender roles is important; and the social awareness that grips us today is terribly important. We begin to see that I cannot achieve identity or I cannot even relate in this total and full way with the person next to me if I am not concerned about the person on the other side of the globe, the person in North Vietnam as well as in South Vietnam. This capacity to respond to the human being, the human condition everywhere, is certainly a mark of our modernity. I think Marshall McLuhan says it very determinedly. He says that we are a global village here; that not only do we have a global village, but also a global way of perceiving it. This sort of total way, I think, was what Jacqueline was getting at yesterday.

Technology today has reached the great point where we have perhaps a possibility of ending our prehistory, as Marx would say. We have a great possibility of ending work in the "toil" sense that Mr. Lecht was talking about yesterday. This to me is not so frightening as it is thrilling. I suggest that we find ourselves not only at the death of an old culture, but at the birth of a great time. That's a great way to end, isn't it?

LOUIS DUPRÉ: You can see that I did not exaggerate in my flowery introduction of my fellow panelists. What you may not know is that I am also on the panel, so I can now quietly abuse the rest of the time and say a few things which I think are important. I think this symposium has been very successful. In my case, this is illustrated by the fact that I had a neatly typed paper which I didn't even take the trouble of getting out of my suitcase this morning, because this symposium has made it completely passé. It's worthless. It deals with particular problems that can much better be solved once we have a better grip on the main problems, once we see them in their context.

What I'm going to do now is basically, I guess, the task of the philosopher, who's really not a specialist in anything but who, when the show is over, mounts the stage and says what it has been all about. In other words, I am using the expertise of everyone else without contributing much of my own, except for placing the problem that we have been discussing in the total dimension of human existence.

What is happening and where are we going? What is happening to women? Where are we going together? Contradictory statements have been made here about how women are completely different from men and how men and women are completely the same. I would like to point out two things we have learned here which may, perhaps, reconcile these seemingly contradictory statements. Most of the time during this symposium, at least since yesterday morning when I arrived, we have been debunking all kinds of myths about woman. In doing so, we were not trying to build up a new image, but rather we attempted to understand better what woman is and has been all along. The new thing which the present experience and our reflection upon it teaches us is the awareness that whatever woman is she is by choice rather than by nature. There is no eternal female nature. It is not possible to say, "This is what a woman looks like or what she's supposed to look like." Even a man with as little insight into womanhood as I have can see that.

A few years ago Simone de Beauvoir wrote her famous book *Le Deuxième Sexe* (*The Second Sex*). It is a very questionable book, and I'm not going to defend it here. Nevertheless it had some merit because of the illusions which it destroyed and the response which it provoked. The most interesting was that of a Dutch psychology professor, F. J. Buitendijk, in a book entitled *La Femme*. In it he pointed out first what I have fully realized at this symposium: woman is not what she *is*, but what she accepts as her role. When I say her *role*, I mean a role that is freely created, either by man or woman or by both, together—unfortunately (and this will be my second point) in the past too much by men alone.

We see that we cannot permanently define a woman by any one role in society, in the sense that the man *always* does this and the woman does that. This is very important. We should never forget, when we speak about human beings, that what we call *human nature* does not really exist at all. Man is the only living being that has no fixed nature, no unchanging essence. He is the only being that makes himself. He is in charge not only of this world, but, as Marx expressed it so well, in creating his world, he also creates himself. This is also true of woman. She makes herself into what she is. She makes herself on the basis of her relation to man.

Be that as it may, whatever we call *feminine* is not something we can consider God-given, like the physiological sexual differences. Beyond those sexual differences, woman is free to create her own differentiation and to define femininity. If she functions as the weaker sex, she does so either because she wants that role or because it has been inflicted upon her. It is not predetermined. She makes herself into a woman.

Unfortunately, and this is my second point, in the past, woman's role has been created too much by man alone, and she may have made herself into a very passive person by trying to accommodate an all-domineering male. This symposium has beautifully illustrated also that any final definition of womanhood is a myth, *myth* in the bad sense of the word. Any such statement as, "This is the way she is," is, a priori, wrong, for the simple reason that it goes against human nature since there is no predetermined human nature.

Once we get rid of the myth, then we can try to come to grips, not only with how woman has created herself, but also with how woman really wants to create herself. How *does* woman like to create herself? I would say that she, more than the male perhaps, likes to create herself in a relational way. She creates her role as a relational role. We should not understand this merely as relating to the male, but also to the children.

This relationality which at first seems to imply losing one's independence—if one sees independence in an insular way—and which may look like weakness, is really the strength of womanhood. To be relational is to be greater than to be insular. The male runs around loose, because there is nothing that keeps him there. He has to invent something to create. That is why he does all kinds of things: he makes machines; he writes poetry; he really has been more efficient when it comes to production than the female has. There's no question about that, although the future may change this. The woman is often not even interested in doing that, because she feels deep down that there is something that is more important than her talents. Even though she may make full use of her talents, even though she may make them productive, she knows that ultimately the main thing is life—existence. That is where she is in charge. This is the most important thing.

Yet presently a new image emerges; something in modern life has changed. It is not only a new awareness on the part of woman, of mankind's power to determine itself and the ability to shape its own existence. In the present society, she will no longer allow her role to be shaped by man and to be inflicted on her. She will no longer tolerate the male telling her what she is going to be. She won't take it, and she can't take it anymore, because she is conscious of her freedom, and nothing can stop the development of consciousness.

That sounds like an abstract principle but it would be very practical if we applied it in politics, economics, and social relations. We cannot stop consciousness. Once something has been discovered, it cannot be halted. The woman has discovered that she really has as much right to be self-creative as the man. She has always known her relational creativity, but now she sees it in a new light: her being related need not include submission. It is an entirely different thing. It means, in fact, a very great amount of independence.

Of course, the male who hears that gets scared. He thinks, "Well, there goes femininity." I don't think men should worry about that. We should worry instead about women who refuse to create their own feminine role and who simply imitate what the man is doing. For example, there is a kind of autonomy that has been inflicted on women in Soviet Russia. It is utterly absurd, of course. It does not include creativity at all. It is another way in which the male, with his heavy boots, has stamped on the female's creative potential, telling her that from now on she must be the same as a male. That is as much an insult as reducing woman to a submissive role.

When we look at attitudes in our society today, we see that many things have changed which allow a woman to be more independent. We have the problems to which I directed myself in my original talk, the problems of contraception and of divorce. These are essentially modern problems. Why? Because morality has disappeared? Certainly not. People are always the same, more or less. One generation is not much better or much worse than earlier generations. There are times which are decadent, but I don't think morality changes.

What has happened, in fact, is this. We first had to take care of the population of the world. That was a demanding task but indispensable because the basis of culture is population. But that job is finished. Teilhard de Chardin said, "Now that we have satisfied all these enormous biological needs that were there, this tremendous power of human creativity, of the human creativity of love, should be used for spiritual creations." In other words, love should be used to strengthen the quality of interindividual relationships, and not to make more people. We don't need any more people for the sake of increasing numbers. That can only degrade our being together in this world. So we are transforming energy which used to be biological into spiritual energy, the energy of love. Marriage has changed because we have changed, and therefore our institutions had to change. So let us not say that marriage is the same as it was in the past and as it always will be. It is already different.

The problem of divorce is similar. A month ago, my wife and I were here to give a common paper on divorce (a rather strange task for a married couple). We pointed out that the attitudes toward divorce reflected in civil law show that in a society which is still unsettled and shaky, man has to put all the emphasis on the establishment of institutions. The stability of the institution of marriage is an important matter, not to be left to individual choice alone. In the complete disarray of Western culture around the fourth and fifth centuries, the Church, the only source of order available at that time, decreed that marriage was to be absolutely indissoluble. The civil law, the common law, as my wife pointed out, followed this whole line of thinking. The institution was always right. As life developed, however, it became increasingly more important to protect the rights of the individuals within and sometimes against the institution. We now say, "Why should the individual always be sacrificed to the stability of the institution?" Indeed, we realize that the institution itself suffers if man tries to make it more stable than it can be. If two individuals can no longer live together, the marriage is *already* a failure, whether they divorce or not.

Such shifts in attitude show how woman, in her relational creativity, is becoming more independent, less submissive, now that attitudes in society are changing. Some of the speakers here have said that this is the end of a culture; others have said this is the beginning of a culture. Whatever be the case, this is a difficult time because we are in transition, and society fights back during transition periods.

As Marx pointed out, social structures are the last things to give in. Their very nature sets them against change. They ought to be that way because social structures are also a protection for individuals. (I realize very well that I'm abusing my role as chairman here to go over my time. I'm sorry and I apologize to my fellow panelists, but I would like to make one final point.) Man tends to fall back on old patterns of morality and religion. He tends to repeat to his children what he has heard. He says, "That's the safe way to live." But we should remember that what was once the safe way to live may not be the safe way anymore.

I don't think we can continually repeat what has been said in the past. We should be open and we should be able to listen. Our moral code is a self-created code. That doesn't mean it's arbitrary. Man creates his own values according to the way in which God has created him, and in that sense, moral values are divinely inspired, but shaped by man himself. We have to be open in our moral perspectives, yet without being irresponsible. We should never go one step further than seems wise in the light of present considerations. We should not make predictions about what marriage will be like 2000 years from now. Will it still be around? I don't know. Something like it will always be with us, but probably not in exactly the same form. So let us remain open to the future and be aware of the relativity of man.

I am not in the least impressed by the current idea that the young are always right. I don't think that's true at all, nor do I think they're better. But I think that the young at least represent one thing—that which will be. To find out what it is, we must listen to them.

The same thing is true of religion. Religion is not morality, but, for those who are religious, religion is the ultimate foundation of their morality. As all foundations, religion tends to be conservative. It establishes absolute guidelines for man. However, these guidelines are absolute only for the time when they are given. The same foundation may, in fact, lead to entirely new ways and entirely new roles. Looking at it from that angle, we have no reason to be alarmed about today's changes or about what is called "the crisis of Western civilization." Every crisis simply means one stage in the process of growing up.

We have reached a turning point. This is always an unpleasant experience, but it gives us also tremendous prospects, prospects of ridding ourselves of so many things that we are now hung up on, such as, for example, fears and questions related to sex and femininity. We still want to hold onto our clichés of the past because we are afraid.

At present we are moving toward a greater state of freedom for man. To be free, we must be willing to be completely open toward the future. To be free is never to say that the future will be the same as the past.

We have a new awareness of what woman is; and we have a new situation in which she can express this new awareness, in which her relational creativity is realized in an independence that has not existed before. That gives unprecedented possibilities and opens up for us all new ways and means of living together and working together. Life may become better than before because it can be much more creative. That's what I want to say.

KERMIT KRANTZ: It is very interesting for me to see that the philosopher and the scientist aren't so far apart.

VIRGINIA JOHNSON: I didn't interpret you that way, Kermit. I was deeply pleased that Louis put this finalization on it. I'm afraid that when you said, "The female should always play it this way," indicating her passivity and her relutance to express her needs (you were a little more concise about it), I was ready to suggest that, as an interpreter of the female, you would make a good hell-fire and damnation preacher!

KERMIT KRANTZ: As I told you, I skipped through some of those things rather rapidly. I think you know me better than that . . .

VIRGINIA JOHNSON: I was hoping I heard you wrong. I thought you were harkening back to the old passive female.

KERMIT KRANTZ: No, I was trying to point out some of the genetic aspects that have come to the fore. Whether these are going to stay the same or not, I don't know.

VIRGINIA JOHNSON: Well, I don't know. I read as much as I can and I am certainly not competent in the area, but this is not the feeling I get in the meetings of geneticists or the biological scientists. I get too much of a feeling in obstetrics and gynecology meetings of a tendency to protect against facing woman as she is, because of the very nature of the discipline, for which I have great compassion. It is not easy to adapt to something that is a forerunner of the freedom that is to come, but nevertheless I feel a little obstetrics and gynecology influence here, and I think this has been the last outpost to view woman as a viable being.

JESSIE BERNARD: Well women, after all, do go to obstetricians in a "tell me what to do" way, and so that is the way obstetricians and gynecologists see them.

CATHERINE CHILMAN: All during this symposium I have been dying to say one central thing. We have talked a great deal about how women must be allowed to be persons. I think we have not said enough perhaps about men being allowed to be persons. I think that we have assigned values to men: that they must be strong and tough and achieving and competent. In bringing them up in the family, in school, in jobs, we have denied the humanity of men, making it very hard for them to be tender and open and not needing to be heroes. If women are going to insist on being persons who have feelings and needs and so on, it's very important, too, to nurture the humanity of men.

JACQUELINE GRENNAN: I thought Dick Cornuelle's remarks, especially toward the end of his speech, were terribly important in tying this together. I wrote down a phrase: "One needs to learn how to love and be loved by a woman." He said you don't learn it theoretically, in abstractions. He then tied it into the whole notion of an institutional evolution. I would hope that this is the consequence of what we are trying to learn at the experiential level. I would still like to say that I think we must watch terribly carefully the filters with which we hear each other. When we're moving away from one kind of standard, from images and stereotypes, so much of the perception is that we move to something else.

In moving to a desirable personalism, in the way Dick means it (a personalism that lets one become more responsible in social structures), one is not at all necessarily moving to hedonism. Mother Gorman's concern with fear is a very important concern. However, unless one is sensitive to the other person, one is obtuse. (Where is that line between fear and sensitivity?) These are all lines that can't be ciphered down, and, in my estimation, this is the anguish and the wonder of being man. We are always trying to resolve these. As Philip Morrison once said at Webster, "A thing is as true as its opposite." He was playing with opposites and using glorious old sayings such as "Look before you leap" and "He who hesitates is lost." Which is truth? He said only the man who believes both of them are true has a chance of being a man. It is the attempt at any moment to resolve those two contrarieties, in the most beautiful sense of paradox, that makes a man moral and responsible.

FATHER JOHN THOMAS: I think our time is up, so I just want to drop one final pearl. We've heard a lot of talk here about being in a transitional state. I say it better be transitional, or we're in a hell of a mess. We've heard a great deal about freedom from, but what the hell are we free for? This is what I say to our young people: "What are we free for?" As we are moving in this transitional stage, I hope we will gradually evolve some of these symbolic values. I do think we have a very serious problem in what we will be committed to, asking ourselves what are we free for?

LOUIS DUPRÉ: I should have made an important point earlier. Many people think, in moving forward, that we can live without structures. I think something of that was perhaps reflected in some of Michael Scriven's idealistic remarks. Here I agree completely with Father Thomas. We can never just drop structures without replacing them, as some theologians do today, by secularizing religion. In Japan and in other Oriental countries we have undermined the religious foundations of morality which we found primitive. This is a dangerous thing to do, because without them nothing else protects the building anymore. The same thing is true for morality in general. I don't think we can live without structures at all. Before we move forward, we should know where we are going. On the other hand, I do not think we should draw a line here.

UNIDENTIFIED WOMAN: I think the great joy is in finding out. We have to live.

LOUIS DUPRÉ: I agree, but we should not remove our structures completely.

MARTHA STUART: Louis, I don't think anyone can know exactly where we are going. After all, what are we? We can't end on this note!

SEVERAL PEOPLE: Let's end on *that*.

LOUIS DUPRÉ: Good question, that last question—What are we?

Index

Abortion
    culture and acceptance of, 47
    for family planning, 2, 23
    rates, 2
Acculturation, behavior and, 47–48
Achievement-orientation of culture, 7–8
Adaptibility
    of females to independence, 58–66
    limits of, 119
Aggressiveness
    effects of female, 110, 111, 257–264
    male vs. female, 12, 15, 110, 111
Aging, sexual response and, 107, 108–109
Alternatives to marriage, 262–264, 265 ff.
Androgyne, Plato's tale of, 126, 127, 128
Anomie, concept of, 29
Artificial insemination, 51

Autocreation, model and, 285
Automation, impact of, 185–194

Behavior
    acculturation and, 47–48
    ambivalence of female, 293–294
    culture and, 4–5, 35–36, 81
    discrepancy between belief and, 39–40
    education and, 272–273
    identification with sex, 55
    interpretation by children, 279
    in literate vs. preliterate societies, 35–36
    social meaning of, 27–28
Belief
    discrepancy between behavior and, 39–40
    levels of, 4–5

Castration concept of vasectomy, 16
Celibacy. See also Virginity
    gender role and, 83

317